New Caseboo

VIC... ...EN
POETS

New Casebooks

New Casebooks

VICTORIAN WOMEN POETS

EMILY BRONTË, ELIZABETH BARRETT BROWNING, CHRISTINA ROSSETTI

EDITED BY JOSEPH BRISTOW

First published 1995 by
MACMILLAN PRESS LTD
Houndmills, Basingstoke, Hampshire RG21 2XS
and London
Companies and representatives
throughout the world

ISBN 0-333-60803-8 hardcover
ISBN 0-333-60804-6 paperback

A catalogue record for this book is available
from the British Library.

10 9 8 7 6 5 4 3 2 1
04 03 02 01 00 99 98 97 96 95

Printed in Malaysia

Contents

Acknowledgements

The editor and the publishers wish to thank the following for permission to use copyright material:

Isobel Armstrong, for an extract from *Victorian Poerty: Poetics and Politics* (1993), pp.332–57, by permission of Routledge; Deirdre David, for 'Art's a Service', *Browning Institute Studies*, 13 (1985), 113–36, by permission of *Victorian Institute Studies*; Sandra M. Gilbert, for 'From *Patria* to *Matria*', PMLA, 99 (1984), 194–211, by permission of the Modern Language Association of America; Elizabeth K. Helsinger, for 'Consumer Power and the Utopia of Desire', *ELH*, 58 (1991) 903–33, by permission of The Johns Hopkins University Press; Margaret Homans, for 'Emily Brontë' from *Women Writers and Poetic Identity* (1980), pp. 104–29. Copyright © 1980 by Princeton University Press, by permission of Princeton University Press; Angela Leighton, for 'Because men made the law', *Victorian Poetry*, 27 (1989), 109–27, by permission of *Victorian Poerty*; Jerome J. McGann, for 'The Religious Poerty of Christina Rossetti', *Critical Inquiry*, 10 (Sept. 1983), 127–44, by permission of The University of Chicago Press; Dorthy Mermin, for 'The Damsel, the Knight and the Victorian Woman Poet', *Critical Inquiry*, 13 (Autumn 1986), 64–80, by permission of The University of Chicago Press.

Every effort has been made to trace all the copyright holders but if any have been inadvertently overlooked the publishers will be pleased to make the necessary arrangement at the first opportunity.

General Editors' Preface

The purpose of this series of New Casebooks is to reveal some of the ways in which contemporary criticism has changed our understanding of commonly studied texts and writers and, indeed, of the nature of criticism itself. Central to the series is a concern with modern critical theory and its effect on current approaches to the study of literature. Each New Casebook editor has been asked to select a sequence of essays which will introduce the reader to the new critical approaches to the text or texts being discussed in the volume and also illuminate the rich interchange between critical theory and critical practice that characterises so much current writing about literature.

In this focus on modern critical thinking and practice New Casebooks aim not only to inform but also to stimulate, with volumes seeking to reflect both the controversy and the excitement of current criticism. Because much of this criticism is difficult and often employs an unfamiliar critical language, editors have been asked to give the readers as much help as they feel is appropriate, but without simplifying the essays or the issues they raise. Again, editors have been asked to supply a list of futher reading which will enable readers to follow up issues raised by the essays in the volume.

The project of New Casebooks, then, is to bring together in an illuminating way those critics who best illustrate the ways in which contemporary criticism has established new methods of analysing texts and who have reinvigorated the important debate about how we 'read' literature. The hope is, of course, that New Casebooks will not only open up this debate to a wider audience, but will also encourage students to extend their own ideas, and think afresh about their responses to the texts they are studying.

John Peck and Martin Coyle
University of Wales, Cardiff

Introduction

JOSEPH BRISTOW

I

If the predicament of the Victorian woman poet might be characterised by any one statement, then it would seem to emerge most
forcefully in the famous declaration made by Elizabeth Barrett
Browning in a letter of 1845. 'I look everywhere for grandmothers',
she despondently observes, 'and see none'.[1] Written the year after
her two volumes of *Poems* received highly favourable reviews, this
memorable remark has led Dorothy Mermin to suggest that 'for
most practical purposes' Barrett Browning ranks as 'the first
woman poet in English literature'. Mermin carefully qualifies her
point by saying that Barrett Browning, born in 1806, was the first
woman to establish herself in the main English tradition (the one
that forms the literary consciousness of other poets and educated
readers of poetry)'.[2] Nothing could uphold this claim more completely than a comment made in the influential *Athenaeum* when
candidates were being sought to fill the post of Poet Laureate after
the death of William Wordsworth in 1850: '[W]e cannot help suggesting that in the reign of a youthful queen, if there be among her
subjects one of her own sex whom the laurel will fit, its grant to a
female would be at once testimonial to the individual, a fitting
recognition of the remarkable place which the women of England
have taken in the literature of the day, and a graceful compliment
to the Sovereign herself.' And the writer went on to add: 'there is no
living poet of either sex who can prefer a higher claim than Mrs

Elizabeth Barrett Browning.'[3] Even if Alfred Tennyson was finally elected to this prestigious post, such commentary is a sure sign of Barrett Browning's considerable standing in a literary world where women writers, more than ever before, had secured a professional foothold for themselves. But Barrett Browning is the 'first woman poet' in another sense as well. For it is in her writing that we discover a pronounced discontent with male chauvinism that would set the tone of much poetry by women in succeeding decades. In the Second Book of *Aurora Leigh*, the protagonist – herself a poet – has to contend with the following contemptuous comments passed upon her professional work by her cousin:

> 'Women as you are,
> Mere women, personal and passionate,
> You give us doating mothers, and perfect wives,
> Sublime Madonnas, and enduring saints!
> We get no Christ from you, – and verily
> We shall not get a poet, in my mind'
> (2.220–5)[4]

It is one of the major tasks of *Aurora Leigh* to show that the woman poet could indeed come into her own against such prejudice. Thus this spirited poem belongs to a discernible 'recreative poetic tradition', which Sandra M. Gilbert sees descending from Sappho and Christine de Pizan and leading in the twentieth century to Renée Vivien, H.D., and Adrienne Rich, among others. Barrett Browning's influence would certainly extend across the Atlantic to inspire the work of Emily Dickinson, while in Britain the force of her writing would most directly feed into the poetry of Christina Rossetti, not least where the female revision of traditionally male-dominated forms was concerned.

Late-twentieth-century feminism has something of a grandmother in Barrett Browning herself. Small wonder, then, that feminist literary criticism has been at the forefront of producing illuminating historical and theoretical contexts in which we may productively re-evaluate what counted among the most influential and widely-read works of poetry during the mid-nineteenth century. Indeed, practically all the essays contained in this volume have their basis in critical methods deriving from the resurgence of feminist politics in the late 1960s. But before examining some of the principles of these recent feminist approaches, it is worth pausing to consider why Barrett Browning felt bereft of a poetic tradition of her own. The main reason stems from the fact that the first developments of an organised feminist movement dated from roughly the time when she was drafting *Aurora Leigh*, itself a new kind of work, marking a new kind of poetry by women. As Barrett Browning notes in her correspondence, she had been reading Bessie Parkes's polemical essays on the 'woman question',[5] and Parkes was the leading light of the women of Langham Place who were among the first campaigners for the rights of women to professional employment.[6] The Victorian 'woman question' covered many currents of thought about women and professional work, female suffrage, single women, and prostitution, as well as the notorious restrictiveness of the doctrine of 'separate spheres' for the sexes which dominated bourgeois domestic ideology at this time. Materials on the 'woman question' have been gathered together in several useful anthologies, and they help to explain the marked discontent with the position of women that we find in the work of many female poets of this period.[7] Much more than in the previous century, educated women were under great pressure to consider why the achievements of their sex were so singularly undervalued. And, in many respects, subsequent literary criticism carried into the twentieth century a great deal of prejudiced thinking about much Victorian women's writing, which was often dismissed for being too sentimental, too limited in formal and intellectual range, and simply too out of date to speak meaningfully to a twentieth-century sensibility desperate to repudiate the worst offences of the Victorian frame of mind. Even though she established a distinctive form of poetry that won a host of admirers in her own time, shortly after her death in 1861 Barrett Browning would for many decades suffer much of the same fate as those grandmothers she sought but could not find. By the time Virginia Woolf was writing on *Aurora Leigh* in 1932, it was only too clear that Barrett Browning was disfavoured since she wrote in an outmoded idiom: 'Nobody reads her, nobody discusses her, nobody troubles to put her in her place ... In short, the only place in the mansion of literature that is assigned her is downstairs in the servants' quarters, where ... she bangs the crockery about and eats vast handfuls of peas on the point of a knife.'[8] Such comments surely prompt us to ask why a Victorian woman poet who once enjoyed great renown should by the 1930s have ended up in the basement of literary history. The first part of this Introduction considers how the cultural conditions of the mid-nineteenth century worked both for and against women poets as ambitious and accomplished as Barrett Browning, Emily Brontë, and Christina Rossetti.

Although each and every era is populated with numerous gifted women poets, almost all of them, one generation after another, have vanished into obscurity. Only through the offices of a scholar such as Roger Lonsdale have we recently been able to obtain a comprehensive picture of how many of Barrett Browning's poetic grandmothers there really were.[9] It is certainly the case that two influential 'mothers', so to speak, still maintained their readerships through the remainder of the nineteenth century. The works of Felicia Hemans (1793–1835) were reprinted on countless occasions right up until 1900, and her experiments with the dramatic monologue collected in *Records of Woman* (1829) would have far-reaching effects on the development of this poetic form throughout the nineteenth century.[10] But by far the most significant of these immediate predecessors for Barrett Browning was a writer four years her senior. Always known by her initials, L.E.L. (Laetitia Elizabeth Landon) was the author of several Byronic romances that have a powerful bearing on aspects of *Aurora Leigh*. In the developing tradition of poetry by Victorian women, the tragic life and sensational writing of L.E.L. would take on a legendary status, and her lingering presence in the poems of later women writers holds an important clue to some of the main concerns of the distinctly female tradition that would subsequently evolve. Found dead in her room at the slave-post of Cape Castle in Benin (to which she had, at the age of thirty-six, accompanied her newly-married husband two months before), L.E.L. was rumoured to have committed suicide (a bottle of prussic acid was supposedly found in her hand). News of her terrible death compounded the many scandals surrounding her comparatively successful career. For L.E.L. had not, to say the least, found it easy as a single woman to establish her professional reputation in the literary world of London. During the 1820s and 1830s, she had been the subject of damaging gossip about her close friendships with three well-known editors and journalists. Seemingly desperate to escape from the vilifications of her London contemporaries, L.E.L. hastily married Captain George McLean, only to discover on arrival in Africa that she was being treated like a household drudge. It would be left to her early-Victorian biographer, Laman Blanchard, to tell several tall tales about what exactly led to her death. But, as Angela Leighton points out, whatever the true circumstances of L.E.L.'s demise, the 'much publicised nature of her end only intensified the punishing moral which lies at the core of the myth'.[11]

That myth was a cautionary reminder about the severe problems into which L.E.L. ran when it came to being a woman, on the one hand, and a poet, on the other. The saddening example of L.E.L. showed that this apparently irreconcilable division between the two could lead only to death. But in her tribute to this poetic 'mother', published in 1844, Barrett Browning looks upon her poetic precursor with a not entirely uncritical eye. In 'L.E.L.'s Last Question', Barrett Browning disparages the monotonous writing of 'love and love' where 'All sounds of life assume one tune of love'. L.E.L.'s failure, according to Barrett Browning, lay in her inability to assume a public voice. Instead of asking 'Do you praise me, O my land?', L.E.L. continued to play her 'silver music' of love, waiting for approval from the world at large. 'Do you think of me as I think of you?' is the 'last question' to which the title of Barrett Browning's poem refers, and it is a question that strikes the younger poet as far too limited in its artistic ambitions. For, we are told, 'little, in the world, the Loving do' but expect the 'echo of their own love evermore'.[12] Given lines such as these, it does not take much to see that Barrett Browning is dissatisfied with the woman poet who only anticipates praise for those feminine skills in singing sweetly. 'L.E.L.'s Last Question', therefore, opposes the older poet's consoling lyricism by suggesting that its romantic idealism was the very thing that sent L.E.L. to her doom.

Indeed, Barrett Browning makes a similar criticism of L.E.L.'s artificial style in a poem dating from 1835. Entitled 'Felicia Hemans', the poem takes issue with the stanzas L.E.L. had recently dedicated to the memory of the late Hemans. Where L.E.L. seeks to sentimentalise Hemans, suggesting that her work freely expressed female suffering, Barrett Browning takes pains to show that Hemans's 'mystic breath ... / ... drew from rocky earth and man, abstractions high and moving'. On this view, Hemans was just as much a visionary poet as any of her male peers. To make her point, Barrett Browning chose a form and a style that were anything but smoothly lyrical. This rather awkwardly written poem – which, as Leighton observes, 'edges on the grotesque in its rough heptameters and over-ambitious abstractions' – ends on what might be read as a reproving, if not indecorous, note.[13] For in the final verse Barrett Browning hopes that her country will commemorate L.E.L. in precisely the same terms as L.E.L. has chosen to remember Hemans:

'May thine own England say for thee, what now for Her it sayeth –
/"Albeit softly in our ears her silver song was ringing,/The footfall
of her parting soul is softer than her singing".'[14] These closing lines
certainly indicate that for Hemans to be honoured for the 'softer'
qualities of one's soul does rather demean the achievements of her
standing as a poet. For many years hereafter, women poets would
continue to struggle with the acceptable feminine connotations
attached to the 'silver music' they were so often expected to sing.

In this respect, the tragic story of L.E.L. was subject to critical
revision by Barrett Browning's most significant heir, Christina
Rossetti, whose first volume of poetry, published in 1862, contains
a poem simply entitled 'L.E.L.' There Rossetti dramatises L.E.L.'s
'silver music' in a rather different mode. Perpetually fascinated by
the private emotions of women, Rossetti adds to the myth of
L.E.L. by voicing her anguish in the repeated line 'My heart is
breaking for a little love' – a refrain that revises and deepens the
strain of Barrett Browning's 'L.E.L.'s Last Question', where L.E.L.
is shown to be 'One thirsty for a little love'. First appearing in
Emily Faithfull's *Victoria Magazine* – a journal edited, printed, and
published by women – Rossetti's 'L.E.L.' accentuates the stark contrast between the 'sport and jest' (l.1) which the woman poet displays in public and the heartbreak she experiences in her 'solitary
room' (l.2). But rather than reprove L.E.L. for pouring her poetic
energies into the lyric sweetness of love, Rossetti has her own point
to make about the predicament of a woman denied the physical
affection she desires. For in her closing stanza, Rossetti announces
the voices of a saint and an angel who insist that the woman poet
must 'Take patience' because 'True best is last' (ll.36, 38).[15]
Committed at all times to the wisdom of Scripture, Rossetti not
uncommonly draws on those passages of the Gospels where Jesus
Christ declares that 'the last shall be first, and the first last' (see,
for example, Matthew 20:16). Acutely aware that many women
are not destined for carnal love on earth, Rossetti time and again
turns her reader's attention to the greater love of God that 'shall
fill thy girth,/ And ... make fat thy dearth' (ll.40–1). This unswerving belief in the superiority of divine over human love is elaborated
in many of Rossetti's poems, perhaps the best and most complex
example being 'The Lowest Room' where the speaker, a single
woman, compares her lot with that of her married sister who
enjoys all the benefits of a rewarding family life. In 'The Lowest
Room', which first appeared in *Macmillan's Magazine* in 1864, the

spinster has to 'learn/ That lifelong lesson of the past': the biblical lesson, that is, of what it means 'Not to be first' (ll.265–6). Everywhere we look in Rossetti's distinguished poetry, we find this lesson of deferred rewards set against the disappointments experienced by women who seek romantic love on earth. And even where women have traditionally been the objects of adoration in poetry, Rossetti suggests that they have to some extent been betrayed by their male suitors.

This point comes most clearly into focus in her preface to the 'sonnet of sonnets' entitled 'Monna Innominata', published in 1881. Partly modelled on the love poetry of Dante and Petrarch, and taking epigraphs from the works of each poet respectively, Rossetti's sequence gives a voice to one of the many 'unnamed ladies' whose praises were 'sung by a school of less conspicuous poets'. 'Had such a lady spoken for herself', writes Rossetti, 'the portrait left us might have appeared more tender, if less dignified, than any drawn even by a devoted friend.' One can detect some tension in the wording of this sentence, for there is surely anxiety here in representing the innermost feelings of a woman. In using an anonymous speaker to articulate a woman's private emotions, Rossetti is aware that what she may be gaining in tenderness she may equally be losing in dignity and moral respectability. Such cautiousness suggests that there were potential dangers for the middle-class woman poet when she turned her female speaker into a lover. Not surprisingly, then, these fourteen sonnets are fraught with contradictory impulses. Take, for example, the fourth poem in the sequence. No sooner has the woman speaker declared that she 'loved first' than her 'friendly cooings' are 'drowned' by the 'loftier song' of her male admirer (4.1–3). Similarly, her love was 'long' where his 'seemed to wax more strong' (4.4–5). Although, in the end, both recognise that 'Rich love knows nought of "thine that is not mine"' (4.12), the poem sustains a strained mood of hesitancy and apprehensiveness. Even if rituals of courtship necessarily involve anyone, man or woman, in states of confusion and uncertainty, Rossetti's persona repeatedly reveals that the expression of love is in itself hazardous. 'I loved and guessed at you', she remarks, 'you construed me/ And loved me for what might or might not be' (4.6–7). It would not be unreasonable to suspect that the happy outcome of their courtship could be put down to serendipity as much as anything else. In any case, however we choose to interpret this sonnet, it is clear to see that Rossetti has shifted the woman poet's writing of love far from the 'silver music' that Barrett Browning implicitly condemned in the work of L.E.L.

Much of the inspiration for 'Monna Innominata' came from Barrett Browning's *Sonnets from the Portuguese* (1850). Masquerading as a translated work, Barrett Browning's impressive sequence of forty-four Petrarchan sonnets obliquely refers to the love of the Portuguese poet Luis de Camões for Catarina, a lady of the court. In fact, the substance of the episodic narrative alludes to her own courtship with the poet Robert Browning during 1845–6, which would in time become something of a legend in itself. In her preface, Rossetti refers to the 'Portuguese Sonnets' written by the 'Great Poetess of our own day and nation'. But having duly praised her precursor, Rossetti subjects Barrett Browning to a criticism that bears not a little resemblance to Barrett Browning's critique of L.E.L.'s 'silver music'. Had Barrett Browning 'only been unhappy instead of happy', writes Rossetti, then 'her circumstances would have invited her to bequeath to us, in lieu of the "Portuguese Sonnets", an inimitable "donna innominata" drawn not from fancy but from feeling.' Sensing that Barrett Browning's poems are some-what artificial in their sentiment, Rossetti seeks to lend realism to the emotional life of the woman whose voice had yet to be heard within the canons of European poetry.[16] And in dramatising the speech of those 'unnamed ladies' celebrated by countless sonneteers in previous ages, Rossetti was devising a form in which a Victorian woman could be understood as one who had the capacity not just to be a passive object of amorous attention but to take the active role of a lover as well.

Rossetti's ambition to speak of a woman's 'feeling' rather than mere 'fancy' led her work increasingly towards introspection, medi-tation, and devotionalism. Where Barrett Browning's poetry became more and more assertive in its public voice – from its courageous use of 'woman's figures' (*Aurora Leigh*, 8.1131) to its less reputable praise of Louis Napoleon III's invasion of Italy in *Poems before Congress* (1860) – Rossetti's later writings were largely religious in subject-matter, tone and sentiment. Although Rossetti's High Anglican faith shapes many aspects to her earliest poetry from the late 1840s onwards, the poems gathered in *Verses* (1893) are com-pletely dedicated to Christian doctrine and festivals. By the time of her death in 1894, Rossetti was often thought of as an exclusively religious writer. Among her books, after all, were several meditative prose works for the Society for the Promotion of Christian

Knowledge. Although these prose writings are to all intents and purposes orthodox works of religious contemplation, modern readers have found in them traces of radical thinking, not least when it comes to the position of Eve in the Christian legend of the Fall. Diane D'Amico points out how in *Letter and Spirit: Notes on the Commandments* (1883) we discover 'the biblical record left enough room for Rossetti to offer an interpretation in Eve's favour'.[17] For there we read that Eve, 'that first and typical woman ... indulging quite innocently sundry refined tastes and aspirations ... [displayed] a feminine boldness and directness of aim combined with a no less feminine guessiness as to means. Her very virtues may have opened the door to temptation.'[18] But Rossetti herself would be rarely credited with the 'feminine boldness' she herself imagined in the figure of Eve. When her *Poetical Works* were published by Macmillan in 1904, her readers could only gain a somewhat negative perspective on her achievement as a writer from the rather condescending memoir furnished by her brother and executor, William Michael Rossetti. There he takes pains to point out how utterly self-abnegating his sister was in their closely-knit family circle. 'For all her kith and kin', he writes, 'but for her mother far beyond all the rest, her love was as deep as it was often silent.' Emphasising her shyness, he somewhat bluntly adds: 'Upon her reputation as a poetess, she never presumed, nor did she ever volunteer an allusion to any of her performances: in a roomful of mediocrities she consented to seem the most mediocre as the most unobtrusive of all.'[19] He wants us to believe that Rossetti did her utmost to shy away from the considerable fame she had won by the mid-1860s. But even if trying to enforce the idea that his sister was not in any respect outwardly special, this extract from William Michael Rossetti's memoir makes a rather contrary impression. To be the 'most mediocre' and 'most unobtrusive of all' may well suggest that she made herself only too noticeable through her reticence. It is certainly this rather eccentric image that captivated Woolf in her short essay entitled 'I Am Christina Rossetti'.[20]

Yet there is perhaps something to be learned about her poetry from the wilfully resigned attitude Rossetti chose to strike. Many of her poems, after all, are preoccupied with issues of secrecy and silence. Indeed, she derives her greatest poetic energy from exploring enclosed forms of female subjectivity, and she examines the experience of being shut out or cut off from the world around her in a mood of striking defiance. 'The Thread of Life', published in 1881,

provides a good example of Rossetti's surprising analysis of the
'prison' of female selfhood (2.1). Giving voice to a speaker who feels
'aloof' and 'bound with the flawless band/ Of inner solitude' (1.5–6),
the poem insists on the impossibility of ever belonging to the 'merry-
making crew' (2.9). One would reasonably expect the poem to
become more and more despondent in tone, given that the speaker's
sense of painful solitude deepens in one line after another. Yet in
Rossetti's writing, to find oneself apart from the community is not
necessarily to feel disempowered or at a loss. For there is, she
argues, no release at any time from the 'self-chain' that binds oneself
to oneself (1.7). Thus the 'prison' of subjectivity is in fact one's 'sole
possession' (3.3). Once recognised in this way, the necessarily embattled self discovers that its very condition allows the possibility of
emphatically declaring 'I am even I' (2.14). It is not uncharacteristic
of Rossetti to show how feelings of exclusion can be resourcefully
transformed into the language of self-assertion. Much of the ingenu-
ity of her writing lies in the resilient manner in which her female
personae come to see how their deep feelings of exclusion are
founded in principles of self-worth. By the close of the 'The Thread
of Life', the woman speaker declares that her 'sole possession' is
God's gift, with whom she shall be reunited at the Last Day.

But teasing out the intellectual complexities of Rossetti's writing
occurred only long after her death. Even in 1972, it was perfectly
possible for Lionel Stevenson, a highly respected scholar of
Victorian poetry, to write that Rossetti's work disappointingly 'contains a minimum of intellectual substance'.[21] Such a view is entirely
continuous with the critical perspectives offered by many commentaries on her writing that date from earlier in the twentieth
century. In an autobiographical essay charting how she became a
feminist reader, Isobel Armstrong examines how and why during
the 1950s contributors to the influential Pelican Guides to English
Literature resorted to a constraining vocabulary to blame rather
than praise Rossetti's poetry. 'Simplicity, modesty, delicacy, good
taste, good manners, shy reserve, tenderness, truthfulness, limited
pretensions, touching sincerity, ladylikeness – all these epithets',
observes Armstrong, 'are in effect coercive.'[22] The regular deployment of demeaning adjectives such as these meant that for years
Rossetti could rarely be understood as anything other than feminine in its most blameworthy Victorian sense. Writing in 1958,
W.W. Robson remarked that it was surely 'significant that one finds
oneself appraising her work in these negative terms'.[23] Such quali-

ties were not always viewed with disdain. Among Rossetti's contemporaries, simplicity and expressiveness counted among the most
distinguished features of her work. But, even then, the manner in
which her Victorian readers praised these attributes set a serious
limit on the ambitions of her work. Reviewing her first four
volumes in 1887 for the *London Quarterly Review*, for example,
Arthur Symons declared that the 'secret' of Rossetti's characteristic
style lay in her 'sincerity, leading to the employment of homely
words where homely words are wanted, and always of natural and
really expressive words'. Yet, he would add, this use of simple language created the 'union of homely yet always select literalness of
treatment with mystical visionaries, or visionariness which is sometimes mystical'.[24] The fact that Symons takes recourse on several
occasions to the adjective 'homely' as a term of praise indicates how
closely Rossetti's writing was associated with the 'proper' domestic
sphere of femininity. In 1891, however, Richard Le Gallienne
would rightly object to the 'obtuseness' of the term 'poetess', stating
that genius transcended the gender of the artist. Such a standpoint
enables him to place Rossetti in the main tradition of English
poetry, regarding her as a 'native descendant of the magician of
"Kubla Khan"', Samuel Taylor Coleridge. Yet, in exalting
Rossetti's supreme lyricism above all her other talents, Le Gallienne
fails to consider the intellectual power of her writing. 'A gift of
simple singing, an artless perfection of art, a pulse of unpremeditated passion, an ideal spiritual exaltation – all these powers',
writes Le Galliene, 'go to the making of these poems, with a spontaneity in their exercise rare indeed in our self-conscious age.'[25] So
keen is Le Gallienne to emphasise the expressive power of Rossetti's
poetry that he draws attention to how her 'artlessness' – which he
knows is a pejorative term – aptly describes the impressive lack
of pretension in these exuberant and plainly written works. It
is a paradoxical evaluation, for it consigns Rossetti's skills to
qualities that one might readily regard as flaws in the works of
other writers.

It would take many years before detailed reassessments of
Rossetti's writing emerged, and these altogether different readings
were to suggest that she was articulating states of consciousness
that were not quite as artless or unpremeditated as some of her
Victorian readers believed them to be. By the late 1970s, a group of
diverse feminist perspectives were shedding light on the sexual, historical, and political aspects of some of Rossetti's better known

poems. In this context, Sandra Gilbert, Susan Gubar, Cora Kaplan, and Ellen Moers were among the first feminist interpreters to explore the strange fantasmatic world of 'Goblin Market' (1862), the disturbing fairy-tale that has subsequently been discussed more than any other of Rossetti's works. In this poem, two sisters are tempted to buy the fruit of each goblin 'merchant man' (l.70). Laura succumbs, while Lizzie resists. Consequently, the tempted sister famishes, and almost expires from the pain. Salvation arrives when Lizzie confronts the goblins, who do their utmost to make her eat the fruit. After subjecting her to torment, they finally leave Lizzie when it becomes clear that she cannot be force-fed. On Lizzie's return home, Laura licks off the fruit that the goblins have brutally smeared across her face. (Indeed, their attack on her is tantamount to an attempted rape.) At this point, the fruit juice miraculously transubstantiates into a 'fiery antidote' (l.559) that restores Laura to her former health. The poem closes with a few words on how these girls grow up to be mothers, teaching their children that there is '"no friend like a sister"' (l.562). Although we must assume in the final section of the poem that Laura and Lizzie are happily married women, at no point do we glimpse their husbands. Thus many critics have noted that this disturbing and alluring narrative – replete with erotic overtones and religious symbolism – contains no positive or approving images of men.

In the most sophisticated of these early feminist readings, Kaplan begins her analysis by discussing how Rossetti and Emily Dickinson use fantasy as a means of exploring distinctly feminine psychological states. Noting how such poems often resist paraphrase, she suggests that other critical methods are required to comprehend how 'dreamform ... either directly stated or implied, becomes an important means of presenting distorted or unclear images with impunity'. Aware that there are dangers in either binding the works of writers into biographical speculations or mistakenly integrating them into pregiven psychoanalytic models of interpretation, Kaplan insists that we must become aware of how these 'texts speak to and about psychic phenomena in ways that are unique in women's writing of the period'. So it follows that Kaplan can claim that 'Goblin Market' 'undoubtedly remains an exploration of women's sexual fantasy which includes suggestions of masochism, homoeroticism, rape or incest'.[26] To be sure, in its exploratory narrative of feasting and famishing upon the goblins' poisonous fruit, the poem gives very free rein indeed to forms of religious and sexual symbolism. But, as countless recent commentaries on 'Goblin Market' attest, the poem refuses to be moulded into a straightforward allegory of either the Fall of Man or female sexualisation. What appears most innocent in this narrative has the troubling potential to be genuinely transgressive.

The sexual suggestiveness of 'Goblin Market' has undoubtedly made it a compelling work for feminist readers concerned with what constitutes a distinctly female imagination. Gilbert and Gubar immediately seize on how, in this narrative of female resistance to male authority, 'Rossetti does ... seem to be dreamily positing an effectively matrilineal and matriarchal world, perhaps even, considering the strikingly sexual redemption scene between the sisters, a covertly (if ambivalently) lesbian world.'[27] If the latter comment seems far-fetched, then it should be borne in mind that in 1973 Rossetti's poem was reprinted, with titillating illustrations, in the soft-porn magazine *Playboy*.[28] This extraordinary appropriation of a poem that has been reprinted time and again in editions aimed at children is intriguing, since it makes us question the extent to which 'Goblin Market' exhibits either a striking knowingness or utter innocence of sexual behaviour. But there are, indeed, historical difficulties with attempts to explain the sexual elements of this remarkable poem from a cultural position informed by Freudian and related kinds of psychoanalytic thought that have done much to consolidate our sense of normative and perverse forms of sexual identification. Subsequent criticism has suggested that the term 'lesbian' is not apposite for the woman-to-woman affections to be found in a work produced in a period when that term did not specify a type of sexual being. Instead, it may seem more advisable to examine how the idea of sisterhood – which is in many ways the focus of 'Goblin Market' – brings together a range of familial and religious meanings that had a special amplitude for a Victorian writer such as Rossetti, in ways that may be obscure to modern readers. Yet any attempt to historicise the desires we find in a poem such as this one needs to be alert to what Lilian Faderman sees as the 'revolutionary potential' in the sisterly relationship that Rossetti depicts.[29] Faderman's point is that we have to be cautious in making any claim that same-sex eroticism does not exist in this poem simply because Victorian readers were unable to see it – and thus condemn it.

This issue raises one highly significant difficulty for late-twentieth-century readers of poetry by Victorian women, since the struggles of such poets for self-representation may seem only too clearly to coincide with our own modern preoccupations with equal opportunities for men and women in all spheres of life. There have indeed been many intractable problems with early forms of feminist criticism that believe poetry by Victorian women anticipates some of the central beliefs of the Women's Liberation Movement, as it developed through the 1970s. The most problematic issue concerns the elevation of the idea that there was a tradition of women's writing that must be recognised as wholly independent from the culture at large. Critical separatism of this kind can be hazardous. Margaret Reynolds cautions feminist readers against establishing ideals of a separate sphere for women's experience, since such beliefs can be founded on precepts that in the Victorian period ensured that women were safely allotted to the private and domestic realm, and thus removed from serious consideration as artists in their own right. Consequently, argues Reynolds, a 'dangerous feminist folk-poetics is ... created – dangerous because it is, in fact, not more than a restatement of the classic values relating to women and poetry'. She sums up the main stumbling-blocks of such an approach as follows: 'Feminist folk-poetics privileges women's experience, especially identifying an oppression common to all women (not allowing scope for their cultural, historical, and ethnic differences); it values the experience of the "self" (unproblematised in all but its contingent relation to patriarchy); it traces a "female" tradition (without any consciousness of the possible interference of a wish fulfilment) inherited from our mothers (qualified to endow by simple biology) which is usually an oral tradition (and consequently without trace) and often a mysterious one, related to a spiritual and moral sphere (which returns women's poetry to its conventional place).'[30] In other words, feminist criticism needs to be wary of duplicating many of the damaging assumptions about femininity that have been long embedded in Western society, and which have done much to consign a marginal place to the cultural achievements of women.

Some of these objections have been levelled at one of the monumental works of feminist criticism dating from the late 1970s. In her attack on the reactionary humanist assumptions informing the work of some Anglo-American feminist critics, Toril Moi remarks that Gilbert and Gubar's *The Madwoman in the Attic* (1979) presents an uncritical 'belief in the true female authorial voice as the essence of all texts written by women'. Moi claims that this belief dangerously 'masks the problems raised by their theory of patriarchal ideology', since '[f]or them ... ideology becomes a monolithic unified totality that knows no contradictions; against this a miraculously intact "femaleness" may pit its strength'.[31] Even if, on reflection, Moi may be somewhat overstating her case, her comments are certainly true in one respect. There is indeed a strong tendency in Gilbert and Gubar's imposing work to foreground the dynamic of self-assertion that we can readily identify in a poem such as *Aurora Leigh* without quite seeing how the creative self that is being established in a narrative of this kind achieves its aims because of its class disposition. Concentrating their minds on the empowerment of the female self, they write: 'Aurora's self-development as a poet is the central concern of Barrett Browning's *Bildungsroman* in verse, but if she is to be a poet she must deconstruct the dead self that is a male "opus" and discover a living "inconstant" self.'[32] What is omitted from their often persuasive analysis is how this narrative of self-development belongs very much to the bourgeois ideology to which Barrett Browning's male peers were espoused. One main current of mid-Victorian liberal ideology, after all, was the doctrine of self-help. This significant current in Victorian ideas underpinned the work of many Victorian women writers, such as Charlotte Brontë, in their desire to represent scenes of female autonomy.

This observation, however, should not serve as an excuse to divert attention away from what is distinctively female in Barrett Browning's aesthetics. There is no doubt that *Aurora Leigh* was exceptionally challenging in its unorthodox use of figurations modelled on the female body. One only has to look at the reviews of the poem to see the amount of consternation they could cause. Writing in the liberal-minded *Westminster Review*, W.C. Roscoe is clearly taken aback by the following passage in the Fifth Book:

> Never flinch,
> But still, unscrupulously epic, catch
> Upon the burning lava of a song
> The full-veined, heaving, double-breasted Age:
> That, when the next shall come, the men of that
> May touch the impress with reverent hand, and say
> 'Behold, – behold the paps we all have sucked!'
> (5.213–22)

The poet's imperative to 'catch the burning lava of a song' in the image of a volcanic woman's bosom made for Roscoe a 'contrast' that was 'almost savage'. 'Burning lava and a woman's breast!', he indignantly exclaimed, 'and concentrated in the latter the fullest ideas of life. It is absolute pain to read it.' Such sentiments he found tinged with a 'sort of forward familiarity', and the 'uneasiness' he felt when encountering this imagery convinced him that '[n]o man could have written it'.[33] This response surely indicates the moral risks Barrett Browning was taking in this ambitious narrative of a gifted woman poet who, like herself, achieves fame and fortune in London.

But, as Deirdre David points out in her contribution to this volume (essay 4), this excerpt should not be read as an entirely idealistic expression of female creative power. In terms of Aurora Leigh's attitude to sexual difference, the lines are perhaps more conflicted than we might initially believe. 'This mammocentric imagery' argues David, 'is ambiguous.' And she continues: 'Aurora, the woman poet, rather peculiarly figures the poet's task in conventionally male terms – as unflinching, aggressive work – and she makes the subject of the poet almost primordially female – full-veined, heaving, double-breasted.'[34] In general, David regards the whole trajectory of this narrative as quite reactionary, suggesting throughout that Aurora Leigh's model of poetic creation presses a 'woman's art' into the moral service of the patriarchy. Indeed, she argues that the doctrine of poetic labour that we find championed in many sections of this poem in fact derives directly from Thomas Carlyle's influential writings on the fundamental meanings of work in all human endeavour. Similarly, the visionary belief in poets as the 'last truth-tellers now left to God' (1.859) places Aurora Leigh very much within the lineage of male Romantic poets to whose ideals she frequently aspires. Yet, even if Barrett Browning's protagonist is not entirely opposed to the male-orientated poetic ideology in which she is working, her narrative broaches new understandings of female creativity. Especially alert to Barrett Browning's innovative female symbolism, Kaplan points to the lines in Book 1 which tell us how Aurora Leigh at the age of thirteen 'suddenly awoke / To full life and life's needs and agonies/ With an intense, strong, struggling heart' (1.205–7). 'Discreet as this passage may sound now', observes Kaplan, 'it is probably the closest any English woman writer had come to an explicit reference to menstruation and the stirrings of sexual desire.'[35] To be sure, the courage of such lines cannot be underestimated.

At first glance, Barrett Browning's commitment to producing distinctly female figurations feels altogether more modern than the sparely written and at times obscure stanzas that we find in the volume entitled *Poems by Currer, Ellis, and Acton Bell,* published ten years before in 1846. In part, the Brontës' idiom feels older. Much of their impressive collection defines itself against the works of the major Romantic poets. Echoes of Byron, Coleridge, Shelley, and Wordsworth are found everywhere in it. But to suggest that the Brontës' poetry should simply be understood as a belated footnote to the achievements of Romantic luminaries can only belittle their specific poetic engagement with a culture which, in the 1830s and 1840s, was becoming more responsive to the distinctive power of women's writing. The Brontës, needless to say, are generally remembered as Victorian novelists, and their prose fictions are often upheld to characterise representative bourgeois responses to the structural transformations that English society was undergoing in the decade in which they were writing. So it needs to be borne in mind that their poems, if written in forms that are conspicuously more taut than those generally employed by Barrett Browning, share very similar preoccupations when it comes to where gender figures in the identity of the poet.

In any case, the Brontës' famous decision to use implicitly male pseudonyms surely suggests that to be read as a woman poet could interfere with the value laid upon a literary work. For a short period, their true identities remained unknown. *Poems* preceded *Jane Eyre* by 'Currer Bell' by one year. Towards the end of 1847, *Wuthering Heights* by 'Ellis Bell' and *Agnes Grey* by 'Acton Bell' were being sent out for review. The usual reason given to explain these writers' decision to pass as male authors lies in a comment made by Charlotte Brontë in the 'Biographical Notice' she furnished for the 1850 joint edition of her sisters' first novels. Aware that critics patronised 'authoresses', they were keen to ensure that their readers assumed their 'mode of writing was not what is called "feminine"'. But no sooner had these novels been put out on sale than critics were beginning to speculate that they must indeed be the work of women writers. Only in July 1848 did Charlotte Brontë and Anne Brontë reveal their true identities to their publisher, George Smith. Immediately London was rife with rumours about who was the real 'Currer Bell', and not before long Charlotte Brontë would become something of a celebrity in the metropolitan literary world. Given the circumstances surrounding the publication and reception of their works, it goes without saying that the issue of gender was central to the production of literary writing at this time.

Altogether less obvious, as Margaret Homans observes (essay 3), is
the thinking behind Charlotte Brontë's comment that their work
should not be considered 'feminine': 'If Charlotte means that later
on they did come to understand that their writing was now "what
is called 'feminine'" it is not clear whether she welcomes this distinction, thinking of "the poetry women generally write", or
whether this distinction was an affront to her sense of identity and
integrity as a woman.'[36]

This point is worth considering at some length, since in their
work the Brontës – for all the diversity between each of their styles
– continually throw into question exactly what constitutes the 'feminine'. In the poetry of Emily Brontë, this issue is extremely vexed,
since her speakers frequently evince a strong identification with
structures of masculine authority. Indeed, many of the works included in *Poems* of 1846 represent personae who are struggling to
locate themselves within a male-defined tradition of visionary
writing inherited directly from the Romantics. But does this mean
that 'Ellis Bell' sought to write like a man? Or are these writings
questioning certain masculine assumptions about the nature of
poetic inspiration and the visionary power claimed by so many
male Romantics? Take, for example, 'The Philosopher'. Structured
as a dialogue between a philosopher and a seer, this complicated
poem counterpoints the voices of reason and vision. In many respects, this is a very commonplace debate between the powers of ratiocination and those of creativity that one can find in a host of late
eighteenth- and early nineteenth-century poems. Here the seer
berates the philosopher for his introspection: 'Too long hast thou
been dreaming/ Unenlightened' (l.3). The seer is right, since the
philosopher declares that he was wracked with internal torments:
'Three gods, within this little frame,/ Are warring night and day'
(ll.17–18). Implying that the godhead is disintegrating within his
soul, the philosopher listens to the wisdom of the seer, who recalls
how a 'spirit sent his dazzling gaze' to blend three rivers of prismatic yellow, blue, and red into pure white light. But such remarks
cannot console the philosopher, who closes the poem by raising his
'coward cry' for death (l.47).

What might we make of this ending? On the face of it, the poem
is stating that the visionary power of the seer is greater by far than
the dry reason of the anguished philosopher. But the dialogic movement of 'The Philosopher' is altogether more deceptive in establishing this point than we might at first imagine. In fact, the ostensible

distinction between the two parties begins to collapse when we hear the philosopher yearning for the 'time' when he 'shall sleep/ Without identity' (ll.7–8). Although he is adamant to annihilate himself, it is the case that the 'wild desires' (l.11) and 'quenchless fires' (l.13) that he continually suffers actually constitute who he is. Identity, in other words, is internally structured by these violent impulses. These fiery desires comprise what he later calls his 'present entity' (l.22). It is not that the philosopher lacks any kind of agency in this world. Instead, he would seem to have too much of it. That is perhaps why the philosopher has sufficient will to wish death upon himself. The seer, in the meantime, does not appear to play an active role in the universe he inhabits. Rather than intervene in his world, he refers to the visionary actions of an unnamed 'spirit' that pieces together those warring forces that threaten to tear the philosopher apart. It might be argued, then, that the seer exists in a state devoid of identity and 'thought'. His condition is simply to watch and wait. It may well be that the seer's visionariness is not necessarily superior or preferable to the agonised voice who possesses a 'sentient soul' and 'living breath' (l.52). But the provisional tone of my commentary should signal how difficult it is to resolve some of the obscurer reaches of this poem. Given its intellectual power, Emily Brontë's poetry remains strikingly resistant to interpretative closure. Instead, her poems drive at the centre of the main questions of knowledge, reason, and vision that fascinated the major male Romantic poets, whose work she had very fully absorbed. But, as Armstrong's opening essay in this volume shows, this is not the only context in which to understand the rationale motivating Brontë's demanding lyrics and verse narratives.

II

In her analysis of the expressive aesthetic explored by many women poets from the 1830s onwards, Armstrong reads 'The Philosopher' as a poem about difference and confinement where 'identity is violently at war'. Emphasising how the question of sexual difference actually becomes noticeable by virtue of its absence, Armstrong argues that here 'the violence of a universe constituted through rigid categories of difference, whether spiritual, moral or sexual, needs to be "lost"'.[37] Indeed, Armstrong claims there is a wilful impulse in this poem to withdraw any 'feminine' associations to the inspirational spirit celebrated by the seer, since such a figure would be conventionally associated with the female muse. Instead, Brontë insists that the 'spirit' is a man. The force of Armstrong's reading drives at further suggestive areas of intellectual struggle at work within what is, on the face of it, a quite simply constructed poem. But like many of the lyrics analysed in Armstrong's discussion of poetry by Victorian women, 'The Philosopher' employs quite commonplace language to extremely complex ends.

If one thread links together the vast range of women poets whose writings Armstrong places under careful scrutiny, it is precisely their continuous exploitation of the special capacity of poetry to express feeling that had been highly praised in the 1830s by John Stuart Mill. To be sure, Mill's interest in the interaction between thought and feeling would make a lasting impression on the specific purpose of poetry in the Victorian period. In 'Thoughts on Poetry and Its Varieties' (1867), Mill would comment that '[w]hat constitutes the poet is not the imagery nor the thoughts, nor even the feelings, but the law according to which they are called up'.[38] In other words, poetry organised the relationship between emotion and cognition in a manner that was discrete from the systematic logic embedded in scientific reasoning. As W. David Shaw comments in his study of Victorian aesthetics: 'Mill is one of the few Victorian philosophers to take art no less seriously than science and logic as a means of enlarging knowledge and of discovering repressed or forgotten truths.'[39] This observation has a significant bearing on how we might comprehend the activity of much expressive poetry by Victorian women, since the apparent simplicity of this style of writing – a style that often uses the form of the hymn or the apostrophising lyric – can make such work appear as if it is lacking in thought.Yet the more we analyse Brontë's and Rossetti's intensely controlled stanzas, in particular, the more they shake our expectations from one line to another. In this respect, 'The Philosopher' is assuredly a philosophical poem – one that keeps pushing against the limits of conceptual possibilities.

But if the Victorian woman poet could find a niche within the lyric tradition generally favoured by critics and male poets alike, she was constrained by the gendered connotations attached to that selfsame expressive aesthetic. This is precisely the difficulty that Mermin explores in her comparative readings of poems by Barrett Browning, Rossetti, and Brontë (essay 2). She demonstrates how their wholehearted wish to participate in literary tradition occurred at a time when 'writing poetry seemed like woman's work'. In making this point, Mermin is focusing on how the favoured emphasis on expressive lyricism increasingly became associated with the feminine domain: a world in which emotion had full rein over ratiocination. Feminine sweetness would become one of the most highly praised qualities of Alfred Tennyson's writing, as a significant review by Coventry Patmore attests.[40] 'The enormous popularity of Tennyson's *In Memoriam* [1850]', writes Mermin, 'owed a great deal to the scenes of domestic pathos – widows, widowers, grieving mothers, and the like – that belong in women's sphere.'[41] This point has been teased out at some length in an essay by Carol T. Christ, which explores the prevailing femininity – both of style and of subject-matter – in much poetry by Victorian men.[42] The Pre-Raphaelite poets Dante Gabriel Rossetti and Algernon Charles Swinburne most fully exploited lyric styles whose incantatory rhythms and feminine endings frequently serve to elevate sensuous female icons. Their work would set certain precedents for the effeminate mannerisms later championed by the protagonists of the Aesthetic Movement in the 1880s, such as Oscar Wilde. That is not to say that there were no dissenting voices to this manifest feminisation of poetry. Robert Browning, who gained notoriety for his robust if not 'grotesque' choice of poetic vocabulary, would remonstrate against the 'effeminacy' of Rossetti's school.[43] The point is that this perception was increasingly widespread by the 1870s. In some respects, one can see this shift towards feminisation within the poetic sphere as the result of more general changes in the structure of Victorian cultural production, where poetry found itself disorientated in a world where some of its guiding precepts – such as the visionariness championed by Romantic writers – seemed altogether less persuasive than they had been in the late eighteenth century. One of the commonplaces of modern criticism has been that Victorian poetry suffered from an 'alien vision',[44] and later commentators have suggested that poetry of the period became culturally marginalised.[45] Both are debatable points. But the upshot of such insights is that women were particularly affected by the gendering of the genre – to the degree that, as Mermin puts it, the 'association of poetry and femininity ... excluded women poets'.[46] It is not that women were unable to write (which would, of course, be nonsense). Rather, Mermin's insight suggests that it was sometimes hard for the woman poet to find a space from which to speak that did not demand that her work was forever embedded in those negative assumptions about femininity which her poetry was frequently attempting to subvert.

Mermin's discussion serves as a useful introduction to many of the issues that Margaret Homans explores in her study of male visitants who enter Brontë's poetry (essay 3). Drawing on aspects of psychoanalytic thought, Homans examines how Brontë 'defends herself from the danger of becoming a feminine object by aligning her poetic self with the stage in feminine development in which the mother is rejected in favour of a turn toward masculine objects'. The problem, however, for Brontë is that this 'turn cannot become an identity'.[47] For it is not unusual for Brontë's speakers to find that whenever they attempt to assert their power over this masculine muse – who at times presents himself as a comforter, at others as a destroyer – he eventually manages to vanquish them. 'The Night-Wind', dating from 1840, depicts this scenario most completely. Here a 'soft wind' (l.96) seeks to seduce the speaker. Even if the wind is not given a male pronoun, its masculine authority is implied in its 'wooing voice' (l.18). It is as if the speaker is being courted by an intimate power that waves her hair, whispers in her ear, and makes its kiss grow warm upon her cheek. At first, she resists its advances: '"Go gentle singer"', she declares, '"Thy wooing voice is kind/ But do not think its music/ Has power to reach my mind"' (ll.17–20). But no matter how much she protests to this 'Wanderer' (l.25), its powers of seduction gradually overwhelm her. '"I'll win thee against thy will"' (l. 28), it declares. And it does. Intensifying its threats, the wind announces that it shall outlive her. Long after her body has been laid in the graveyard, this Wanderer shall 'have time enough to mourn' (l.36). Since his 'song' emerges from the silence of the night, this 'gentle singer' can only continue his music as long as the female speaker is dead. If we build on Homans's suggestive analysis, such lines prompt us to consider how Brontë sensed that the largely male poetic tradition in which she was working demanded the negation of a woman's voice. But the poem, of course, admits other interpretative possibilities – such as Irene Tayler's more orthodox suggestion that 'The Night-Wind' concludes with 'a jolting *carpe diem*' whereby the wind commands the speaker to 'embrace earthly pleasures now'.[48] The deathly note on which the poem ends, however, makes it seem difficult indeed to accept the wind's advice to live for the moment. Death, I would suggest, has finally annihilated Brontë's initially resistant female speaker.

The issue of poetic inspiration lies at the centre of the generally divergent readings of *Aurora Leigh* presented in the next two essays by Deirdre David and Sandra Gilbert respectively (essays 4 and 5). Given that David finds 'male terms' configured even within Barrett Browning's controversial 'mammocentric imagery', it is not surprising to discover her conclusion that the poem depicts 'a woman's voice speaking patriarchal discourse – boldly, passionately, and without rancour'. David focuses our attention on Barrett Browning's avowed belief in her correspondence that women were intellectually inferior to men, a view that at first glance would seem to clash with the creative prowess of Aurora Leigh herself. But David's point is that this vibrant female protagonist can only discover fulfilment by 'melting the purity of art and sexuality ... into [her cousin] Romney's vision'.[49] The marriage between the two that marks the culmination of the narrative is completely of a piece with the most enthralling kinds of Victorian romantic fiction. Yet the degree to which the drive for emotional satisfaction diminishes the feminist ambitions that we can often witness in Aurora Leigh's art remains a source of considerable dispute. Gilbert, by contrast, amasses a remarkable amount of evidence to indicate how Aurora Leigh does her utmost to challenge Romney Leigh's 'authoritarianism', pointing out that he regards his cousin's poetry as mere '"woman's work"' (2.234) because she exists '"as the complement/ Of his sex merely"' (2.435–6). Little wonder, then, that so much of the first book of the poem places an emphasis on the need for 'mother-love' as a means of tempering the emotional cruelty of detested kinds of masculine behaviour. There is, without doubt, plenty of material in *Aurora Leigh* to support Gilbert's view that the protagonist derives distinctly female forms of strength from her mother's Italian line of descent. But by 1860, when *Poems before Congress* appeared, the more Barrett Browning contemplated the much desired unification of a female-identified (and idealised) Italy, the more it seemed that this ideal could only be realised by the intervention of the very kind of authoritarian masculine force she had been so ready to resist in *Aurora Leigh*. Gilbert claims that in praising Louis Napoleon III as 'Emperor/Evermore' Barrett Browning was 'admitting the dependence of the matriarchal south on the patriarchal language of the rigid north'.[50] So even if Gilbert lends a very different kind of emphasis to the resources of female creativity to be found in Barrett Browning's work, her concluding remarks have a not insignificant congruence with the general line of argument pursued by David.

The two essays that follow, by Jerome J. McGann and Elizabeth K. Helsinger (essays 6 and 7), focus on Christina Rossetti's poetry, and here, too, the Victorian woman poet's desire for an idealised world of her own comes to the fore in both analyses. Analysing some of the chief components of Rossetti's religious poetry, McGann focuses on how Rossetti's work adheres to the adventist theology of William Dodsworth through which she was able to devise her unique and disquieting vision of 'Soul Sleep'. Although Rossetti never used this term anywhere in her writings,[51] it is certainly the case that many of her lyrics explore complex dream-visions of how after death the soul waits in a state of suspension that shall only come to an end at the Last Day – when God and humankind are finally reunited. McGann's persuasive argument is that the complicated manner in which Rossetti imagines states of dreaming after death permits her to admit her dissatisfactions with worldly life by expressing her yearning for spiritual rewards, and his discussion points towards one of the most vexed areas of her writing. First of all, this perspective on Soul Sleep enables us to see how Rossetti employs a quite specific Christian doctrine to legitimate her own poetic vision – to join, in fact, the visionary tradition that Brontë also sought to enter. But, at the same time, her work is constantly haunted by fears of the 'vanity' of human wishes denounced in Ecclesiastes (1:2). Even in a poem such as 'Sleep at Sea', where the sleepers aboard the ship are being driven forward towards their heavenly destiny, we are reminded that 'Vanity is the end/ Of all their ways' (ll.87–8). Internal to many of her poems is a rigorous force of doctrinal self-examination that is quick to undercut any false idealism or mark of indulgence. That is why the well known lyric beginning 'When I am dead my dearest' proves to be so equivocal in the attitude it strikes towards death. In that ostensibly simple poem, the woman speaker who charges her lover not to sing any 'sad songs' (l.2) for her after she is dead and buried sounds a paradoxical note when she declares she may 'haply' remember or 'haply' forget the man who has loved her (ll.7, 8, 15, 16). Soul Sleep, in other words, may be a realm of loss as much as it is one of spiritual recuperation. In Rossetti's haunting dreamscapes, the afterlife which she glimpses time and again seems in many ways rather like the world from which her speakers strive to escape. In such a distant universe there too may be betrayals.

With points such as these in mind, McGann's historicist approach does much to retrieve Rossetti as a powerfully intellectual writer whose stylistic restraint meant that her work did not readily lend itself to the protocols followed by the New Critics of the 1930s which favoured the experimental religious poetry of Gerard Manley Hopkins instead. Hopkins's ostensibly avant-garde poetry bore all the hallmarks of the kind of neo-Metaphysical poetry whose vibrant linguistic experimentation made him seem unorthodox for his time. It is undoubtedly a sign of Rossetti's standing in the late nineteenth century that she exerted considerable influence on Hopkins himself. (Hopkins's 'A Voice from the World' is a carefully studied reply to Rossetti's 'The Convent Threshold'.) Yet such a fact remained obscure to the New Critics who had, as McGann argues, an exclusive interest in poetry that got stylistically 'worked up at the surface'.[52] By putting the New Criticism in its own mid-twentieth-century context, McGann is exposing how and why any critical method which refuses to come to terms with the historical forces that define the pattern of a poet's work necessarily operates with a limited system of values.

McGann remarks that New Historicist methods, which seek to provide informing cultural contexts for the literary works under analysis, have a 'natural ally' in feminist criticism.[53] But rather than concentrating on religious discourse, feminist readers have understandably fixed their attention on questions of gender in Rossetti's writing. In this respect, 'Goblin Market' has become a most productive source of inquiry into many issues about Victorian middle-class femininity. But we would do well not to forget that 'Goblin Market' is exceptional in Rossetti's oeuvre since it certainly does display a dramatic exuberance that her adventist lyrics often control by the principle of 'reserve' she would have known from the poetics of an earlier devotional writer such as John Keble.[54] By examining the 'critical potential' of 'Goblin Market' as 'an account of women's relation to capital', Helsinger subjects this frequently discussed poem to an exacting and searching analysis that assuredly advances earlier feminist accounts of its transgressive subtext. Helsinger's essay draws its critical perspective from contemporary cultural studies – cultural history, the sociology of gender, and Marxist interpretations of capitalist relations – and considers how the story of Laura and Lizzie presents a distinctive critique of women's position as consumers within the marketplace. Where Marx in the 1844 Manuscripts views male capitalists and consumers alike, as dupes who seduce each other by preying on each other's 'weaknesses', Rossetti demonstrates that women can in fact have power as consumers, and that they can spend their money how and when they wish. This point comes most clearly into focus in Helsinger's essay when we remember how Lizzie defeats the goblins to save her sister. Unlike Laura, Lizzie travels to the market with a penny in her pocket, and she has learned from her sister's experience that she must not 'pay too dear' (l.311). But the goblins, not to be outwitted, refuse her terms by trying to make her eat the fruit that has poisoned Laura. Having attempted to force-feed her, they throw back her penny. The significance of this episode lies in how Lizzie's entry into the marketplace reveals her not just as one who is asking her own price but also as a female consumer who is buying for someone other than herself. And in making her bid for her sister, she manages to resist the very forms of emasculation resulting from the rapid circulation of commodities that appalled Marx. The implications of the sisters' withdrawal from the market encourage Helsinger to suggest that perhaps the poem is masking 'the desire, not to give and nurture, but to hoard – goods, words, sex, children, and even money (Lizzie's jingling coin)'.[55] Such a concealed desire is in itself ambiguous. For in seeking to abstain from market relations, it is none the less built upon the very system of economic relations that it attempts to spurn. Lizzie's penny, after all, has emerged from the relations of production, suggesting that there is no escape from 'each merchant man' whose seductive siren songs always threaten to touch the hearts of 'modest maidens' (l.209).

It almost goes without saying that the goblins, emanating from a strange assembly of animal forms, have been read on countless occasions as male seducers whose poisonous fruits transmit sexual diseases from which unsuspecting young women may die. Barely beneath the narrative surface of 'Goblin Market' is what was frequently stigmatised as the 'great social evil' of prostitution in mid-Victorian society. And it has been suggested that Rossetti may have read her poem aloud to the women confined to the home for fallen women in which she served as a volunteer until 1870.[56]

The final essay in this volume, by Angela Leighton, provides a comprehensive account of how Victorian women poets approached a topic on which so many male commentators would infamously pontificate in deeply moralistic terms. Convincingly tracing a line of development from Barrett Browning's *Casa Guidi Windows* (1851) and *Aurora Leigh* to Adelaide Anne Procter's 'A Legend of Provence' (1855) and Rossetti's 'Goblin Market', Leighton shows

how the woman poet's resistance to the vilification of the prostitute
gathers in strength as unfair laws were devised to prohibit soliciting
on the streets. After the passing of the pernicious Contagious
Diseases Acts of the 1860s, under which women in garrison towns
and ports could be arrested on the very suspicion of working as
prostitutes, Josephine Butler mounted her attack on the 'double
standard' which put the burden of blame onto female sex workers
and not their male clients. The hypocrisy of this situation emerges
forcefully in Augusta Webster's magnificent dramatic monologue,
'A Castaway', published in 1870. Webster wrote many monologues
of equal rhetorical power, and it is not surprising that Rossetti
herself regarded this poet as one of her most formidable rivals. But
for all the fine reviews she received, and her sometime popularity –
her works went into several editions – Webster's voice has largely
gone unnoticed this century. Mermin has remarked that in her fine
dramatic poems Webster 'exploits without subterfuge the assault on
poetic tradition that her predecessors began'. 'But', she adds, 'that
tradition has had its revenge: despite their excellence, her poems
remain almost entirely unknown.'[57] Even if Webster may strike us
as the most dispiriting example of a sorely neglected talent in a still
under-researched field of inquiry, this *New Casebook* presents us
with arguments and insights that already have done much to
explain how and why, in the Victorian period, to be a woman and a
poet at the same time was a special challenge to which many
powerful writers would rise.

NOTES

1. *The Letters of Elizabeth Barrett Browning*, ed. Frederic G. Kenyon, fourth edition, 2 vols (London, 1898), I, p. 232.

2. Dorothy Mermin, *Elizabeth Barrett Browning: The Origins of a New Poetry* (Chicago, 1989), pp. 1–2.

3. *Athenaeum*, 1 June 1850 (no. 1179), 585.

4. Quotations from *Aurora Leigh* are taken from Margaret Reynolds's definitive variorum edition (Athens, OH, 1992). Book and line numbers appear in parentheses.

5. In this context, Reynolds draws attention to an unpublished letter by Barrett Browning to Isa Blagden, dated 20 October 1856, held in the Fitzwilliam Museum, Cambridge; see 'Critical Introduction' to Barrett Browning, *Aurora Leigh*, p. 18.

6. On the significance of Langham Place in the development of the organised feminist movement, see Jane Rendall, *The Origins of Modern Feminism: Women in Britain, France and the United States, 1780–1860* (Basingstoke, 1985), pp. 307–20.

7. The most comprehensive introductions to the Victorian 'woman question' are by Elizabeth K. Helsinger, Robin Lauterbach Sheets, and William Veeder, *The Woman Question: Society and Literature in Britain and America, 1837–1883*, 3 vols (Chicago, 1989), and Janet Horowitz Murray, *Strong-Minded Women and Other Lost Voices from Nineteenth-Century England* (Harmondsworth, 1984).

8. Virginia Woolf, '"Aurora Leigh"', *The Common Reader*, second series (London, 1932), pp. 202–3.

9. Roger Lonsdale (ed.), *Eighteenth-Century Women Poets: An Oxford Anthology* (Oxford, 1989).

10. Hemans's writing has been the subject of increasing critical attention in recent years. See, in particular, Marlon B. Ross, *The Contours of Masculine Desire: Romanticism and the Rise of Women's Poetry* (New York, 1989); Norma Clarke, *Ambitious Heights: Writing, Friendship, Love – The Jewsbury Sisters, Felicia Heman and Jane Welsh Carlyle* (London, 1990); Angela Leighton, *Victorian Women Poets: Writing against the Heart* (Hemel Hempstead, 1991); and Tricia Lootens, 'Hemans and Home: Victorianism, Feminine "Internal Enemies", and the Domestication of National Identity', *PMLA*, 109:2 (1994), 238–53. On the development of the dramatic monologue in the Victorian period, see Ekbert Faas, *Retreat into the Mind: Victorian Poetry and the Rise of Psychiatry* (Princeton, NJ, 1988).

11. Leighton, *Victorian Women Poets: Writing against the Heart*, p. 57. The story of L.E.L.'s last years in Benin is reported in Laman Blanchard, *Life and Literary Remains of L.E.L.*, 2 vols (London, 1841).

12. Elizabeth Barrett Browning, *The Poetical Works of Elizabeth Barrett Browning* (Edinburgh, 1904), pp. 399–401.

13. Leighton, *Victorian Women Poets*, p. 43.

14. Barrett Browning, *Poetical Works*, pp. 398–9.

15. Quotations from the poetry of Christina Rossetti are taken from *The Complete Poems of Christina Rossetti*, ed. R.W. Crump, 3 vols (Baton Rouge, LA, 1979–90). Line references appear in parentheses.

16. For a detailed exploration of the intertextual links between Rossetti and Barrett Browning, see Antony H. Harrison, 'In the Shadow of EBB: Christina Rossetti and Ideological Estrangement', in Harrison, *Victorian Poets and Romantic Poems: Intertextuality and Ideology* (Charlottesville, VA, 1990), pp. 108–43.

17. Diane D'Amico, 'Eve, Mary, and Mary Magdalene: Christina Rossetti's Feminine Triptych', in David A. Kent (ed.), *The Achievement of Christina Rossetti* (Ithaca, NY, 1987), p. 178.

18. Rossetti, *Letter and Spirit: Notes on the Commandments* (London, 1883), p. 17.

19. William Michael Rossetti, 'Memoir', in Christina Rossetti, *Poetical Works* (London, 1904), pp. lv–lvi.

20. Woolf, '"I Am Christina Rossetti"', in *The Common Reader*, second series, pp. 237–44.

21. Lionel Stevenson, *The Pre-Raphaelite Poets* (Chapel Hill, NC, 1972), p. 88.

22. Isobel Armstrong, 'Christina Rossetti: Diary of a Feminist Reading', in Sue Roe (ed.), *Women Reading Women's Writing* (Brighton, 1987), p. 122. For an overview of critical attitudes to Rossetti's poetry, see Edna Kotin Charles, *Christina Rossetti: Critical Perspectives 1862–1982* (Selinsgrove, PA, 1985).

23. W.W. Robson, 'Pre-Raphaelite Poetry', in Boris Ford (ed.), *From Dickens to Hardy*, Pelican Guide to English Literature, vol. 6 (Harmondsworth, 1958), p. 364.

24. [Arthur Symons,] 'Miss Rossetti's Poetry', *London Quarterly Review*, 88 (1887), 338–9.

25. Richard Le Gallienne, Review of Christina Rossetti, *Poems, Academy*, 7 February 1891, pp. 130–1.

26. Cora Kaplan, 'The Indefinite Disclosed: Christina Rossetti and Emily Dickinson', in Mary Jacobus (ed.), *Women Writing and Writing about Women* (London, 1979), pp. 61–2, 69. Kaplan is explicitly building on the analysis of 'Goblin Market' given by Ellen Moers in *Literary Women* (New York, 1976), pp. 100–7.

27. Sandra M. Gilbert and Susan Gubar, *The Madwoman in the Attic: The Woman Writer and the Nineteenth-Century Literary Imagination* (New Haven, 1979), p. 567.

28. Rod Edmond draws attention to the reprinting of 'Goblin Market' in *Playboy: Affairs of the Hearth: Victorian Poetry and Domestic Narrative* (London, 1988), p. 170.

29. Lilian Faderman, *Surpassing the Love of Men: Romantic Friendship and Love between Women from the Renaissance to the Present* (London, 1985), p. 171.

30. Reynolds, 'Critical Introduction' to Elizabeth Barrett Browning, *Aurora Leigh*, p. 10. By focusing on Victorian women poets, the present volume may appear separatist in intent. It is not. Its aim is to

examine how and why the distinctive contributions of women to mid- and late-nineteenth-century poetry were critically ignored for years.

31. Toril Moi, *Sexual/Textual Politics: Feminist Literary Theory* (London, 1985), p. 63.

32. Gilbert and Gubar, *The Madwoman in the Attic*, p. 19.

33. [W.C. Roscoe,] Review of *Aurora Leigh*, *National Review*, 4 (1857), 245.

34. See below, p. 116.

35. Kaplan, 'Introduction' to Elizabeth Barrett Browning, *Aurora Leigh and Other Poems* (London, 1978), pp. 19–20.

36. See below, p. 87.

37. See below, p. 36.

38. John Stuart Mill, 'Thoughts on Poetry and Its Varieties', in Joseph Bristow (ed.), *The Victorian Poet: Poetics and Persona* (Beckenham, 1987), p. 44. This essay, published in 1867, revises and brings together two essays, 'What is Poetry?' and 'The Truth of Poetry', that Mill published in the *Monthly Repository* in 1833.

39. W. David Shaw, *The Lucid Veil: Poetic Truth in the Victorian Age* (London, 1987), p. 12.

40. See, for example, [Coventry Patmore], 'Tennyson's *Maud*', *Edinburgh Review*, 102 (1855), 498–519. Patmore's anxieties about the feminine sweetness of lyrics written by his male contemporaries, especially Tennyson, are discussed in Bristow, 'Coventry Patmore and the Womanly Mission of the Mid-Victorian Poet', *Victorian Studies* (forthcoming).

41. See below, p. 67.

42. Carol T. Christ, 'The Feminine Subject of Victorian Poetry', *ELH*, 54 (1987), 385–401.

43. Robert Browning, 'To Isa Blagden', 18 June 1870, *Dearest Isa: Robert Browning's Letters to Isabella Blagden*, ed. Edward C. McAleer (Austin, TX, 1951), p. 336. The applicability of the term 'grotesque' to Browning's poetry was first elaborated at length by Walter Bagehot in 'Wordsworth, Tennyson and Browning; or Pure, Ornate, and Grotesque Art in English Poetry', *National Review*, 19 (1864), 27–57.

44. The study that set this trend was E.D.H. Johnson, *The Alien Vision of Victorian Poetry* (Princeton, NJ, 1952).

45. On the marginalisation of poetry within Victorian culture, see Alan Sinfield, *Alfred Tennyson* (Oxford, 1986), pp. 10–21.

46. See below, p. 67.

47. See below, p. 86.

48. Irene Tayler, *Holy Ghosts: The Male Muses of Emily and Charlotte Brontë* (New York, 1990), p. 45.

49. See below, p. 125.

50. See below, p. 161.

51. Linda H. Marshall disputes McGann's use of the term 'Soul Sleep' to define the 'suspensive interim between death and the Second Advent'. Marshall claims that Rossetti's 'patient and intensely inward attendance on apocalypse ignored premillenarian computations of the last days', and that her poetry and meditative prose depicted the sleeping dead in terms accommodated by conventional Anglican eschatology: 'What the Dead Are Doing Underground: Hades and Heaven in the Writings of Christina Rossetti', *Victorian Newsletter*, 72 (1987), 55.

52. See below, p. 171.

53. See below, p. 173.

54. John Keble wrote in 1838: '*Poetry is the indirect expression in words, most appropriately in metrical words, of some overpowering emotion, or ruling taste, of feeling. The direct indulgence whereof is somehow repressed*' (Review of the *Life of Sir Walter Scott* by J.G. Lockhart, in *Occasional Papers and Reviews* [Oxford, 1877], p. 6).

55. See below, p. 215.

56. This suggestion is made by D.M.R. Bentley, 'The Meretricious and the Meretorious in *Goblin Market*: A Conjecture and An Analysis', in Kent (ed.), *The Achievement of Christina Rossetti*, pp. 57–81.

57. Mermin, *Godiva's Ride: Women of Letters in England, 1830–1880* (Bloomington, IN, 1993), p. 80. Leighton provides a detailed analysis of Webster's work in *Victorian Women Poets*, pp. 164–201.

1

'A Music of Thine Own': Women's Poetry

ISOBEL ARMSTRONG

[Felicia] Hemans wrote overtly of politics, of Greece, emigration, the Pilgrim Fathers (the first 'trade unionists'), and declared a Byronic response to liberty. But the politics of women's poetry in this century cannot necessarily be associated with the uncovering of particular political positions but rather with a set of strategies or negotiations with conventions and constraints. It is remarkable how resourcefully the three Brontës, each of them highly individual writers (though Anne and Charlotte at least, politically conservative), follow Mrs Hemans in exploring consciousness under duress, imprisoned within limit, or how Anne Adelaide Procter (to be associated with radical thinking in the mid-century) follows Letitia Landon in exploring the alien rituals of another culture in her tales, and the demands of either moral or affective conventions in her shorter lyrics. It is not necessary to assume a direct relationship between these poets, though in some cases that can be ascertained, to see that they share common strategies. They also share a capacity to produce a poem with a simple moral or emotional surface which actually probes more complex questions than its simplicity suggests. Three poems by the Brontës and a group of poems by Adelaide Anne Procter indicate how Victorian women poets could exploit the legacy left by late Romantic writers such as Letitia Landon and Felicia Hemans, in particular the poem of the affective moment and its relation to moral convention and religious and cultural constraint. This will suggest the basis on which a women's tradition can be constructed – necessarily briefly in a chapter of this length –

and provide an introduction to the way in which expressive theory could be allied with a feminine poetics.

Anne Brontë, a poet of great subtlety and far wider range than is often thought, negotiated the sobriety of the religious and didactic lyric to suggest precisely where its conventions are most painful and intransigent by *not* breaking these conventions, but by simply following through their logic. In this way a poem on the inevitability of suffering can end with a challenge to God either to provide the strength to endure or to release the sufferer through death ('If this be all'). 'Song' ('We know where deepest lies the snow'), a poem on the inevitability of oppression even when master and slave, hunters and hunted, reverse their positions and displace one another, chooses the trembling life of the hare rather than the cruelty of the hounds, and ends almost triumphantly by asserting the knowledge that only oppression can bring. Intransigently, it refuses the knowledge brought by power. But it is in a more overtly conventional poem such as 'The Arbour' that her gift for turning an orthodox position can be seen. It is a pastoral poem both of the affective moment and the moral lesson. It depends on the discovery of a deceptive perceptual and psychological experience which is withheld from the understanding of the reader in the same way that the discovery of the writer's mistake is delayed until it is recognised. The security, protection and fecundity of an arbour, with its 'thickly clustering' trees, 'green and glossy leaves', sunshine and blue sky, prompts a moment of release into emotion and reverie, in which the past becomes imbued with autumnal pleasure and the future invested with the fulfilment of summer: memory and desire are devoid of pain. But a perceptual trick or misprision has occurred; what has seemed 'summer's very breath' occurs when 'snow is on the ground'; 'How can I think of scenes like these?'

> 'Tis but the *frost* that clears the air,
> And gives the sky that lovely blue;
> They're smiling in a *winter's* sun,
> Those evergreens of sombre hue.
>
> And winter's chill is on my heart –
> How can I dream of future bliss?
> How can my spirit soar away
> Confined by such a chain as this?[1]

The conclusion reproaches the speaker for factitious sentiment, which attaches feeling to conventional metaphors of the seasons and provides an escape into fantasy from the demands of the chill winter present. Nevertheless it is an interrogative conclusion: 'How can.... How can...' not only implies the reproach, how could I? but also asks the question, how is it possible?; it may well be that it is the moral reproach which is profoundly conventional and narrow, refusing the possibility of imaginative transformation and accepting the orthodox symbolism of winter as constraint, restriction and dearth too facilely. For the frost and the winter's sun *were* transforming. Shifting slightly the context of the feminine metaphor of breath and breathing, Anne Brontë allows that the 'whispering' of boughs 'through the air'(l.8) may not have been 'summer's very breath' (l.17), but they nevertheless nourished the body and soul, enabling the ear to 'drink[s] in' sound, and the soul to 'fly away', a statement repeated and modulated in the last stanza when the 'spirit', another form of breath, can 'soar away'. The confinement of the frosty arbour – 'Confined by such a chain as this' – is seen in two ways by the end of the poem. The wintry enclosure is a material imprisonment, holding the soul in thrall. On the other hand, it is a paradoxical context of rebirth, in which the soul can soar precisely because it is chained to the material world whose wintry 'evergreens' may be more reliable auguries than the transient leaves of summer. In this context the words 'confined' and 'chain' strangely dislodge the connotation of imprisonment and take on the generative implications of the womb and the birth cord in another feminine pun on the cord which tethers and the chord from which the breath or air of life and of music is created. This seemingly docile poem is a sustained pun on the sense of confinement as imprisonment and confinement as gestation in the womb, one sterile, the other creative.

Confinement is the structural figure in both Charlotte Brontë's 'The Lonely Lady' and in Emily Brontë's 'Enough of Thought, Philosopher', though they work respectively through psychologised experience and symbol. Charlotte Brontë's poem is ostensibly a study in 'Mariana'-like hysteria and unreciprocated sexual desire. Confined and alone, insomniac, weary with the women's tasks of lace-making and music-making, the tension of the lady's feeling is expressed through the 'quivering strings' of the harp she abandons. The intensity of her emotion meets no recognition, and, in a brilliant verbal displacement, this condition is externalised in the sounds of the clock which mechanically records time and listens to itself doing so, and to the *cessation* of its own responses which vibrate – the characteristic feminine metaphor appears again – nothing: 'the clock with silver chime did say/The number of the hour, and all in peace/Listened to hear its own vibration cease' (ll.6–8).[2] The setting sun casts a lurid, blood-red crimson blush on the lady's face, and until the last stanza this appears to be the psychological counterpart of violent feeling which can only return upon itself. In the last stanza an army in battle, too, 'leagues away' (l.40), sees the sunset, 'The last ray tinged with blood' (l.45), and the way in which the light gives all the features of the landscape the semblance of gore, just as it had to the features of the lady's face. But the sunset is no longer simply the extension of hysterical feminine sexuality. The syntax of the last stanza affirms that the literal burning of the battle is the cause of the bloody light. The lady's hysteria is accounted for by her anxiety and ignorance as to the state of the battle. And yet there is no simple distinction here between feminine emotion and masculine violence. Feminine sexuality becomes horribly dependent upon and implicated in male aggression and warfare. It is the battle, certainly, which makes the sunset not a symbolic but a literal portent of disaster, and it is the raging battle which has caused the lady's isolation: yet she is committed to a vicarious experience of it in which hysteria and warfare have an uncanny affinity. The metaphor gives them a blood relationship.

Emily Brontë's poem rages too, but again simple opposition is deceptive, and a poem which appears to be caught in a familiar dilemma, a 'cruel strife' between 'vanquished Good' and 'victorious ill', actually breaks the restrictions of this confining oppositional and binary terminology altogether. 'The Philosopher' is a monologue which includes a dialogue within itself, and this makes problematic the 'identity' which the poem longs to lose.[3] 'O for the time when I shall sleep/Without identity' (stanza 2). Identity means both that which is in unity with itself and without difference and that which is uniquely different and the founder of difference. The Philosopher who speaks these lines is an aspect of the speaker's self, and the 'I' which resounds through the poem splits and fragments into separate experiences and definitions. The Philosopher describes a vision of a 'Spirit' in contradistinction to the listening 'man' or speaker, and the 'man' or speaker replies by addressing the Philosopher as 'seer', assimilating him to spirit and juxtaposing the two terms – 'And even for that spirit, seer,/I've watched and sought my lifetime long' (stanza 5). 'Man' appears to comprehend seer, philosopher and spirit just as philosopher comprehends seer, spirit and man. Thus the speaker's earlier statement (stanza 3) that 'Three gods, within this little frame,/Are warring, night and day' becomes easier to understand. And similarly, the second stanza's fierce assertion that the stark Manichean oppositions between heaven and hell are categories whose simple dualism cannot contain the energies of desire or will is related to this. But the identity is violently at war, it seems, precisely because a universe founded on rigid categories of binary difference constantly excludes the third term. The narrator him or herself is also committed to the epistemology of opposition, so habitual is it, seeking the 'spirit', or breath, in 'heaven, hell, earth and air', and thus, not surprisingly, 'always wrong' (stanza 5). In the same way the narrator has earlier brought 'spirit' and 'man' into relationship but excluded 'woman', the unmentioned term of the poem. The vision of the spirit, on the contrary, offers a revelation of another universe, a world of 'three rivers' 'Of equal depth, and equal flow'. The rigid antitheses are broken. These are rivers of gold, blood and sapphire, retaining prismatic difference but transformed from their black confluence to the unifying whiteness of light by the spirit's agency. The specific symbolism of these rivers, reaching back to Revelation, matters less, perhaps, than their triple nature, their capacity to include the third term. Gold, sapphire and blood could signify Father, Son and ungendered Holy Ghost, or spirit, matter and the human, or divine, satanic and human, or androgyne, male and female. What matters is that the violence of a universe constituted through rigid categories of difference, whether spiritual, moral or sexual, needs to be 'lost'. The spirit, which is also comprehended in 'this living breath' (stanza 5) of the narrator and by the 'air' of earth, is otherwise murderous and destructive. There seems to be an attempt to remove the 'spirit' and 'this living breath' from the categories of gender and a refusal to consent to the 'feminine' associations of this figure. On the other hand, the powerful energies of Emily Brontë's poetry, which push the hymn-like form of her stanzas towards violence, tend to reaffirm terrible alternatives despite the move to the third term – heaven or hell, spirit or man, male or female, a gendered or an ungendered world: the negations sound with the force of affirmation, and the affirmations with the force of negations.

Adelaide Anne Procter, writing between the mid-1840s and the 1860s, takes up the figures and forms associated with the thematising of feminine issues and virtually typifies the woman poet's interests at this time. Like Mrs Hemans before her and like her contemporaries, Dora Greenwell and Elizabeth Barrett Browning, she wrote of political matters, particularly on the oppression and the suffering of the poor (for instance, 'The Cradle Song of the Poor', 'The Homeless Poor') and on the complexities of the master–slave relationship (for instance 'King and Slave'). She also wrote some magnificently humane lyrics on the Crimean war, refusing superficial heroism and narrow patriotism ('The Lesson of the War', 'The Two Spirits'). Like Letitia Landon, she worked with the external narrative poem and with the didactic lyric. Her narrative poems, dealing with the movement beyond the boundary, with escape, with ex-patriotism and return, are deeply preoccupied with displacement, and through this with the woman's 'place' or displacement in a culture. As so often with women writers, the more conventional the didactic lyric, the more accepting of its conventions the writer is, the more it can be used as a way of looking at conformity from within. Writing with a boldly simple directness and immediacy, Adelaide Anne Procter developed increasing strength here. A series of lyrics redefine the emotional space of sexual love arrestingly, by a conventional refusal of the role of exclusively sexual passion in a love relationship with a man in a way which outflanks conventionality. Neither 'A Parting' nor 'A Woman's Answer' retreats to celibacy or virginity as an alternative to marriage. 'A Parting' thanks the man who has rejected the woman's passion and, half ironically, half seriously, expresses gratefulness for a 'terrible awaking'. The poem conventionally redirects desire towards divine love; but that desire is explicitly affirmed as the intense power of sexual love, 'all too great to live except above'.[4] It is neither sublimated nor repressed. 'A Woman's Answer' professes to promiscuity by redefining love as intense libidinal passion in many spheres – for knowledge, the natural world, art, books (*Aurora Leigh* in particular) – and not simply the sphere of sexual love. 'Envy', a terse, abruptly economical lyric, is another poem which expresses a conventional moral position, but dramatically turns the commonplace. The speaker is envious of envy, always losing to him: 'He was the first always: Fortune/Shone bright in his face./I fought for years; with no effort/He conquered the place'. Envy wins the competition every time, and even dies first: 'God help me!/While he is at rest,/I am cursed still to live; – even/Death loved him best'.[5] The startling combat with envy comes about because it is both a traditional Christian allegorical combat

against envy, an attempt to defeat a moral and psychological condition, and a representation of envy itself, a jealous fight *with* envy
for possession of all that we envy – success, mastery, recognition –
on envy's own terms. This constantly reproduces jealousy even
when it is seemingly 'conquered'. Even the death of jealousy is
something to be jealous of. Envy, the successful combatant, is gendered as 'him'; the speaker is a shadowy other, the bleeding subject
of loss, the one 'without', even to the extent of being without a
coffin. Ironically Envy engenders envy, and the *speaker* is actually
forced to become the personification of envy. The submerged
phallic symbolism here testifies savagely to the dominance of male
power and to the *anger* of loss.

Adelaide Anne Procter began her writing career by publishing in
Household Words and *All the Year Round*, journals which were associated with popular radicalism, and was converted to Roman
Catholicism in 1851. Tractarian or Anglo-Catholic aesthetics, enun-
ciated through Keble in particular, paid special attention to developing an expressive theory of poetry as the vehicle of hidden
emotion, and that may be why Procter's poetry takes up the feminised expressive figures of the musical vibration as the epitome of
feeling, and breath or breathing, air and spirit, as the representation
of the imprisoned life of emotion needing to escape or to take form.
Her poems of displacement, and the exploration of the 'place' of
women in several senses, particularly 'A Tomb in Ghent', provide a
context for the exploration of expressive feeling and its relation to
the feminine and lead to a fuller consideration of the importance of
expressive aesthetics to women's poetry. This is required especially
for the work of Dora Greenwell, Christina Rossetti and Jean
Ingelow, who seem to have been consciously aware of this theory as
a problematic model of the feminine.

The longer narrative poems frequently use travel and change of
place to examine the degree to which institutions are capable of
flexibility. In 'Homeward Bound', a long-lost sailor, anticipating
Tennyson's *Enoch Arden* (1864), returns to find his wife with
another man and his child and refuses to claim her back rather than
endanger her happiness or reputation. A mother transposed from
one environment to another sacrifices her child to a second marriage in 'The Sailor Boy', a motif of the second marriage also explored in 'A New Mother'. In 'A Legend of Provence', a novice
elopes with a wounded knight but returns to her place when marriage fails. An exiled Tyrolean girl returns to her country from

Switzerland to warn of the Swiss intention to attack Austria in 'A Legend of Bregenz'. The return to roots, the testing out of the limits of the shaping and determining agencies in a culture, these seem to be at the heart of the narrative poems.

'A Tomb in Ghent' charts the commitment to a new culture by a skilled mechanic who has emigrated to Belgium, and an enforced withdrawal from it by his granddaughter, who returns to England when her father dies, attempting to find a place, to be assimilated into what is now an alien culture. This unsolved dilemma forms the frame to the story of her parents who achieve, it seems, a kind of self-expression, communication and mutuality unknown either to their parents or their children. The tale is prefaced by the legend of the dragon given to Bruges but stolen by Ghent. The story goes that the dragon will one day spread its wings and return to Palestine, where the Crusaders stole it. The legend within the legend achieves a number of purposes: exactly where the dragon belongs, and to whom, is problematical; it is displaced, like the characters, and implicitly questions the idea of the nation and the boundary. Its status as military trophy also questions the martial values and gender-bound rituals of war. The exiled son abrogates conventional roles and releases his own being through music, eventually playing the organ in the great cathedral. Music in this poem replaces the flight of the dragon and its aggression with the feminised flight of sound, analogy for the language of the spirit, a flight parallel but antithetical to that of the totem of war. Waves of sound break 'at heaven's door' bearing 'the great desire' of spiritual feeling on 'eagle wings'.[6] The expressive figuring of the feminine is associated with a male experience, but in fact this expression is enabled or inspired by the statue at the 'White Maiden's Tomb'. The player can make the organ 'answer' and 'thrill with master-power the breathless throng' – give the congregation breath or inspiration – because he in turn is handed passion through the 'expectant' statue who 'holds her breath' with parted lips, and through the wife who is an image of the statue. Again the figure is many-sided in its implications.[7] There is a frank assimilation of mystical and musical experience to sexuality: on the one hand male creativity emerges out of female silence and becomes its gift; on the other hand the gift is returned to the woman as song, and the daughter is endowed with the power of expressive singing. Music, or the 'air', literally circulates in and between the group and the congregation, cancelling the fixities of gender and social division and releasing the stony categories from their rigidity. Momentarily, in an alien country and in the safe space of the cathedral, expressive song reconfigures relationships – but only in a place of safety untouched by national boundaries rather than transcending them.

But there are a number of poems – some of her finest – in which Adelaide Anne Procter writes with anxiety about the nature of expression. 'A Lost Chord' is the perfect harmony which eludes discovery; 'Hush!' turns on the deathly silence which displaces the sounds envisaged by the internal imagination; 'Unexpressed' speaks of the failure of articulation and the ephemeral nature of language, which dissipates and recedes 'Like sighings of illimitable forests,/And waves of an unfathomable sea'.[8] In 'Words', language is so fragile – 'the rose-leaf that we tread on/Will outlive a word' – and yet so powerful that it can transform the course of a life.[9] Nevertheless words can remain imprisoned in the self, and though each has its own 'spirit' or breath it is externalised only as *echo*, as representation without substance, dissociated from its hidden originary experience, the shadow of a sound, inveterately secondary. Thus the expressive moment is by no means unproblematical. The figure of overflow is warily explored by contemporaries such as Greenwell and Barrett Browning and by the slightly later poets, Rossetti and Ingelow. To see how these poets negotiate the dominant poetics of expression and deal with its ambiguities it is necessary to look more closely at the expressive aesthetic. The incipient sexual implications of the recurrent figurings of feminine discourse, the receptive vibration of the musical chord in sympathy, the exhalation or release of feeling which moves ambiguously between the body and the spirit, are present in the metaphors of expressive aesthetics, but they are given both a negative or pathological and a positive or 'healthy' signification, a hysterical and a wholesome aspect, often implicitly gendered respectively as 'feminine' and 'masculine'. Expressive theory becomes morbid either when the overflow of feeling is in excess or when it is unable to flow at all and repressed into a secret underground life. For expressive theory is above all an aesthetics of the *secret*, the hidden experience, because the feeling which is prior to language gives language a secondary status and is often written of as if it cannot take linguistic form at all. The politics of women's poetry emerges in its transactions with this orthodoxy and, strangely, the hermeneutic problem of discerning a feminine discourse in the structure and language of a poem can be approached by addressing a theory which often tries to do without an accout of language. This account of the poetics of expression is illuminated by the terms of Dora Greenwell's essay, 'Our single women', where the negative aspects of expressive aesthetics belong to the language which gives an account of the feminine.[10] The essay enables one to see how Greenwell, Barrett Browning, Rossetti and Ingelow deal with the structural implications of expressive metaphors in relation to gender, and how far later poets, Mathilde Blind, Augusta Webster and Amy Levy, were able to depart from the expressive model.

Victorian expressive theory is affective and of the emotions. It is concerned with feeling. It psychologised, subjectivised and often moralised the firm epistemological base of Romantic theory, though its warrant was in Wordsworth's spontaneous *overflow* of feeling. The idea of overflow, of projection and expression, a movement of feeling out of the self, develops metaphorically from a cognitive account of consciousness, in which mediation between subject and object was the constitutive structure of mind, and the idealist implication that the subject constructs the other as a category of mind. This can be shifted to describe projection, empathy, a moving out of the self in which the barriers and limits of selfhood are broken, a liberation of feeling almost like love, and certainly like breathing, which finds or invents forms and images to which it is attached. Expansion, movement outwards, the breaking of barriers, is the essence of poetry and the essence of *healthy* poetry. To Sydney Dobell, the function of poetry is to express a mind: 'To express is to carry out'; 'to express a mind is to carry out that mind *into some equivalent*'.[11] For Arthur Hallam the movement outwards into 'energetic love for the beautiful' was a moral activity because it educated the self in a liberation from the bonds of the ego. He praised, in Tennyson's work, 'his power of embodying himself in ideal characters, or rather moods of character', so that the

> circumstances of the narration seem to have a natural correspondence with the predominant feeling, and, as it were, to be evolved from it by assimilative force ... his vivid, picturesque delineation of objects, and the peculiar skill with which he holds all of them *fused*, to borrow a metaphor from science, in a medium of strong emotion.[12]

There is a perfect chemistry here in which empathy is called forth by objects while correspondingly subjective life moves beyond the self to fuse objects in feeling. There is also a perfect reciprocity because emotion does not master objects, and neither do objects take priority over feeling. But it is not altogether clear whether feeling is simply displaced or represented and verbalised in some way, and for some critics there is an almost inevitable hiatus between the movement of feeling and the form in which it is embodied. In 1842 G.H. Lewes quoted with approval John Stuart Mill's account of poetry from the *Monthly Repository* of 1833, where Mill assumed a disjunction between emotion and its form of expression. Poetry 'is the delineation of the deeper and more secret workings of human emotions'. It is 'feeling confirming itself to itself in moments of solitude and embodying itself in symbols which are the nearest possible representations of the feeling'.[13] The assumption is that ideally there should be a perfect match between feeling and symbol but that the correspondence is necessarily impossible and imperfect. Emotion remains secret, inaccessible, hidden. There is always a barrier to its expression. Lewes more confidently seizes on those aspects of Hegel's thinking (whose work he was reviewing) which enable him to speak of the representative medium which allows those emotions 'which fill and expand the heart' to be expressed. He quotes Hegel on mourning and the need to be 'relieved' by seeing grief in 'external form'. Tears, of course, are the model of the expressive moment, the visible, literal expression of the 'oppressed heart'.[14] He reads Hegel unashamedly as an expressive theorist but he also acknowledges that expression is bound up with repression. He thinks of Greek art, for instance, with Goethe, as a volcano burning beneath a covering of ice. Once the representation of emotion fails to be adequate to it the representation itself becomes a barrier. And this is where expressive poetics moves to the pathological. Keble's sense that the secret and hidden currents of feeling resist expression to the point of driving the poet mad, even though he has theological reasons for endorsing their repression, is not an extravagant form of expressive theory. Feeling for him is always pressing for a release which cannot be granted. One might say that the poet becomes hysterical in these circumstances, like a woman.

> What must they do? They are ashamed and reluctant to speak out, yet, if silent, they can scarcely keep their mental balance; some are said even to have become insane.[15]

The problem is accentuated for Tractarian aesthetics by the theological necessity of a due 'reserve', a refusal to bring forth an excess of feeling and an assent to hidden meaning. Keble's theory of symbol speaks of the *concealing* as well as the *revealing* nature of symbol. Christian meaning should not be carelessly *exposed* to misprision (and to democratic reading).

So there are two related aspects of Victorian accounts of expressive projection. First, if the mind cannot be 'carried out' into an equivalent of itself and find a form in representation, there will be a disjunction between the secret feelings of the mind and the form of the representation. The representation then becomes the barrier feeling is designed to break. Secondly, since the representational symbol is both the *means* of expression and the *form* of its repression, *ex*pression and *re*pression, although in conflict with one another, become interdependent. They constitute one another, so that expression is predicated upon repression. The overflow of secret and hidden feeling creates the barriers which bind and limit it, while the limits enable the overflow of feeling. This is not willingly acknowledged by the writers I have mentioned, but it follows from their thinking. Indeed, it is their willingnss to construct an opposition between expression and repression rather than to allow the structural interdependence their theory implies, which accounts for the uneasiness and frustration of their thought and its ambiguities. People have noticed the superficial resemblance of this theory to Freud's account of repression, but it is radically different because it assumes a consciously *known* experience which is inexpressible because the verbal forms of language are inadequate, ineffable. Freud, on the contrary, assumed that representation is part of a symbolic structure of displacement which is a manifestation of the *unknowable* unconscious. Thus he places emphasis on the importance of the material sign or symbol where Victorian expressive theory does not. Expressive theory does have something in common, however, with Julia Kristeva's account of the opposition of the semiotic and symbolic in language. Syntax operates as a symbolic law of the paternal function in exercising grammatical and social constraints, while the instinctual drives of the semiotic and the primal processes of condensation and displacement refuse to be accommodated by the symbolic and subvert and dissolve it.[16] Kristeva is worth mentioning because she provides a way of thinking of expressive theory in terms of language. On the other hand, it is the assumption of expressive theory that language fails to embody or symbolise primal feeling which precisely defines its difficulties. It cannot account for language. For Kristeva both the semiotic and the symbolic do have linguistic form.

It is interesting that in her remarkable essay on single women (first published in the *North British Review*, 1860) Dora Greenwell, who had sympathies towards Quakerism rather than to Tractarianism, adopts the language of secrecy when she is speaking of women but, in a surprising move, compares the withholding and suppression required of women in social life with the expressive openness of their art. In poetry the female subjectivity is to be defined by its capacity to create through writing a self which is commensurate with the 'secret' identity concealed in social dealings. And yet, paradoxically, this self is constituted by secrecy, and thus the poem is an expression of feminine subjectivity through its very capacity to conceal as well as to reveal: the secret is an open secret – and a closed one.

> It is surely singular that woman, bound, as she is, no less by the laws of society than by the immutable instincts of her nature, to a certain suppression of all that relates to personal feeling, should attain, in print, to the fearless, uncompromising sincerity she misses in real life; so that in the poem, above all in the novel – ... a living soul, a living voice, should seem to greet us; a voice so sad, so truthful, so earnest, that we have felt as if some intimate secret were at once communicated and withheld, – an Open Secret, free to all who could find its key – the secret of a woman's heart, with all its needs, its struggles, and its aspirations.[17]

The theological language of the open secret of the Gospel is directly, and with extraordinary boldness, related to women's experience, so that through this language women become the prime bearers of the Christian message (we shall see that in the same way Barrett Browning identifies the fallen woman with Christ). In terms reminiscent of Letitia Landon's justification of and apologia for the introduction of the affective into the hardness of phallocentric society, Dora Greenwell defends the introduction of feminine sensitivity into art and into life, but with the difference that modern life makes it increasingly difficult to give that feminine subjectivity *expression*, thwarting and obstructing it so that there is a disjunction, just as in expressive theory itself, between internal experience and external form.

> The conditions of life grow continually less and less severe, yet more and more complicated: the springs of thought, of love, lie deeper. Conscience grows more exacting, responsibilities wider. Women's whole being is more sensitive. It may now, perhaps, be harder for her than it has ever yet been to make her wishes and her fate agree – 'to

bring her external existence into harmony with her inner life' [my emphasis].[18]

The affective and expressive vocabulary continues throughout the essay: Dora Greenwell asks for *'a more perfect freedom and expansion* in that which is already their [women's] own' (my emphasis).[19] She quotes Mrs Jameson on the particular nature of the 'feminine and religious element' in women's identity, and argues for the superior capacities of sympathy in women, the expressive capacity to project themselves into different psychological conditions – 'In such a task, the complicated play of sympathies ever at work within her – the dramatic faculty by means of which she so readily makes the feelings of others her own – find full expression. To her, *sympathy is power*, because to her it is knowledge.'[20]

The essay challenges Mill on the subjection of women a number of times, claiming that women accept subordination, and adopts a flagrantly essentialist account of feminine consciousness. Women are innately passive, responsive and nurturing rather than original and creative.

> In imaginative strength she has been proved deficient; she unfolds no new heaven, she breaks into no new world. She discovers, invents, creates nothing. In her whole nature we trace a passivity, a tendency to work upon that which she received, to quicken, to foster, to develop.[21]

Intellect becomes as one-sided as feeling in women: no woman remains single from choice; the true oneness of men and women in love is – the sense of loss combined with the phallic language is poignant here – 'like the healing of some deep original wound'.[22] And yet neither the essentialist conformism nor the poignancy should be allowed to obliterate the boldness of this essay. Dora Greenwell certainly wanted the 'power' granted by imaginative sympathy for women. Though she saw that it would be necessary to appeal to the agency of men to enable women to use their energies in productive work, she attacked the conservatism and conventionality of contemporary accounts of women, and what she advocated is striking. Though she concentrated on nursing, she wanted women to be able to work together in groups, in collaborative projects (she advocated a museum of women's arts): she wanted women to be able to enter the ministry of the church with a clear and defined and officially recognised status, participating in 'aggressive' moral reform, and she believed that in undertaking unpaid work among the poor, female labour could democratise society and erase class difference; she praised the moral qualities of working-class women. A 'certain mingling of classes on one ground' could take place.[23] In working in hospitals and with fallen women, middle-class women could assuage differences because they were egalitarian in their sympathies and did not *'come down'* to the poor.[24]

The mixture of the conventional and the unconventional in this essay is surprising and often unpredictable; it consents to a passive account of women and simultaneously subverts it, seeing the expressive model of femininity as one of struggle and limit. Rather like her own double poems, the essay is both conservative and subversive. If she could assert the virtues of passivity she could also castigate and question the 'self-complacent idolatry of the safe and mediocre, in the fullness of which we once heard a lady thank Heaven that her daughters were not geniuses. True apotheosis of the commonplace!'[25] The truth is that expressive accounts of consciousness sanctioned both the 'aggressive' movement of self outwards (here made safe by being associated with the church) and the hidden, secret life of feeling, expression and repression, energising movement and hysteria, concealment and revelation, silence and speech. Thus the woman poet's negotiation of the aesthetics of secrecy and its contradictions is highly complex, and always deeply concerned with struggle and limit, transgression and boundary, silence and language.

Christina Rossetti took up this theme directly in relation to poetry in another extraordinary documenting of the cultural dilemma of women, her Preface to a fairly late poem, *Monna Innominata*. In this brief discussion, and with characteristically 'secret' obliquity and indirection, she claimed, like Greenwell, expressive rights for the unmarried woman in poetry. She claimed, not only the freedom of the unmarried woman to express her sexuality, but also the freedom to be absurd, undignified, if feminine sexuality necessitated this.

She calls Elizabeth Barrett Browning 'the Great Poetess of our own day and nation' and yet implicitly offers a critique of her position.[26] Beatrice and Laura, she writes, dismissing a whole mythology of women, may have been immortalised by Dante and Petrarch, but they come down to us 'scant of attractiveness'. The reason is that they and the 'unnamed ladies' who preceded them were the objects of sexual love and religious feeling but could not express it themselves. They come down to us as remote and unpassionate beings. In the same breath she makes a characteristically oblique and ambitious historical statement: 'in that land and that period which gave birth to Catholics, to Albigenses, and to Troubadours', Renaissance Italy, in other words, were generated the forms of thought and feeling and the religious and sexual conflicts which have conditioned the nineteenth-century culture evolving from them. In both periods it was impossible for a lady to 'have spoken for herself'. Elizabeth Barrett Browning, the 'Great Poetess' of her period might, she continues, have achieved another kind of art than the 'Portuguese Sonnets' 'had she only been unhappy instead of happy'. The mysterious indirectness here (for *Sonnets from the Portuguese* is hardly a happy poem) is to be understood by remembering that in Victorian terminology to be 'happy' was to be married. And when the euphemistic terms are reversed, to be 'unhappy' is to be a spinster. Spinsters are not free to write of sexual love or passion as the 'happy' married woman is. The claims are striking. Elizabeth Barrett Browning might have been a different and perhaps a greater poet if she had remained single. Correspondingly, the unmarried woman has something important (perhaps more important?) to say about sexual feeling, but is blocked by convention from saying it. No wonder such spinster poetry might be 'less dignified', if just as honourable, than that written *to* her. She would be writing of the 'barrier', implicitly both hymenal and societal in this prose, between women and men, between herself and the object of her passion, sexual or divine. The barrier 'might be one held sacred': she would be writing of taboo subjects, unfulfilled feminine desire and rejection.[27]

The 'barrier' as the topic of expressive theory is explored, necessarily indirectly, by Rossetti, Greenwell and Ingelow. These poets worked inside the religious lyric and the love lyric and radically redefined them by exploring their limits. How they do this, and how they not only metaphorise but establish the barrier as a structural principle of their poems, is perhaps more fundamental to the nature of Victorian women's poetry than any of the direct accounts of women's experience to be found in their poems.

Of course, overt polemic about women can be found in the work of these poets, but these are less fundamental than their indirections. Certainly Christina Rossetti's work yields enough, at the level of direct statement, about sexual, social and economic matters for one to be sure that she thought of herself as a 'woman' writer and indeed saw that she was marginalised as one by the very nature of her situation. She contributed to *The Germ* but her sex naturally excluded her formally from the Pre-Raphaelite *Brother*hood.

> *The P.R.B.*
> The two Rossettis (brothers they)
> And Holman Hunt and John Millais
> With Stephens chivalrous and bland,
> And Woolner in a distant land –
> In these six men I awestruck see
> Embodied the great P.R.B.
> D. G. Rossetti offered two
> Good pictures to the public view;
> Unnumbered ones great John Millais,
> And Holman more than I can say.
> William Rossetti, calm and solemn,
> Cuts up his brethren by the column.[28]

This poem, dated 19 September 1853, might have been even tarter if she had known that William was to cut up his sister by the column when he edited her poems in 1904.

Illegitimacy, fallen women, the fierce legal bond of marriage, the sexual fate of the woman who waits, while the male is given social licence to experiment, the experience of exclusion, all this is to be found particularly in Christina Rossetti's earlier work. Her poems constantly define the lyric writer as shut out, outside, at the margin. 'Shut Out' is the title of a poem which makes the condition of exclusion paradoxically that of being shut in. 'At Home' is a poem about being not at home in this woman's place, ironising the visiting-card title – 'When I was dead my spirit turned/To see the much frequented house'. 'The Iniquity of the Fathers upon the Children' (1866) clearly emerges from her well-known interest in fallen women: ballads about prohibition, possession, rivalry, the rigour of the law, bonds and legal forms ('Love from the North', 'Cousin Kate', 'Noble Sisters', 'Maude Clare') testify to her awareness of the social and economic circumstances of women. She is fierce about the dependency of marriage in 'A Triad' for instance. There three kinds of passion are envisaged. The last, institutionalised sexuality in marriage, is enervated and passive – 'One droned in sweetness like a fattened bee'. And yet Rossetti's generalised lyric seems almost created to resist and circumvent such analyses. The seeming sourcelessness and contextlessness of lyric, its impersonal reserve, its *secrecy*, is the form Rossetti chose. On the other hand, the intransigently enigmatic, by declaring itself as such, allows itself an

extraordinary openness. Reserve and intensity, constraint and exposure, belong together because, as Dora Greenwell recognised,
reserve is necessarily built upon its opposite. Once you have let it be
known you have a secret you allow that there is something to give
away.

Part of the secret of 'Goblin Market', the title poem of Christina
Rossetti's first volume, is the questioning feminine discourse it
masks. Two girls, ambiguously children and adolescents, seemingly
autonomous and without parents, crouch as if nesting in the rushes
as they hear the goblin's cry, 'Come buy'. Distorted, half-animal
creatures, resembling cats, rats, wombats and snails, offer a collection of fruits (which violate all seasonal patterns) for sale in a jingle
of plenitude, 'All ripe together'. The poem has the unplaced contextlessness of a fairy tale. Arthur Symons called it 'the perfect realisation of those happy and fantastic aspects of the supernatural
which we call fairy land'. It was to him 'naïve and childlike', but he
added that it was also 'fantastic and bewildering' in its 'faery' at-
mosphere (this archaic spelling often indicates discomfort in
Victorian writers).[29] The consummate metrical virtuosity of the
jingle sophisticatedly deflects the poem into the 'naïve' aural and
oral tradition, a literary way of masking the literary, perhaps (and
there is something of an astringent, sharpened almost ironised Keats
here), but one which does propose that the tracks of the poem are
in some way covered. It proposes to the reader precisely a deferral
of placing. It is 'bewildering'.

> Morning and evening
> Maids heard the goblins cry:
> 'Come buy our orchard fruits,
> Come buy, come buy:
> Apples and quinces,
> Lemons and oranges,
> Plump unpecked cherries,
> Melons and raspberries,
> Bloom-down-cheeked peaches,
> Swart-headed mulberries,
> Wild free-born cranberries,
> Crab-apples, dewberries,
> Pine-apples, blackberries,
> Apricots, strawberries; –
> All ripe together
> In summer weather, –
> Morns that pass by,

Fair eves that fly;
Come buy, come buy:
Our grapes fresh from the vine,
Pomegranates full and fine,
Dates and sharp bullaces,
Rare pears and greengages,
Damsons and bilberries,
Taste them and try.'[30]

This is a deeply, insatiably oral poem in another way. The words
'fill the mouth' as the goblins' figs do, with a materiality which is
taken up in the 'tingling cheeks' of the listening girls. And when
Laura is forced not to take but to *buy* the fruit by giving up part of
herself (a lock of her hair is exchanged instead of money), she
'sucks' it.

She sucked and sucked and sucked the more
Fruits which that unknown orchard bore;
She sucked until her lips were sore.[31]

It is tempting to literalise the sexuality of such lines, but it is important to be sceptical about doing so. What can be said is that the
poem is not, in Rossetti's words, 'dignified'. Laura's orgiastic
sucking, the passionate fury of her loss when she can have the fruit
no more ('she gnashed her teeth for baulked desire and wept'[32]),
the assault of the goblins upon Lizzie, who resists the fruit which
they smear and crush upon her face, Laura's eager kissing of her
sister to regain the juice of the fruit, such passages are not only not
'dignified' but transgress and outrage in their violence and agony.

Kicked and knocked her,
Mauled and mocked her,
Lizzie uttered not a word;
Would not open lip from lip
Lest they should cram a mouthful in:
But laughed in heart to feel the drip
Of juice that syrupped all her face,
And lodged in dimples of her chin,
And streaked her neck which quaked like curd.[33]

But what can be made of this narrative? Laura never sees or hears
the goblins again. Pining and starvation follow fierce agony and
rage, that most poignant condition. Lizzie, seeing that Laura is near
to death from deprivation, searches for the goblins. Wiser than

Laura, she has her silver penny in her pocket. Something happens to her: 'And for *the first time in her life*/Began to listen and to look' (my emphasis).[34] Once she finds the goblins she bargains in order to be able to carry the fruit to Laura but they, refusing to accede to the take-away principle, attack her, grind the fruit against her face, literally expressing the juice, and smear her with it. Laughing with glee, her silver penny still intact, she returns dripping to Laura, who expects to see her 'goblin-ridden'. Laura licks the fruit from her face, and this secondary experience induces paroxysms of pain. But she recovers. The poem ends almost perfunctorily, celebrating the love of sisters and declaring that the tale is handed onto the children when the sisters marry.

Payment for forbidden fruit, prohibition, taboo, punishment, the consumption of what is itself dangerously consuming, the harsh moral exclusion of the erotic, all these are in play here. The difficulty is to place them. Some critics have literalised the poem in terms of masturbation: menstruation and faeces would do as well because the images are so enigmatically precise that they are open-endedly generalisable. Some critics see a lesbian passion between the two girls: some have seen fantasies of the colonial other at work in their response to the goblins; some have been tempted to see Laura and Lizzie in conflict and moral opposition to one another, in a cautionary tale of freedom and repression. All these readings are possible. But why the strange collusion in which Lizzie displaces the pulped fruit for Laura's consumption, a 'sacrifice' which leaves her not merely untouched but gleeful and energised? Why the recovery in which light dances in Laura's eyes? Is the fate of Jeanie, who went to her death before marriage on encountering the goblins, an attempt to reinforce the harsh moral intransigence of a cautionary tale or an indication that it is not an analogue for the central episode? The harshness of the poem is not so much in its sense of retribution as the cruel way in which the fruit is offered as a saleable commodity and arbitrarily withdrawn. It has to be bargained for, but it belongs to a mystified economy to which both girls are inalienably subject. You exchange or sell something for it but the exchange is unequal. The fruit is *made* into temptation according to arbitrary laws. Some of these questions can be clarified by recourse to the aesthetics of expressive theory.

How does expressive theory return upon 'Goblin Market'? Boldly and dramatically Christina Rossetti transfers the structure of aesthetic thought, with all its uneasiness and ambiguities, directly to the sexual and erotic conflict bound up in the forbidden fruit. Sexual and moral conflict is metaphorically incipient in expressive theory but Rossetti exposes this through the context of the goblins' temptation. Laura is like one of Keble's poets. She will go mad or die unless she can carry out her desires and consume the fruit once more. The dissipation of her energies when they have no means of expression and find no meaningful object in formerly happy tasks is extreme. In anorexic grief,

> She no more swept the house,
> Tended the fowls or cows,
> Fetched honey, kneaded cakes of wheat,
> Brought water from the brook:
> But sat down listless in the chimmey-nook
> And would not eat.[35]

Desire without an object, which has been summarily and cruelly removed, cannot move out of the self. To go back to the aesthetic terms, feeling can find no equivalent for itself, no form or object to invest or 'fuse' with emotion. The object isn't there. It isn't there because it is mysteriously forbidden. Either to have the object or to represent it is a transgression. So feeling thrusts against barriers or expends itself on nothing. Laura's representations of her experience to Lizzie ('You cannot think what figs/My teeth have met in') only make her more desperately aware both of her loss and of the disjunction between her symbolic expression and the experience itself. 'She dreamed of melons, as a traveller sees/False waves in desert drouth ... /And burns the thirstier in the sandful breeze'.[36] The symbolic representation turns out to be illusory, the false equivalence of a dream.

One way of reading Lizzie's anxious ethical care for Laura, her sense of the rules, her escape from the consequences of the goblin fruit, is to see it in neat moral opposition to Laura's experience. The answer to Laura's suffering is a punitive medicinal exorcism, in which pleasure turns to pain, effecting Laura's moral transformation and reincorporation into social life. Part of the complexity of the poem arises because this is one feminine discourse allowed by the work – the agony of repression, denial and sacrifice. But it is at this point that the questions which have been asked make their claims. And the ambiguities of expressive theory help here. If expression is predicated upon repression, if they are interdependent as much as in antithesis, the structure of the poem shifts. The interdependence of Laura and Lizzie becomes a possibility. It is not a question of choosing either Laura or Lizzie, freedom or prohibition. Laura and Lizzie are doubles of one another. Rossetti has seized on the interdependence of the overflow of feeling and the barrier. Each reciprocally enables and disables the other. It is only through Lizzie's resistance that Laura is able to gain access to the (significantly) expressed fruit. It is only through Laura's longing that Lizzie finds herself resisting the goblins. Laura is liberated by repeating the tasting of the fruit but it is only through a process of displacement that the fruit can be regained. As if to endorse this doubling, Lizzie's resistance to and Laura's assimilation of the fruit are represented by the same traditional images of virginity under attack. Lizzie resists like a lily or a stone assaulted by the surging currents of the sea, or a town under attack, 'Made to tug her standard down',[37] and the breaching current of feeling becomes the force of aggression. Laura is *carried* by the force of her experience 'Like a caged thing freed', 'like a flying flag when armies run'.[38] Like a town in an earthquake, a mast or a tree in a tempest, she is overwhelmed.

The passages have the metaphor of current, surge, overflow, which is constantly present in Victorian poetics to describe the force of expressive feeling. The condition of Laura's freedom seems to be an *assent* to being overwhelmed by the power of the fruit rather than a resistance to it, a reversal of what one would expect of a 'moral' reading of the poem. For if we pursue the metaphor, the barriers of virginity are breached. And yet the situation is paradoxical. Her freedom is in proportion to, and depends upon, her resistance to it. On fire, 'she loathed the feast' and 'Gorged on bitterness without a name'.[39] The energy of resistance is the condition of the energies of expression. They partake of one another so that expression *is* 'mortal strife'.[40] Laura's liberation does not rest on the elimination of constraint but on a consent to its power.

The poem is deeply ambiguous here, reproducing the ambiguities at work in the poetics of expression, for one reading of this passage reasserts the simple opposition between free unbound sexuality and bitter constraint. It slips into conventional ethics. The fruit becomes a medicinal punishment, a 'fiery antidote', as it is later called, which purges Laura of her poisons and restores her innocence. 'Laura awoke as from a dream,/ Laughed in the innocent old way'.[41] She is made ready to accept the institutionalised conventions of marriage and passes on her 'fears' to her children. Certainly this is one

feminine discourse in the poem, an acceptance of patriarchy and
the rigour of repression. But there is another working against the
simplicities of the first. If we accept the structural dependence of
expression and repression upon one another, Laura's recovery of
energy – her grey hair disappears, her locks gleam and light dances
in her eyes – becomes a function of her acceptance of the full power
of sexuality. It is not a second fall but a *new* second innocence. The
words 'gorged on bitterness' recall Milton's Eve, who 'greedily
engorg'd' the apple from the tree of knowledge of good and evil.
And yet in a bold rereading of Milton, Laura's second taking of the
fruit is not a fall but a recovery and consolidates the power of the
fruit. Sexuality is neither freedom nor constraint, but both. As such
its energies are ambiguous – 'sweeter than honey from the rock' and
'wormwood' to the tongue.[42] That is why the power of the fruit is
'without a name'. No single representation of it can be adequate
or, indeed, it *can't* be represented. Rossetti's representation of sexuality is not in the names or images she finds but in the structure of
the whole poem with its repeated tasting. It is important to the intransigence of the poem that Laura does not *do* anything with her
acceptance. It simply enables her to stay alive. She is absorbed into
the female patterns of marriage, 'beset with fears' for her children,
for what is celebrated in 'Goblin Market' is also to be feared.[43]
And, to become a Victorian parent is to be dogged by fear of sexuality. The syntax of the first jingle allows that to buy the fruit is also
to buy 'Morns that pass by,/ Fair eves that fly', loss and fulfilment,
delight and fear. Sexuality itself is defined by, locked into, the institutions in which it has its being. It is governed by money and a
principle of exchange. It is construed as temptation.

'Goblin Market' is Christina Rossetti's most remarkable long
poem. She was also a writer of consummate lyrics. What can be
called the feminine discourse which responds to the aesthetics of
expression and repression, overflow and barrier, in 'Goblin Market',
is also at work in her short poems. Her lyrics of love or devotion
are written with a curious intensity and authority and the traditional forms she chooses, pastoral, song, incantation, riddle, allegory, ballad, make them into quintessences of themselves. They are
offered as if – Symons' word is right here – they are 'naïve' forms of
known conventional lyric. They have at first sight a crystal ingenu-
ous openness, inviting the simple reading. Yet in them a rigorous
reserve and economy is under pressure. The 'naïve' lyric becomes a
way of being secret. The theological concept of reserve, of keeping

back, which is openly accepted by Keble as a poetic principle seems
to be a principle of these lyrics, and yet they disclose the struggle
and difficulty Greenwell described as the founding moment of feminine consciousness. They come to be *about* reserve, the struggle to
express and not to express, to resist and not to resist. All her work
is adamantly locked in repetition. Doubling of words, phrases, pat-
terned iteration and duplication, create the spareness of her lyrics.
Repetition works as a barrier. It is a way of setting up a pattern, resisting or confirming it. The shifting and deflecting which goes on in
and through the process of repetition indicates a play in and *with*
limit, which is set up, violated, transgressed, confirmed. The formal
constraint, as with rhyme, enables a play with regularity and irregularity. Her early games of bout rimés (the Rossetti family game, an
exercise which is described interestingly in *Maude*, Christina
Rossetti's adolescent tale of religious hypochondria) were fundamental to her poetry.[44] Refrain is another way of defining and
redefining barriers, because it falls inside and outside the poem
simultaneously. These strategies of restriction achieve startling
shifts and realignments, just as Rossetti's conventional language
produces arresting collocations – 'bloodless lily', 'fattening rain',
'chill-veined snowdrop'. Through them her lyrics experiment with
boundaries and the transgression of boundaries in such a way that a
seemingly conventional lyric moves into a questioning of convention. Conventions are arbitrary in themselves and the poetry
becomes a questioning of the arbitrary.

Christina Rossetti's response to the aesthetics of overflow is not
unique, though it is explored in a uniquely original way. It is shared
by the other poets I have mentioned, Greenwell and Ingelow, who
are compulsively concerned in form and content with the implications of expressive thought. It is useful to put some of their work
against hers. An early poem bears a striking resemblance to Dora
Greenwell's 'Qui sait aimer, sait mourir'.

> 'I burn myself away!'
> So spake the Rose and smiled; 'within my cup
> All day the sunbeams fall in flame, all day
>   They drink my sweetness up!'
>
> 'I sigh my soul away!'
>   The Lily said; 'all night the moonbeams pale
> Steal round and round me, whispering in their play
>   An all too tender tale!'

'I give my soul away!'
The Violet said; 'the West wind wanders on,
The North wind comes; I know not what they say,
And yet my soul is gone!'

Oh Poet, burn away
Thy fervent soul! fond Lover at the feet
Of her thou lovest, sigh! dear Christian, pray,
And let the world be sweet!
                              (Dora Greenwell)[45]

She sat and sang alway
    By the green margin of a stream,
Watching the fishes leap and play
    Beneath the glad sunbeam.

I sat and wept away
    Beneath the moon's most shadowy beam,
Watching the blossoms of the May
    Weep leaves into the stream.

I wept for memory;
    She sang for hope that is so fair:
My tears were swallowed by the sea;
    Her songs died on the air.
                    (Christina Rossetti, 'Song')[46]

In Greenwell's poem the Rose, the Lily and the Violet, conventional
symbols of erotic love, are given speech, as if the role of the
'unnamed ladies' mentioned in Rossetti's Preface is reversed. They
are no longer objects but agents. They are explicitly compared to
the poet who, like them, breaks the limit of selfhood, burning, and
to the male lover, sighing. The sigh, the exhalation, is an appropriate image for that moving of being beyond itself and indeed takes
up the poet's projection of self which is often described as the
empathy of love in Victorian criticism. Rose, Lily and Violet,
however, are consumed or dissipated in the expressive act. The
male lover has an object. As if aware of its dangerous implications,
the poem ends as Christian prayer in which the overflow of feeling
has a transcendental object. Rossetti's poem, characteristically con-
densed and terse, is based not upon a triad but an antithesis – 'She
sat and sang alway ... I sat and wept away'. With near repetition
'away' shifts from an intensifier to reflexive – I wept myself away.
Expressive feeling momentarily finds a correspondent image in the
world as the May blossoms 'weep leaves into the stream' but the

representation cannot contain the overflow of feeling which is dispersed in an unresponding universe. Antithesis is superseded by a new parallelism. Both tears and songs dissipate, swallowed by the sea, dying on the air. Because it can find no equivalent or limiting form the expressive act is a death. There is no Christian resolution.

Goblin Market and Other Poems was published in 1862. Dora Greenwell, already an established poet, published another volume of *Poems* in 1867. These later poems in particular return repeatedly to a language of burning and blushing, exposure, overflow, sighs, breathing, exhalation, and to a structure in which hidden and secret feeling kills and is killed if it finds no expression but expires in the expressive act. 'A Song' is a virtual pun on the idea of expiration, the sigh, a death. A cloud can neither condense 'To fall in kindly rain', nor project its colours onto the world. It exists merely as that which 'sighed': 'What could it do but die?'[47] The golden heart of the rose 'o'er flows' and decays in 'Amid Change Unchanging'. In 'One Flower' the blush, the tear, the smile, the sigh, achieve a transitory moment of expression, breaking out of limit but dying in the act. 'Thy soul has burst its sheath,/Oh, is it love or death,/Sweet flower, that thou hast won?'[48] 'A Picture' plays with expression both as a physical embodiment in eye, cheek, smile and lips and expression as an unbodily, fleeting manifestation of hidden and intangible spiritual being: 'And on her lips that, like an opening rose,/Seemed parting some sweet secret to disclose'.[49] The pun on 'disclose' makes expression both released and withheld. The physical form is both the means of expression and its obstruction. This is a love poem to a woman by a woman. Or, more complexly, perhaps, by a woman envisaging a love poem by a man. In 'Reserve', the problem is dealt with directly, as the speaker longs to gain access to 'thy Being's overflow' and liberate the 'deeper' 'tide/Of feeling' from 'the bar' of constraint. 'Bar' is a pun on both barrier and music, as if the representation of feeling becomes its barrier in a way characteristic of expressive theory.[50] The virtuosic 'A Scherzo' is about the overprotected and yet constricted heart which longs to escape 'Anywhere, anywhere, out of this room!'[51] It is not surprising that Dora Greenwell's remarkably detailed and humane essay 'On the Education of the Imbecile', published in the *North British Review* in 1868, sees idiocy as potential feeling and intelligence which has been blocked.[52] Idiots *are* educable and capable of love and mental effort, even though it is as if 'a secret finger had been laid upon some hitherto unsuspected *stop* in the great organ'. 'Fast-bound', 'bondage', 'captivity', 'clogged', are the words she uses to describe their condition. She compares the idiot to the maniac, 'who has at least *lived*'.[53] The idiot, blocked from expression, has something in common with women, though she does not say so. It shares the same experience of constraint.

If Dora Greenwell's work is concerned with expression obstructed or dissipated in the act, Jean Ingelow, also publishing in this decade (*Poems*, 1863), deals with expressive metaphor as passionate overflow, flood, outpouring. 'The High Tide on the Coast of Lincolnshire', a narrative historical ballad of disastrous flood, is emblematic of her work. The river Lindis breaks its banks as the result of a huge, unforeseen tidal wave, sweeping away Elizabeth, the cowherd's wife, and her two children.

> Then bankes came downe with ruin and rout –
> Then beaten foam flew round about –
> Then all the mighty floods were out.[54]

Water, or light, forcing a passage outwards, but hurrying towards extinction and destruction, flows through her poems. The 'Star's Monument' turns on the eclipse of a star which had fulfilled its existence simply by giving out light. Passion and outpouring, however transient, is celebrated as meaningful.[55] In 'Requiescat in Pace!', sunset, uncannily flushing landscape and sky, is an image of the expenditure of Christ's life in the Passion, a transformation of matter by spirit. This is a metaphor of flow and *influence*, feeling justified in and by itself. Its language of light and flush owes much to Tennyson and the rhythms of *Maud*.

> Below me lay the wide sea, the scarlet sun was stooping,
>   And he dyed the wasted water, as with a scarlet dye;
> And he dyed the lighthouse towers, every bird with white wing
>   swooping,
>   Took his colours, and the cliffs did, and the yawning sky.
>
> Over grass came that strange flush, and over ling and heather,
>   Over flocks of sheep and lambs, and over Cromer town;
> And each filmy cloudlet crossing drifted like a scarlet feather
>   Torn from folded wings of clouds, while he settled down.
>
> When I looked, I dared not sigh: – in the light of God's splendour,
>   With his daily blue and gold, who am I? What am I?
> But that passion and outpouring seeming an awful sign and tender,
>   Like the blood of the Redeemer, shown on earth and sky.[56]

Interestingly, God's expressive act supersedes and extinguishes the writer's: 'I dared not sigh'. It provokes the question 'who am I? What am I?' Both Greenwell and Ingelow present the female subject in extinction, as obliterated. Uncontained by it, unable to find representation, or without an object, overflow and flood are self-extinguishing. These poets appropriate the dominant aesthetic of expression, take over its metaphor and linguistic forms and work within it, but they explore its impossibilities.

Dora Greenwell's *Poems* (1867) are dedicated to Elizabeth Barrett Browning, and some of the poems in that volume are clearly influenced by her. 'A Song to Call to Remembrance', subtitled 'A Plea for the Coventry Ribbon Weavers', engages in direct political writing: 'When anxious fathers have no work, the children dare not play'. It is an indication of Elizabeth Barrett Browning's independence that *Aurora Leigh* does not negotiate with the terms of expressive theory. Expressive metaphor, the flow of milk and love, for instance, is present in *Aurora Leigh*, but without the tensions it has in the work of Greenwell and Ingelow. The terms of expressive theory are more nearly present in *Sonnets from the Portuguese,* and there, in the hesitating affirmations of these poems, Elizabeth Barrett Browning is interested in a dialectic of subject and object which attempts to represent the struggle for identity in passion between two people and the struggle for *language. Sonnets from the Portuguese* is about idolatry, dependency, the temptation to disappear before the object of adulation. It is ambitious because it attempts to discover a language to represent and go beyond the structure of an unwilling master–slave relationship. It is a language of dissolving categories which attempt to coalesce into new forms. Though its language is very different, its preoccupation is the same as those of Greenwell and Ingelow, the dissolving of selfhood.

The aim of *Sonnets* is to redefine 'the whole/Of life in a new rhythm', as Elizabeth Barrett Browning puts it in Sonnet VII, and the sliding cadences, the deliberate elisions and metrical freedoms which break away from the established regularities of the sonnet form are clearly intentional.[57] The late caesuras and enjambement declare an attempt to dissolve the customary forms and restrictions. Language goes into a flux, as if enacting the dissolution of categories. In XV, for instance, an adjective acts with a double function, as both adjective and noun – 'Love's *divine*' (l.6), shut 'in a *crystalline*' (l.7). The effect is of expansion, a going beyond the limit of definition. In the same way the lover's gaze attempts not to be 'shut

... in' or subordinated by the gaze of the other, but to look away and move beyond the definition of the other's sight – 'As one who sits and gazes from above,/Over the rivers to the bitter sea' (ll.13–14). But to gaze 'from above' is simply to invert the relationship and this seems only to circumvent the 'rivers' of feeling by looking beyond them to death and the 'oblivion' (l.12) of the 'bitter sea'. The sonnets chart the struggle of the feminine subject to take up a new position which is free of dependency. They struggle with their own dissolve as they try to break into new areas of being. The door and the threshold, that peculiarly Victorian image of barrier, of lines crossed and partition established, determined space, are the incipient images of these sonnets. In Sonnet IV the expressive model is reversed as the poet experiences the overwhelming power of the other as *in*fluence, a breaking in, a shattering of the doors of the self – 'My cricket chirps against thy mandolin' (l.11). The 'voice within' (l.13) can only be retrieved in solitude and paradoxical silence. The male poet's expression is music falling 'In folds of golden fullness at my door' (l.8). Music materialises as the folds of a curtain and de-materialises as space, 'folds ... of fullness'. Colour, texture, space, the reconfiguring of categories, denotes new dimensions and possibilities. Elizabeth Barrett Browning is attempting to reconfigure the expressive act as music so that it finds not a representation, for non-referential music cannot be that, but releases itself from contradiction by going beyond the barrier of equivalences and inventing new forms and experiences independent of them. So *Sonnets* moves towards language as a self-referring or self-creating act. This is one way out of the impasse of expressive theory. The poem does not always measure up to its ambitions but it is a fertile experiment.

From Isobel Armstrong, *Victorian Poetry: Poetry, Poetics and Politics* (London, 1993), pp. 332–57.

NOTES

['"A Music of Thine Own": Women's Poetry' is extracted from the long chapter of the same name in Isobel Armstrong's major study of Victorian poetry. In its original form the excerpt reprinted here is placed after an introductory section which discusses the impact of Felicia Hemans's and Leititia Landon's poetry on the tradition of poetry by women as it evolved after 1830. The concluding section of her chapter examines how women poets in the second half of the nineteenth century develop a 'poetics of myth and mask'. Included in this latter part of the discussion are poets, such as Augusta Webster, who produced distinctive and powerful dramatic monologues, and Mathilde Blind, whose *Ascent of Man* (1880) engages with Darwinian theory.

Armstrong's work is characterised by a painstaking attention to form and language, in an effort to accentuate how poetic representation mediates changing historical forces. Responsive to recent developments in feminist cultural theory, Armstrong places questions about femininity and poetry in relation to a range of prominent Victorian debates about aesthetics and politics. In particular, she is interested in how poetic language organises categories of knowledge. This is a point central to the argument of her previous book, *Language as Living Form in Nineteenth-Century Poetry* (Brighton, 1982). Ed.]

1. Anne Brontë, *The Poems of Anne Brontë: A New Text and Commentary*, ed. Edward Chitham (Basingstoke, 1979), pp. 110–11, 21–8.

2. Charlotte Brontë, *Poems of Charlotte Brontë*, ed. Tom Winnfrith (Oxford, 1984), pp. 202–3.

3. Emily Brontë, 'The Philosopher', in *The Complete Poems*, ed. C.W. Hatfield (London, 1923), pp. 5–6.

4. Adelaide Anne Procter, *Legends and Lyrics and Other Poems* ([1858] London, 1906), pp. 111–13.

5. Ibid., p. 151.

6. Ibid., pp. 45–52, 47.

7. Ibid., pp. 48–9.

8. See ibid.: 'A Lost Chord', p. 159, 'Hush!', pp. 131–2, and 'Unexpressed', pp. 137–8.

9. Ibid., pp. 85–6.

10. Dora Greenwell, *Essays* (London, 1866), pp. 1–68.

11. Sydney Dobell, a Spasmodic poet, describes expressive theory in his impressively complex lecture on 'The Nature of Poetry', *Thoughts on Art, Philosphy, and Religion* (London, 1876), pp. 3–65. The poet's problem is to make the poem a representation of mind: '*a perfect Poem is the perfect expression of a Perfect Human Mind*' (p. 7). Metaphor is crucial to expressive poetry, which is based on transposition and substitution (of words for the contents of consciousness). 'To express is to carry out. To express a mind is to carry out that mind into some equivalent' (p. 13).

12. Arthur Henry Hallam, 'On Some of the Characteristics of Modern Poetry', *Englishman's Magazine*, 1 (1831), 616–28, reprinted in Isobel Armstrong, *Victorian Scrutinies: Reviews of Poetry 1830–1870* (London, 1972), p. 93.

13. [G.H. Lewes] 'Hegel's Aesthetics', *British and Foreign Review*, 13 (1842), 1–49.

14. Ibid., p. 22.

15. John Keble, *Lectures on Poetry, 1832–1841*, ed. Edward Kershaw Francis, 2 vols (Oxford, 1912), I, p. 20.

16. Julia Kristeva, *Revolution in Poetic Language*, trans. Margaret Waller (London, 1984). See in particular ch. 2.

17. Greenwell, *Essays*, pp. 3–4.

18. Ibid., p. 4.

19. Ibid., p. 19.

20. Ibid., p. 45.

21. Ibid., p. 27.

22. Ibid., p. 8.

23. Ibid., p. 43 ('aggressive action', p. 33).

24. Ibid., p. 59.

25. Ibid., p. 58.

26. Christina Rossetti, *The Complete Poems*, ed. R.W. Crump, 3 vols (Baton Rouge, LA, 1979–90), II, p. 86.

27. Ibid.

28. Ibid., III, p. 332.

29. Arthur Symons, 'Christina G. Rossetti, 1830–94', in A.H. Miles (ed.), *Poets and Poetry of the Nineteenth Century*, 11 vols (London, 1905–7), IX, p. 5.

30. Rossetti, *The Complete Poems*, I, p. 11.

31. Ibid., I, p. 14.

32. Ibid., I, p. 18.

33. Ibid., I, p. 22.

34. Ibid., I, p. 19.

35. Ibid., pp. 18–19

36. Ibid., I, pp. 14, 18.

37. Ibid., I, p. 22.

38. Ibid., I, p. 24.

39. Ibid.

40. Ibid.

41. Ibid., I, pp. 26, 25.

42. Ibid., I, pp. 14, 24.

43. Ibid., I, p. 25.

44. Rossetti, *Maude*, ed. William Michael Rossetti (London, 1897), p. 17.

45. Dora Greenwell, *Poems* (London, 1867), pp. 139–40.

46. Rossetti, *The Complete Poems*, I, p. 58.

47. Greenwell, *Poems*, pp. 175–6.

48. Ibid., pp. 168, 170–1.

49. Ibid., pp. 179–80.

50. Ibid., p. 195.

51. Ibid., pp. 172–3.

52. 'On the Education of the Imbecile', reprinted from the *North British Review* (1868), edited for the Royal Albert Idiot Asylum, Lancaster, 1867.

53. Ibid., p. 8. For the vocabulary of blockage, see pp. 11, 37.

54. Jean Ingelow, *Poems* (London, 1863), p. 150.

55. Ibid., pp. 76–104.

56. Ibid., p. 43.

57. Elizabeth Barrett Browning, *Sonnets from the Portuguese: A Variorum Edition*, ed. Miroslava Wein Dow (New York, 1980), p. 23, lines 6–7. Further line references appear in parentheses.

2

The Damsel, the Knight, and the Victorian Woman Poet

DOROTHY MERMIN

Looking back at her childhood from the vantage point of fourteen years old, Elizabeth Barrett wrote that at four-and-a-half, 'my great delight was poring over fairy phenomenons and the actions of necromancers – & the seven champions of Christendom ... beguiled many a weary hour. At five I supposed myself a heroine and in my day dreams of bliss I constantly imaged to myself a forlorn damsel in distress rescued by some noble knight.'[1] Which was she in these daydreams: the forlorn damsel, or the noble knight? 'I supposed myself a heroine', but 'I imaged *to* myself a damsel rescued...' The knight is more distant – 'some noble knight' – and the fact that the daydreams arose as an escape from weary hours suggests an unwilling identification with the damsel. But from an early age Elizabeth Barrett despised sentimental young women and wanted to dress as a boy and run away to be, perhaps, 'poor Lord Byron's PAGE': a daydream that tries to defer gender identification by deferring adult sexuality, but cannot defer it indefinitely.[2] In her earliest literary imaginings, then, we find her hovering between two mutually exclusive and equally unsuitable literary roles – one precluded by the need for activity and self-assertion, the other precluded by gender. This is the predicament in which the two best Victorian women poets, Elizabeth Barrett Browning and Christina Rossetti, found themselves when they looked for a place where a woman could situate herself without self-contradiction and in which she could not just daydream, but speak.

A study of their encounters with this problem can help us answer the question that puzzles and teases the feminist critic of Victorian poetry: why were there so few good women poets in nineteenth-century England when there were so many excellent women novelists? Victorian critics thought it was probably because the female imagination cannot go beyond the personal and superficial. Now, of course, we find a different kind of explanation. Most women lacked the classical education that served as the rite of initiation into high culture. Traditional conceptions of the poet's role – as priest, for instance – were inherently masculine. Publication seemed like unwomanly self-display, or even sexual self-exposure, and could be justified more easily if one wrote novels to make money rather than poems just for glory. With less prestige than poetry, and a less formidably male tradition, novel writing was more accessible, as new occupations often are, to women. It is sometimes said, too, that women could not summon up the sense of self and the self-assertiveness that poetry requires, and that they were too repressed to write strong lyrics.[3] Of course, many of the hindrances to women poets also hindered men. Fear of self-exposure and the felt lack of a central, stable self with an existence independent of its relations to others were problems for male Victorian poets too. Sexuality and rage do not seem to be significantly more repressed in Barrett Browning's or Rossetti's works than in Matthew Arnold's or even Tennyson's. Nor did the men of a self-consciously prosaic and doubting age find bardic or priestly robes more comfortable than women did. But for women, cultural and psychological barriers were reinforced by the difficulty of situating themselves within the inherited structures of English poetry.

Barrett Browning records in two narrative poems her early realisation that as a woman poet she would have to play two opposing roles at one time – both knight and damsel, both subject and object – and that because she can't do this she is excluded from the worlds her imagination has discovered. The speaker in 'The Deserted Garden' had as a child loved to read and dream in an abandoned garden, a secret and magical place that she entered with 'Adventurous joy' and where as she read her 'likeness grew' 'To "gentle hermit of the dale",/ And Angelina too.'[4] But as if in consequence of this impossibly doubled identification with figures of romance, she 'shut the book', she grew up, and the garden was again deserted. A later and longer work, 'The Lost Bower', tells how as a child the speaker once made her way through thickets and brambles to a lovely bower but never could find it again. Discovering the bower is even more of an adventure than penetrating the deserted garden: it is a heroic exploit, an accomplished quest; but the traditional plot that the child is enacting requires the bower to contain a female figure, and there is no one to be that figure except herself. So she says: 'Henceforth, I will be the fairy/Of this bower ... the dream-hall I have won' (ll. 241–2, 245). That is, she will be both the quester and the object of the quest. It's an awkward arrangement, and it doesn't work. When she looks for the bower again, she can't find it, because, as she realises, she is now being the prince in the story of the Sleeping Beauty, and there is no Beauty in the bower to draw the prince on with the light of her dreaming spirit. She can't be two people at once, both the questing prince and the dreaming princess, both a poet and his fairy inspiration, and so she never arrives. This was the 'first of all my losses' (l.300), the speaker says, and it prefigured many more. It is the loss of a poetic world and a poetic subject, lost because she can't fill both roles that the story requires. The speaker describes herself at the poem's end as weary and waiting, just as four-year-old Elizabeth Barrett was when she 'beguiled many a weary hour' with daydreams of romance, and as Rossetti's speakers typically are: this is the state which for both women, apparently, induces poetry. But she has found that there is no place for herself in her daydreams. Barrett Browning said that the incident described in 'The Lost Bower' had really happened, and her poems testify that, metaphorically at any rate, it really had.[5]

The same patterns appear in crucial places in Rossetti's poetic career. The necessary pairing or doubling of damsel and knight is the subject of the two enigmatic lines of her first recorded verse, composed before she could write: 'Cecilia never went to school/Without her gladiator.' And in 'The Dead City', which opened her first collection of poetry, the speaker moves like a questing prince into the heart of imaginative experience and is balked just when it is time to find and rescue the Sleeping Beauty. Like the speakers of 'The Deserted Garden' and 'The Lost Bower', she (or perhaps he) wanders boldly through the woods alone 'with a careless hardihood'; she eventually finds within an empty city a palace decked for feasting that anticipates in its particular luxuries the world of Pre-Raphaelite sensuousness and art that Rossetti was later to describe in 'Goblin Market'. Everyone at the feast has been turned to stone, but she cannot revive them with a kiss: all the young people are paired off already and their gaze is strange and unwelcoming. She averts her eyes in fear, the palace vanishes, and the poem ends with the assertion that this imaginative quest was not for her: 'What was I that I should see/So much hidden mystery?'[6]

The problem is not only or even primarily one of narrative, although it is articulated most clearly in terms of plot. The Victorian woman poet has to be two things at once, or in two places, whenever she tries to locate herself within the poetic world. Her problem may be said to begin, oddly enough, with the fact that for the Victorians writing poetry seemed like woman's work, even though only men were supposed to do it. Critics liked simple, homely poetic subjects and language and sincere, spontaneous expressions of feeling – the artless spontaneity, in short, which is still assumed by critics who should know better to be characteristic of women. The enormous popularity of Tennyson's *In Memoriam* owed a great deal to the scenes of domestic pathos – widows, widowers, grieving mothers, and the like – that belong in women's sphere. Male Victorian poets worried that they might in effect be feminising themselves by withdrawing into a private world. Arnold tried to exorcise this fear in *Sohrab and Rustum*. Bulwer-Lytton enraged Tennyson by jeering at him with the epithet, 'School-Miss Alfred'. But Tennyson's most potent figures for the artist are female; the poor mill girl in Browning's *Pippa Passes* is a Shelleyan poet; and Shelley himself in Arnold's memorable formulation becomes a 'beautiful and ineffectual angel' – just like a woman.[7]

The association of poetry and femininity, however, excluded women poets. For the female figures onto whom the men projected their artistic selves – Tennyson's Mariana and Lady of Shalott, Browning's Pippa and Balaustion, Arnold's Iseult of Brittany – represent an intensification of only a part of the poet, not his full consciousness: a part, furthermore, which is defined as separate from and ignorant of the public world and the great range of human experience in society. Such figures could not write their own poems; the male poet, who stands outside the private world of art, has to do that for them. The Lady of Shalott could not imagine someone complex and experienced enough to imagine the world beyond range of her windows, or to imagine *her*. A woman poet who identified herself with such a stock figure of intense and isolated art would hardly be able to write at all. Or, like the Lady of Shalott preparing her death-ship, she could write only her own name, only herself. For a man, writing poetry meant an apparent withdrawal from the public sphere (although honour and fame might in time return him to it), but for a woman it meant just the opposite: a move toward public engagement and self-assertion in the masculine world. She could not just reverse the roles in her poetry and create a comparable male self-projection, since the male in this set of opposites is defined as experienced, complexly self-conscious, and part of the public world and therefore could not serve as a figure for the poet. (When Elizabeth Bishop makes the reversal in 'The Gentleman of Shalott' the result is a very un-Victorian sort of comedy.) We can formulate the problem like this: a man's poem which contains a female self-projection shows two distinctly different figures, poet and projection; in a woman's poem on the same model, the two would blur into one.

Furthermore, it's not really *poets* that are women, for the Victorians: *poems* are women. The cliché that the style is the man arises more readily and with much greater literalness and force when the stylist is a woman, and it is often charged with erotic intensity. The young lovers in Gilbert and Sullivan's *Iolanthe* describe their perfect love by singing that he is the sculptor and she the clay, he the singer and she the song. Ladislaw in *Middlemarch* tells Dorothea that she needn't write poems because she *is* a poem. Edgar Allan Poe remarks in a review of Barrett Browning's works that 'a woman and her book are identical'. In her love letters Barrett Browning herself worried about the problem of her identity – was she her poems, were they she, which was Browning in love with? 'I love your verses with all my heart, dear Miss Barrett', he had written disconcertingly in his first letter, ' ... and I love you too.' When Aurora Leigh crowns herself with an ivy wreath in secret anticipation of poetic fame, she looks to the admiring Romney like a work of art, not the artist she means to become (see *Aurora Leigh*, 2, ll.59–64). Dante Gabriel Rossetti describes a woman and a sonnet as interchangeably self-enclosed and self-admiring: the woman is 'subtly of herself contemplative'; the sonnet is 'of its own arduous fulness reverent'.[8] How does one tell them apart? Christina Rossetti was an artist's model as well as an artist, and she says in a sad little poem called 'A Wish': 'I wish I were a song once heard/But often pondered o'er' (ll.3–4). As we can see in Tennyson's *The Princess*, the lyric in particular seemed female to the Victorians – private, non-logical, purely emotional – and it is surely no accident that large numbers of English and American women began to publish poetry in the nineteenth century, when the lyric established its dominance. Victorian poems like Victorian women were expected to be morally and spiritually uplifting, to stay mostly in the private sphere, and to provide emotional stimulus and release for overtasked men of affairs.[9] All this may have encouraged women to write poetry, but at the same time it made writing peculiarly difficult because it reinforced the aspects of conventional Victorian femininity – narcissism, passivity, submission, silence – most inimical to creative activity. Since women already *are* the objects they try to create, why should they write?

Where male writers have two figures in poems, for women it often happens either that one of the two disappears and ruins the economy of the poem, like the Sleeping Beauty in 'The Lost Bower' and 'The Dead City', or else that the two collapse into one. A simple example of the collapsing of subject and object is women's use of flowers, which traditionally represent female objects of male desire. Women poets tend to identify with the flower. Barrett Browning flatly equates a fading rose with a failed poet in 'A Lay of the Early Rose' and sympathises equally with both. Rossetti's 'The Solitary Rose' congratulates a flower that is fortunate enough to be unseen and therefore unplucked; the rose is like Wordsworth's violet by a mossy stone considered from the violet's point of view, and the poem is a literal presentation of what Rossetti's great *carpe diem* poem, 'The Prince's Progress', later presents figuratively – a 'gather ye rosebuds' from the point of view of an ungathered rose. On a larger scale, however, as Margaret Homans has shown, nineteenth-century women writers fear and resist identification with nature: nature for women is not the maternal other, in relation to whom the Romantic poet defined his poetic identity, but – as the mother – always a possible self.[10] But nature doesn't write, just as mothers don't write (in the world as Rossetti and the young Elizabeth Barrett experienced it), and poems don't write, and the forlorn damsel can't rescue herself. In 'Winter: My Secret' Rossetti identifies with the teasing incommunicativeness of the season: like winter, her speaker won't speak.

When the woman poet looks for something that can stand in the same relation of significant difference to her within a poem that a female figure stands in to a man, the equation often reads: a male poet is to a woman as a female poet is to a child or an animal.

Tennyson in *In Memoriam* compares his loss to that of a girl whose lover has died, and calls the girl a 'meek, unconscious dove'.[11] Barrett Browning, in contrast, writes about real doves ('My Doves'), which like Tennyson's young woman are less intellectual and closer to God and nature than the poet is. When her cocker spaniel, Flush, appears in her poems he behaves like a woman, spending long days indoors, filled with love and sympathy, watching tenderly and patiently by a bedside, a 'low' creature who 'leads to heights of love' ('Flush or Faunus'). Rossetti's animals are generally male, like Flush, but like the women portrayed by Pre-Raphaelite men they are compellingly attractive and yet somewhat repulsive, mysterious, and inhuman: the lover whom Rossetti affectionately compares to a blind buzzard and a mole in 'A Sketch', the sexy, self-satisfied crocodile in 'My Dream', and the goblins in 'Goblin Market'. Animal poems have helped to confine Barrett Browning and Rossetti to the women's and children's section of the literary world. But the animals don't come just from emotional hunger, or sexual repression, or cultural pressure toward certain acceptable female subjects: they are generated by the need in certain kinds of poems for someone or something to take the woman's role in relation to the speaker.

Barrett Browning and Rossetti both wrote long poems in which they make the poet a questing male figure and then take the side of the passive female object against the ostensible protagonist. In Barrett Browning's 'The Poet's Vow', a woman deserted by a male poet posthumously denounces him, and in Rossetti's 'The Prince's Progress' our sympathies are directed toward the waiting princess who dies before the dilatory, self-indulgent prince arrives. But such a strongly gendered identification with imagination's object, in direct antagonism to the questing figure or the poet who imagines, takes it for granted that poets and questers are male. Recent women poets have taken a more radically revisionist approach to traditional stories of this sort, making poems precisely out of the act of revising – from a woman's point of view – the male versions of the stories;[12] but Barrett Browning and Rossetti don't do this. In their revisionary stories the crucial shift in point of view is incomplete and usually concealed, and Victorian readers apparently never saw it.

In 'Lady Geraldine's Courtship' Barrett Browning makes an interesting attempt to split her identification between a male poet and a female object, but as a result the poem loses the articulation and psychological tension that is generated by difference. She tries to equalise the two figures and participate equally in both. The poet is poor and lowly born, but male and a poet, and he is the speaker. Lady Geraldine is rich and noble and the active agent of the plot, but she is the object of desire and represents the subjects (nature, beauty, and the like) about which poems are written. She *owns* a garden of art. In the centre of that garden, moreover, there is a statue of a sleeping woman, representing Silence, but Lady Geraldine argues that the statue represents the power of meaning to '"exceed the special symbol"' (l.121) embodying it: that is, a silent work of art in female form says more than speech does. Lady Geraldine herself is both a singer and a song: 'Oh, to see or hear her singing', says the enamoured poet-narrator, 'For her looks sing too' (ll.173–4). This is the only one of Barrett Browning's ballad-narratives with a happy ending: the lady takes the initiative, the lovers marry, the two roles merge. This may be the ultimate narcissistic fantasy of the nineteenth-century woman poet, in which she imagines herself enacting both roles perfectly at the same time rather than, as in 'The Lost Bower', failing in both. That the poem represents a fantasy of wish fulfilment is suggested by the fact that it was written very easily, much of it in a last-minute rush to meet a printer's deadline, and perhaps too by its enormous popularity.[13]

It is in Barrett Browning's and Rossetti's amatory sonnet sequences, however, that we find speakers who most clearly locate themselves in two opposite parts of the poems at once. Here the woman poet-speaker plays both roles whose opposition had traditionally generated such sonnets: the self-asserting speaker and the silent object of his desire. The speaker in Barrett Browning's *Sonnets from the Portuguese* speaks and desires like a male sonneteer, but she is also responding as a woman to male voices – not just her lover's but those of a long poetic tradition. This relation to tradition is even clearer in Rossetti's 'Monna Innominata', since each poem is preceded by a quotation from the sonnets of Dante and Petrarch. In both sequences the roles often jarringly conflict: as object of love, the woman should be beautiful, distant, and unquestionably desirable, and she disturbs and embarrasses the reader when she presents herself as subject as well as object of desire and when her sense of her inadequacy as an object of love is expressed in the self-denigrating humility that traditionally belongs to the male lover-speaker.[14] Elsewhere, Rossetti suggests that it is a transgression for a woman to speak her love. 'But this once hear me speak', a woman says to her lover, although she knows that 'a

woman's words are weak;/You should speak, not I' ('Twice',
ll.7–8). Instead of listening, however, the lover looks – he looks at
her heart and breaks it.

A similar but usually less problematic merging of roles appears
when the speaker's voice comes from in or beyond the grave to
which men's poetry so often relegates women. The poet is necessarily doubling roles whenever she speaks from the place where only
silence should be – the place of poetry's object, not that of the
speaking subject – but these poems, unlike the amatory sonnet sequences, are constructed more fully in response to male poems than
in imitation of them. Barrett Browning gives a narrative context to
such a situation in 'The Poet's Vow', where the woman whom a
male poet abandoned because he loved nature more writes out an
accusation and has it sent to him with her corpse.

> 'I left thee last, a child at heart,
>   A woman scarce in years.
> I come to thee, a solemn corpse
>   Which neither feels nor fears.
> I have no breath to use in sighs;
> They laid the dead-weights on mine eyes
>   To seal them safe from tears.'
>   (ll.416–22)

She is responding, of course, to Wordsworth:

> A slumber did my spirit seal;
>   I had no human fears:
> She seemed a thing that could not feel
>   The touch of earthly years.
>
> No motion has she now, no force;
>   She neither hears or sees;
> Rolled round in earth's diurnal course,
>   With rocks, and stones, and trees.[15]

She appropriates Wordsworth's speaker's power of language and
applies to herself his descriptions both of the woman (she does not
feel or see or move) and of himself (she does not fear, her eyes are
sealed as his spirit was). But she is dead.

Like the woman in 'The Poet's Vow', Rossetti's speakers are often
situated at or beyond the border between waking and sleeping, life
and death: a place where the female object of desire can become,
for a long transitional moment, subject and speaker. A paradigm of

this appears in the first issue of the Pre-Raphaelite magazine, *The Germ*, which contains two poems on facing pages: Dante Gabriel Rossetti's 'My Sister's Sleep', which tells how the speaker's sister died in her sleep, and his own sister's 'Dream Land' – about a woman who has travelled to a deathlike land of dreams in a progression like that which is described with unctuous delectation in 'My Sister's Sleep'.[16] And in what may be Rossetti's most famous lyric, 'Song: When I Am Dead, My Dearest', the speaker thinks about what would happen if she were to die and becomes a legitimate object of song:

> When I am dead, my dearest,
>   Sing no sad songs for me;
> Plant thou no roses at my head,
>   Nor shady cypress tree.
>   (ll.1–4)

She won't hear the songs or see the flowers; and she won't care. The strangeness of the poem comes from the fact that it centres not on the mourning lover's consciousness but on that of the dead beloved, in which the memory of the lover will have ceased to matter and might even disappear.

> And dreaming through the twilight
>   That doth not rise nor set,
> Haply I may remember,
>   And haply may forget.
>   (ll.13–16)

We miss the full resonance of this lyric unless we recognise it not just as self-pity or self-abnegation, but as a response to the long tradition of songs in celebration of women who are dead and silent. Rossetti in tacit reciprocity writes about the indifference of corpses, the grievances of ghosts, and women whose sleep of death will end in a happy resurrection beyond all earthly loves. The speaker in 'Remember' will not mind – 'if the darkness and corruption leave / A vestige of the thoughts that once I had' (ll.11–12) – that her lover forgets her; 'At Home' is the lament of a ghost shut out from the home that has forgotten her; in 'After Death' the speaker recalls with pleasure that a man who had not loved her during her life pitied her when she died; the eponymous ghost in 'The Poor Ghost' is drawn back by her lover's tears only to discover that his grief has abated and he would prefer her to stay in her grave; and 'Sleeping at Last' finds solace in the thought of being 'out of sight of friend and of lover' in the grave. Many of Rossetti's most interesting and successful poems merge the traditionally opposite roles of the poetic speaker and the silent object in this way, and they may seem self-enclosed and solipsistic – as if the speaker were speaking only to herself, as in a sense she is – unless we reinstate the silent other who is present only by implication: the male poet who spoke first.

One might expect women to be more comfortable in devotional poetry, where gender would seem not to matter and where male speakers often take an essentially feminine role. But the difficulty arises here in a different form: religious poetry reinforced the impulses toward self-effacement and self-suppression that threatened women's very existence as writers. For Barrett Browning and Rossetti, Christ can be a maternal as well as a masculine figure, and their submission to God the Father places them in the childish position from which Victorian women artists had to struggle to escape if they were to write at all. This throws their poems badly off balance, in comparison to poetry by men. For George Herbert, for instance, to recognise that he is God's child does not make him childlike in other ways – that he is normally adult and self-dependent is in fact what gives meaning and dramatic force to the recognition. But for Victorian women there is no such clear disjunction between their religious and their social roles. In the writings of both Rossetti and Barrett Browning, religion sanctions the life-weariness, the acceptance of inactivity, and the willing subsidence toward death which often appears in poems by male Victorian poets too, but which the men present with a countering element of resistance that is expressed either tonally or through a dramatic frame – in 'Tithonus' and 'Tears, Idle Tears', for instance, 'Andrea del Sarto', or *Empedocles on Etna*. Here again, where men's poetry has two aspects, women's has only one. (It's no accident that Rossetti's most successful religious poem is 'Up-Hill', which is composed entirely of a dialogue between speakers of no apparent gender.) Oppositions are more drastic in the women's religious poetry, choices more absolute. When they conceive of the world that stands in opposition to God as female, it appeals to them not as a sexual opposite, a possible object of desire, but as an unacceptable potential self; Rossetti describes the world as a beautiful woman who is revealed at night to be a hideous fiend and wants to make the speaker equally hideous: 'Till my feet, cloven too, take hold on hell' ('The World', l.14). Like the male Victorian poets, speakers in Rossetti's religious poems lament their emotional aridity; unlike their male contemporaries, however, they lament their speechlessness too: 'I have no wit, no words, no tears' ('A Better Resurrection', l.1); 'What would I give for words, if only words would come!' ('What Would I Give!' l.4). If she could, she would speak her own sinfulness, but 'if I should begin/To tell it all, the day would be too small/To tell it in' ('Ash Wednesday ["My God, my God, have mercy on my sin"]', ll.2–4) – and so she does not tell it.

It is perhaps surprising that neither of these women poets made much radical use of the dramatic monologue, the primary generic innovation of the Victorian period, which exploits the problematic nature of the speaking subject and would therefore seem to offer an opportunity either to escape or to explore problems of gender. But the women's dramatic monologues are different from the men's. The women seem usually to sympathise with their protagonists, and neither frame them with irony as Browning does nor distance and at least partly objectify them like Tennyson by using characters with an independent literary existence. The women did not find figures in literature or mythology or history through whom they could express in an apparently dramatic and impersonal manner feelings that they did not wish directly to avow. Nor do they show off their own virtuosity the way Browning does in 'My Last Duchess', for instance: we are not made aware of the poet signalling to us from behind the speaker's back. Once again, that is, we find that where men's poems have two sharply differentiated figures – in dramatic monologues, the poet and the dramatised speaker – in women's poems the two blur together. Browning's dramatic mono- logues usually create a collusion between poet and reader that pre- supposes shared values and responses which enable the reader to spy out the poet signalling from behind the mask; women could not expect to evoke such collusion and seldom tried. In fact, unless a woman poet's mask was male, or exceedingly bizarre (Barrett Browning's infanticidal black American slave, for instance, in 'The Runaway Slave at Pilgrim's Point'), she might not be perceived as wearing a mask at all. How could she be, if women are poems, not poets, and speak spontaneously and sincerely? When Rossetti assumed a dramatic mask of her own invention to complain about woman's lot in 'The Lowest Room' and 'A Royal Princess', her brother Dante Gabriel objected because the voice in the poems was not the voice that he was accustomed to think of as her own, and he didn't like it – 'falsetto muscularity', he called it, and said that it derived from Mrs Browning;[17] and yet he didn't think of the poems

as dramatic either. He didn't want his sister to speak in any voice
except the one he chose to consider her own. Like their other
works, the women's dramatic monologues were expected to be, and
were almost always perceived as being, univocal.

Emily Brontë, whose poetry was almost unknown in the nineteenth
century and seems in most respects totally detached from the
Victorian context in which Barrett Browning's and Rossetti's is so
thoroughly embedded, nonetheless presents the woman poet's situation in similar ways. The speaker in 'I saw thee, child, one
summer's day', for instance, is a vision-bestowing spirit; and while
many of Brontë's poems appear to be dramatic lyrics spoken by
characters in the Gondal saga, that context is available to us, if at
all, only through scholarly reconstruction, and the poems generally
offer even fewer indications of authorial distance than Barrett
Browning's or Rossetti's. The story of the damsel and the knight,
Sleeping Beauty and the questing Prince, provides much of the basic
structure of the Gondal world of Byronic exile, wandering, captivity, and ambiguous rescue. And although the same roles can be
taken by both men and women and the gender of speakers is often
unclear, two of the latest, longest, and best poems describe the
rescue or awakening of a woman as an imposition of male imaginative dominance. In 'Ah! why, because the dazzling sun', the
speaker's visionary experience is dispelled when the stars that have
looked into her eyes in a happy mutuality are driven away by the
sun's violent intrusion into her bedroom: 'Blood-red he rose, and
arrow-straight / His fierce beams struck my brow.'[18] She hides her
closed eyes in the pillow, but

> It would not do – the pillow glowed
> And glowed both roof and floor,
> And birds sang loudly in the wood,
> And fresh winds shook the door.
> (ll.33–6)

She is forced to become the centre of Nature's awakening by the
'hostile' and 'blinding' light of an alien imagination which destroys
her own.

Essentially the same story is told and retold six months later as a
Gondal episode in 'Silent is the House – all are laid asleep', which
begins with a brief, mysterious struggle for the position of central

consciousness. The first stanza introduces in the third person the speaker of the second and third stanzas: a woman, apparently, who waits at her window every night for 'the Wanderer' (l.8) and speaks defiance of those who may scorn and spy but will never know about the 'angel' (l.12) who nightly visits her. Her defiance appears to be vain, however, since she is immediately displaced as speaker by a man named Julian who tells how he found in his dungeons a beautiful prisoner, A.G. Rochelle, whom at first he cruelly scorned. Julian reports Rochelle's account of the '"message of Hope"' (l. 67) who has come to her every night, like the Wanderer-angel to the speaker of the opening stanzas, bringing visions of '"the Invisible, the Unseen"' (l.81); but then he takes over as narrator again to tell how he 'watched her' (l.93) like the spies defiantly imagined by the earlier speaker, fell in love, overcame the temptation to keep her imprisoned, and finally freed her and won her love – and (although he doesn't mention this) ended her visions. As in 'Ah! why, because the dazzling sun', the woman's visionary power disappears under the gaze of an intruder-rescuer – is it rescue or rape? – that objectifies and transforms her. For Brontë, the story of the damsel and the knight is the story of the female subject's displacement into the position of the erotic object of male imagination, and she makes poems out of the struggle between them.

In America the same situation produced different results. The contradiction in the double role of the woman poet appears in Emily Dickinson's work less as a difficulty to be evaded or overcome than as an essential organising principle; Dickinson read Barrett Browning's work with great attention, and perhaps it taught her how to go beyond itself. Even more than Rossetti, Dickinson likes to situate her speakers in or beyond the grave, and they characteristically identify with flowers, children, smallness, powerlessness, and silence; but at the same time they implicitly or ironically assert their power in revolt against the patriarchal universe, and the tension between these opposing attitudes is essential both to the poems' meaning and to their form – the smallness and apparent childishness of the verses (and the fact that Dickinson did not publish them) in conjunction with their explosive force. Furthermore, Dickinson went far beyond her British counterparts in exploring the possibility of an absolute equality, or even identity, between subject and object; her explorations suggest that the result would be a horrifying stalemate and may help us to understand why Barrett Browning and Rossetti (who psychologically and poetically were much more conventional than Dickinson) and even Bronte never dropped the essential point of difference that is created in poetry by gender.

> Like Eyes that looked on Wastes –
> Incredulous of Ought
> But Blank – and steady Wilderness –
> Diversified by Night –
>
> Just Infinites of Nought –
> As far as it could see –
> So looked the face I looked upon –
> So looked itself – on Me –
>
> I offered it no Help –
> Because the Cause was Mine –
> The Misery a Compact
> As hopeless – as divine –
>
> Neither – would be absolved –
> Neither would be a Queen
> Without the Other – Therefore
> We perish – tho' We reign – [19]

Since both are the damsel waiting for rescue as well as potential knights, neither can rescue the other and they remain frozen in an intensified and more terrible version of the changeless, eventless condition in which Barrett Browning daydreamed and Rossetti's speakers wait for God. In 'I would not paint – a picture' Dickinson considers the problematic position of the woman poet in her own art: is she artist, or audience, or instrument, or the work itself? She would like to be everything at once – the situation that Barrett Browning and Rossetti found both inevitable and impossible for most kinds of lyric poetry. Dickinson imagines this situation as highly precarious, offering the possibility of an exhilarating self-sufficiency that ends in self-destruction.

> Nor would I be a Poet –
> It's finer – own the Ear –
> Enamored – impotent – content –
> The License to revere,
> A privilege so awful
> What would the Dower be,
> Had I the Art to stun myself
> With Bolts of Melody! [20]

Being both poet and audience, both subject and object, would mean turning eroticism and aggression inward: both to marry ('dower') and to 'stun' oneself, to be 'impotent' and yet to wield the tools ('bolts') of violence – and to wield them against oneself.

Recent American women poets have found other ways both to use and to evade the problematic situation of the woman poet as the Victorians experienced it. Subjects and emotions new to serious poetry and new ways of experiencing such familar ones as love, exclusion, enclosure, and longing provide escape from patterns of relationship embedded in the structure of traditional English poetry. Sylvia Plath expresses rebellion and rage of a kind that Barrett Browning and Rossetti either turn inward against themselves, producing depression that sometimes comes close to despair, or else express indirectly in narrative and political poetry. Anne Sexton and others have done explicitly, aggressively, and forthrightly what Rossetti and Barrett Browning more timidly and unobtrusively tried to do, reinterpreting old stories from a woman's point of view. Elizabeth Bishop transforms the passivity and the sense of enclosure, exclusion, frustration, and impotence that debilitated so much of the work of nineteenth-century women poets into images of exile and travel in which the poet becomes an endlessly questing spirit; and exotic animals and peasants serve the function in Bishop's poetry that animals and children do in Barrett Browning's and Rossetti's, standing in the relation to the woman poet that women have stood in to men. And in writing about love between women it may be possible to escape the shadow cast by the traditional relations between subject and object in amatory poetry.

Rossetti and Barrett Browning, however, were hindered and often debilitated by a situation which Dickinson and later poets were able to exploit or transcend. They sometimes tried to use the problematic nature of woman as speaking subject in an attempt to explore and to protest against women's roles both in poems and in society, but since the surface of their poetry – diction, subject matter, and (at least apparently) tone – did not contradict what Victorian women were expected to say, their shifts in point of view and revisions of old stories generally went unobserved and unencouraged. Rossetti stopped trying to rebel: in her devotional writings she finds an appropriate place for a conventional Victorian woman's voice. Barrett Browning, on the other hand, turned after *Sonnets from the Portuguese* away from the old poetic situations – that is, from the lyric tradition – to narrative form and highly topical contemporary subjects and made her revisionary view of the world defiantly, if incompletely and intermittently, explicit. In *Aurora Leigh* she works the problem through in terms of plot. At the beginning of the poem

Aurora is the forlorn damsel, a dispossessed orphan in a rigidly patriarchal world, but by the end she has become a poet and a knight.
First she rescues Marian Erle, a damsel in distress, and then she
rescues – by marriage, as knights and princes used to do – Romney
Leigh, the man who had tried at various times to rescue both
Marian Erle and Aurora herself, and had been rebuffed by both of
them. But the humiliation, blinding, and subjugation of Romney
that makes the happy ending possible is not a solution to the
woman poet's difficulties; it is her fantasy of revenge. It suggests
that for women to speak, men must be forcibly silenced; for women
to be heard rather than looked at – to be artists rather than works
of art – men must be blinded. Similarly, in Rossetti's 'Goblin Market'
a girl ventures forth and rescues her sister from the thralldom of
goblin sexuality, and later the two sisters with their daughters set
up a society that apparently excludes men. Neither of the two
major Victorian women poets developed any better solution than
this punitive reversal of roles or rejection of men on the one hand,
enacted in narrative rather than lyric, or the retreat into feminine
submissiveness and self-suppression represented by Rossetti's devotional poetry on the other. They could imagine an androgynous
ideal – Barrett Browning celebrated George Sand in two bold
sonnets as a mixture of male and female qualities, and Rossetti
wrote movingly of the one escape from the restrictions of gender or-
dained by Christianity: 'in Christ there is neither male nor female,
for we are all one'[21] – and they sometimes blurred the gender of
their poetic speakers. In narrative and political poetry they could
thematise and redefine the terms in which the speaking subject
located herself within a poem. But despite the substantial although
flawed success of *Sonnets from the Portuguese* and 'Monna
Innominata', and the many excellent lyrics in which Rossetti implicitly responds to the male tradition, neither Barrett Browning nor
Rossetti fully solved within their lyric poetry the problem of the
damsel and the knight.

From *Critical Inquiry*, 13 (Autumn 1986), 64–80.

NOTES

[Dorothy Mermin's essay is reprinted in the complete form in which it originally appeared. Brief passages from the essay are to be found in Mermin's
major study, *Elizabeth Barrett Browning: The Origins of a New Poetry*

(1988), and *Godiva's Ride: Women of Letters in England, 1830–1880* (1993). Both of these studies pay special attention to the gendering of the literary sphere in Victorian England. Ed.]

1. Elizabeth Barrett Browning, 'Glimpses into My Own Life and Literary Character' (1820), in 'Two Autobiographical Essays by Elizabeth Barrett', ed. William S. Peterson, *Browning Institute Studies*, 2 (1974), 123.

2. Barrett Browning to Mary Russell Mitford, 22 July 1842, *The Letters of Elizabeth Barrett Browning to Mary Russell Mitford 1836–1854*, ed. Meredith B. Raymond and Mary Rose Sullivan, 3 vols (n.p. 1983), II, p. 7.

3. Sandra M. Gilbert and Susan Gubar offer most of these suggestions in *The Madwoman in the Attic: The Woman Writer and the Nineteenth-Century Literary Imagination* (New Haven, 1979), pp. 545–9. The distinguished Victorian critic R.H. Hutton answers the question with the assertion that women's imaginations cannot abstract themselves from 'the visible surface and form of human existence' ('Novels by the Authoress of "John Halifax")', *North British Review*, 29 1858], 467).

4. Barrett Browning, 'The Deserted Garden', *The Complete Works of Elizabeth Barrett Browning*, ed. Charlotte Porter and Helen A. Clarke, 6 vols (New York, 1900), ll.17, 69–72; all further references to poems in this edition, identified by line number, will be included in the text. The ballad of Edwin and Angelina appears in Oliver Goldsmith's *The Vicar of Wakefield* (1976), ch. 8.

5. Barrett Browning to H.S. Boyd, 4 October 1844, *The Letters of Elizabeth Barrett Browning*, ed. Frederic G. Kenyon, 4th edn, 2 vols (London, 1898), I, p. 201.

6. Christina Rossetti, 'The Dead City', *The Poetical Works of Christina Georgina Rossetti*, ed. William Michael Rossetti (London, 1911), ll.2, 273–4; all further references to poems in this edition, identified by line number, will be included in the text. The verse about Cecilia is given in Williams's introductory memoir, p. xlix. 'The Dead City' first appeared in *Verses*, printed by Rossetti's grandfather, G. Polidori (London, 1847).

7. Donald S. Hair notes the critical enthusiasm for *In Memoriam*'s domestic themes and images in *Domestic and Heroic in Tennyson's Poetry* (Toronto, 1981), pp. 7–10. Bulwer-Lytton jeered at Tennyson in the 'The New Timon', and Tennyson responded with similar insults in 'The New Timon, and the Poets'. Matthew Arnold's phrase about the angel first appeared in his essay 'Byron'; see *The Complete Prose Works of Matthew Arnold*, ed. R.H. Super, 11 vols (Ann Arbor, MI, 1960–77), IX, p. 237. As Ellen Moers points out: 'The spontaneous, the instinctive, the natural, the informal, the anticlassical, and the

artless: all these terms of art have been associated with the woman's voice in literature from the beginning of time. They are also applied to the start of modern literature that we call Romanticism, and that cannot be separated from the raising of the woman's voice in letters' (*Literary Women* [Garden City, NY, 1976), p. 163).

8. See W.S. Gilbert and Arthur Sullivan, *Iolanthe: or, The Peer and the Peri*, arranged by Berthold Tours (London, n.d.), pp. 19–22; see George Eliot, *Middlemarch* (Cambridge, MA, 1956), p. 166; Edgar Allan Poe, 'The Drama of Exile, and Other Poems', *The Complete Works of Edgar Allan Poe*, ed. James A. Harrison, 17 vols (New York, 1902), XII, p. 1; Robert Browning to Elizabeth Barrett, 10 January 1845, *The Letters of Robert Browning and Elizabeth Barrett Barrett 1845–46*, ed. Elvan Kintner, 2 vols (Cambridge, MA, 1969), I, p. 3; Dante Gabriel Rossetti, 'Body's Beauty', 'Introduction' (in 'The House of Life'), *The Works of Dante Gabriel Rossetti*, ed. William M. Rossetti, rev. edn (London, 1911).

There are many similar examples. Eris S. Robertson coveted a fine copy of Katherine Philips's poems: 'I indulged myself with another peep at the "matchless Orinda", still longing to possess and love what so many reverent hands had fondled' (*English Poetesses: A Series of Critical Biographies, with Illustrative Extracts* [London, 1883], p. 2). An unidentified earlier critic wrote: 'Beauty is to a woman what poetry is to a language, and their similarity accounts for their conjunction; for there never yet existed a female possessed of personal loveliness who was not only poetical in herself but the cause of poetry in others' ('The Female Character', *Fraser's Magazine*, 7 [1833], 601); that the latter part of this sentence says the opposite of what it apparently intends reflects the silliness of the thought.

Gubar discusses the conception of women as works of art in '"The Blank Page" and the Issue of Female Creativity', *Critical Inquiry*, 8 (1981), 243–63.

9. John Woolford points this out in 'EBB; Woman and Poet', *Browning Society Notes*, 9 (1979), 4.

10. Margaret Homans, *Women Writers and Poetic Identity: Dorothy Wordsworth, Emily Brontë, and Emily Dickinson* (Princeton, NJ, 1980). For brief discussions of women poets' use of flowers, see Cora Kaplan, *Salt and Bitter and Good: Three Centuries of English and American Women Poets* (New York, 1975), pp. 20–4, and Alicia Ostriker, 'Body Language: Imagery of the Body in Women's Poetry', in Leonard Michaels and Christopher Ricks (eds), *The State of the Language* (Berkeley, CA, 1980, pp. 256–7).

11 Alfred Tennyson, *In Memoriam*, 6, l.25, *The Poems of Tennyson*, ed. Ricks (London, 1969).

12 Ostriker discusses the remaking of old myths by twentieth-century women poets in 'The Thieves of Language: Women Poets and Revisionist Mythmaking', *Signs*, 8 (1982), 68–90. She notes that

'feminist revisionism differs from Romantic revisionism' in that 'it accentuates its argument, in order to make clear that there is an argument' (p. 87) – which is just what Barrett Browning and Rossetti do not do.

13 To make the two volumes of *Poems* (1844) of equal length, 'there was nothing for it but to finish a ballad poem called "Lady Geraldine's Courtship", which was lying by me, and I did so by writing, i.e. composing, *one hundred and forty lines last Saturday*! I seemed to be in a dream all day! Long lines too – with fifteen syllables in each!' (Barrett Browning to H.S. Boyd, 1 August 1844, *The Letters of Elizabeth Barrett Browning*, I, p. 177). On the poem's popularity, see Alethea Hayter, *Mrs Browning: A Poet's Work and Its Setting* (London, 1962), pp. 85–6.

14 See my 'The Female Poet and the Embarrassed Reader: Elizabeth Barrett Browning's *Sonnets from the Portuguese*', *ELH*, 48 (1981), 351–67; Homans, '"Syllables of Velvet": Dickinson, Rossetti, and the Rhetorics of Sexuality', *Feminist Studies*, 11 (1985), 569–93; and Moers's discussion of nineteenth-century women's love poetry in *Literary Women*, pp. 162–72.

15 William Wordsworth, 'A Slumber Did My Spirit Seal', *The Poetical Works of William Wordsworth*, ed. E. de Selincourt, 2nd edn, 5 vols (Oxford, 1952), II, p. 216.

16 See *The Germ: Thoughts towards Nature in Poetry, Literature and Art*, 1 ([Jan. 1850] Portland, Maine, 1898), pp. 20, 21. Jerome J. McGann attributes Rossetti's idea of the sleep that follows death to the millenarian doctrine of 'Soul Sleep' in 'The Religious Poetry of Christina Rossetti', *Critical Inquiry*, 10 (1983), 133–41. [Reprinted in this volume, pp. 167–88 – Ed.]

17. Dante Gabriel Rossetti to Christina Georgina Rossetti, 3 December 1875, *Letters of Dante Gabriel Rossetti*, ed. Oswald Doughty and John Robert Wahl, 4 vols (Oxford, 1967), III, p. 1380.

18 Emily Brontë, 'Ah! why, because the dazzling sun', *The Complete Poems of Emily Jane Brontë*, ed. C.W. Hatfield (New York, 1941), ll.21–2; all further references to poems in this work will be included in the text. Homans gives a somewhat different analysis of Brontë's poems about visionary visitants in *Women Writers and Poetic Identity*, pp. 110–22. [See extract reprinted in this volume, pp. 84–107 – Ed.]

19 Emily Dickinson, 'Like Eyes that looked on wastes' (l.458), *The Poems of Emily Dickinson*, ed. Thomas H. Johnson, 3 vols (Cambridge, MA: 1965).

20 Dickinson, 'I would not paint – a picture' (l.595). *The Poems of Emily Dickinson*.

21 Christina Rossetti, *Seek and Find: A Double Series of Short Studies of the Benedicite* (New York, [1879]), p. 32.

3

Emily Brontë

MARGARET HOMANS

To be told by her own brother that she is like nature, and implicitly or explicitly that she cannot have her own subjectivity, would seem to be the most compelling of reasons for a woman to feel dislocated from the poetic tradition in which these opinions originate. To receive these views personally as a sister and not just generically as a woman prevents Dorothy Wordsworth even from wishing to seek a way around them. And yet it appears that Dorothy's difficulties as a poet result not just from her unique personal situation, because although Emily Brontë proceeds much further toward the establishment of authentic poetic identity, her poems just as much as Dorothy's reveal that the sources of poetic power are not felt to be within the self. Brontë is troubled by the apparent otherness of her mind's powers, which she imagines as a series of masculine visitants who bring visionary experience to her. As the alien centres of imaginative power, they repeat, in a general way, Dorothy's implicit picture of her brother as a centre of an imaginative power that is never hers. The major and obvious difference between these two configurations is that Brontë's masculine figures for poetic power are invented and contained within her poems, where William Wordsworth has his own irreducible existence, and that consequently they do share their power with the poet, if grudgingly, rather than keeping it perpetually apart.

Brontë's masculine visitants are comparable to a masculine poet's muse. The development of a masculine muse by a woman poet should not logically be surprising, but the phenomenon is new with Brontë (and recurs in Dickinson) and represents a first step toward the internalisation of poetic power. There is no such thing, however, as a simple reversal of roles; unlike the usual situation in which a female muse's power exists to be overcome, the poet's ability to master her muse is in this case genuinely in question. Instead of invoking a visitant's aid and then proceeding with a poem on a chosen subject, Brontë often makes her entire poem an extended invocation. Many of her poems dwell on the masculine figures of alien power, elevating them from the status of agency to that of the major subject. This arrest itself suggests that she is not confident of having obtained the visitants' support, and the content of these poems is a continuous effort to wrest the visitants' power away from them and make it her own. It is not inherent in the concept of a masculine muse that he should take and keep more power than does the traditionally feminine muse, but in Brontë's poems he does.

Two comments about the poet's character by those who knew her suggest a biographical analogy for what the poems reveal. These comments share the assumption, hardly questionable in the nineteenth century, that power is synonymous with masculinity, in regard both to character and to accomplishment. Her French teacher in Brussels, M. Héger, said that 'she should have been a man – a great navigator',[1] and Charlotte Brontë writes that under a simple exterior 'lay a secret power and fire that might have informed the brain and kindled the veins of a hero'.[2] What is interesting here is not that Emily's strength of character should be considered manly, but that both these observers should compare this quality in her character to the character of a man of action, a hero or a navigator, rather than to that of a great author, even though Charlotte's words were written to accompany an edition of *Wuthering Heights*. This circumstance suggests that this sternness was not, or at least did not seem to be, fully integrated into Brontë's character, but stood apart. An inflexibility of will seemed to have her in its power, and to harm her more than it helped.

We can never know how far this lack of integration existed in Brontë's own character, but when Charlotte turns to discussing the novel itself, in the preface to her edition of *Wuthering Heights*, she continues in the same vein:

> Whether it is right or advisable to create beings like Heathcliff, I do not know: I scarcely think it is. But this I know; the writer who possesses the creative gift owns something of which he is not always master – something that at times strangely wills and works for itself ... Be the work grim or glorious, dread or divine, you have little choice left but quiescent adoption.
>
> (*WH*, p. 12)

Possessed by a power not her own, the writer is 'the nominal artist' and deserves neither praise nor blame. In the guise of defender, Charlotte does her sister considerable injustice, if she means that Emily was literally not in control of what she wrote. But as a conscious artist Emily does create a myth of imaginative possession. The account in Charlotte's preface is a literalisation of figurative events in Emily's poems on the imagination, and although she betrays herself to be an insensitive reader of her sister's work, there is a certain truth in her misinterpretation.[3]

Brontë makes those visionary visitants an overt, even a major, subject of her poetry, but she also identifies another alien power of poetry that, perhaps because it is a more profound threat to her own identity, is less willingly acknowledged and therefore less apparent than the visionary power. This power belongs to nature, who inspires and endeavours to control the poet's speech in much the same manner as the visionary visitants. Nature is sometimes, though not always, characterised as feminine. For Dorothy to be identified by her brother with nature is to be silenced, because nature's language is not human; here, even though nature is a speaking object, the result is the same forfeiting of subjectivity that Dorothy experiences. As in Dorothy's 'A Winter's Ramble in Grasmere Vale', Brontë portrays nature speaking in place of or in competition with the poet's own speech, and the poet must silence or turn away from nature in order to speak in her own right. Both Brontë's ambition and her success are greater in this regard than Dorothy's, but in her eagerness to defend against this alternate power of poetry, the poet overvalues and distorts the visionary experience offered by male figures without, however, decreasing her sense of its foreignness. Cutting herself off from one source of poetic identity, and not quite believing in the other, she finds nowhere a settled identity. The poet defends herself from the danger of becoming a feminine object by aligning her poetic self with the stage in feminine development in which the mother is rejected in favour of a turn toward masculine objects, but that turn cannot become an identity. Only in the novel, where she is free to displace the traditional feminine character of nature, can she return to what the reader senses is a more authentic belief.

What is of interest here is not so much the sexual identity of the mind presented in the poems, but the question of whether the poet can claim poetic identity at all, or whether the right to that identity is lodged in external powers, be they masculine or feminine. But the

Brontës were also aware of the problem of sexual identity as it is represented textually. Charlotte shared a general cultural prejudice against 'the poetry women generally write' (WH, p. 4), and all three sisters must have defined themselves against this paradigm, consciously or not. In Charlotte's account of their choice of the sexually ambiguous pseudonyms, Currer, Ellis, and Acton, she says that they did not want to declare themselves women, because of a tendency among critics to condescend to 'authoresses', 'without at that time suspecting that our mode of writing and thinking was not what is called "feminine"' (WH, p. 4). Contemporary reviewers of Wuthering Heights spoke of Ellis Bell's 'power' and 'mastery'. If Charlotte means that later on they did come to understand that their writing was not 'what is called "feminine"', it is not clear whether she welcomed this distinction, thinking of 'the poetry women generally write', or whether this distinction was an affront to her sense of identity and integrity as a woman. They did not want to abdicate their proper identity and assume 'Christian names positively masculine', yet they could hardly wish, in the world in which they lived, to be grouped with authoresses.[4]

The pseudonyms were 'veils', and perhaps insignificant in themselves, but it is impossible to imagine that the sisters could have questioned such a fundamental aspect of self-presentation without having felt, previously or at the time, a less trivial uncertainty about their sexual identity as writers. These considerations are as relevant to the poet's textual sense of identity as to her manner of presenting her works to the public, because the sense of literary identity is established through reading and through the poet's sense of her place in literary tradition. The choice to be named 'Ellis', assuming that Emily participated in the decision, must represent the poet's wish not to have, as a writer, a determinate sexual identity. This wish may result partly from the desire not to be judged on the basis of gender, but sexual identification is problematic also because the two origins of poetry that she perceives as being available to her are sexually defined, and she can consider neither to be identifiable with the self. Feminine nature and forms of the masculine Word present her with a choice she does not wish to make. The arrangement of this choice is of course her own, but it may express her frustration at the sexual restriction of so many aspects of literary tradition and practice. Brontë's separation from the two sources of her power may be, then, the result not of any fragmentation of her own sense of identity, but of her uneasiness about their sexual orientation. She may not be able to, but also perhaps does not wish to, claim identification with either one.[5]

The history of the poet's negotiations for poetic identity is traced in a sequence of poems that forms the core of Brontë's canon. In 1844 Brontë made two books of transcriptions, for which she selected poems written at different periods in her life. She copied these poems into two notebooks, in a book-like printing and format that indicates that these were the poems that she considered to be her best. One notebook is a collection of poems about Gondal, the fictive land that in her adolescence she had invented and peopled, and whose sagas she continued to elaborate up to the year of her death. The other notebook, considered here, bears no title but consists largely of poems that are either explicitly or implicitly about imaginative experience. Of the poems that she published in the 1846 *Poems by Currer, Ellis, and Acton Bell,* five were chosen from the Gondal notebook and fifteen from the non-Gondal group. In making these transcriptions, Brontë retained many of the dates on which the poems were written, though arranging the poems in a new sequence that is roughly but not entirely chronological. The apparent care with which the poems were chosen and arranged indicates that, in the non-Gondal notebook, she is consciously developing a myth of the imagination; consequently this reading follows her arrangement of the poems rather than the chronological sequence.[6]

The pattern of borrowing an identity began very early, in the make-believe world of the Brontë children's 'Young Men's Play', in which Emily represented the polar explorer, Sir Edward Parry.[7] In subsequent 'plays' (the precursors of Gondal), in which the children invented nations and populations engendering lengthy prose tales and then poetry, the mobile adoption of fictive roles proliferates. In a child this borrowing is by itself unremarkable, and for an adult poet it is part of the procedure of any fictional writing to adopt various personae, but Brontë retains this pattern of supplanting identity even when it begins to produce sinister effects. It has been argued that in the conventional heroic posing of the Gondal poems (the first was written in 1836, when the poet was seventeen) she is concealing or suppressing her own identity, to the detriment of the poems, because she has difficulty representing her own genuine powers.[8] The figures she creates in the Gondal poems are often borrowed from gothic or Byronic sources,[9] and these borrowed personae are often themselves possessed by passions that they do not control, as for example in these lines from a poem of 1837:

The burning tears that would keep welling,
The groans that mocked at every tear
That burst from out their dreary dwelling
. . . .
Sometimes a curse, sometimes a prayer
Would quiver on my parchèd tongue.
(P 15)

In other early poems, the speaker is bound by 'a tyrant spell', possessed in dreams by 'the shadows of the dead', and in many places
overwhelmed by despair and by harrowing memories.

The possession of these early poems is emotional rather than
creative, but when Brontë turns from the melodrama of Gondal to
poems about her own mind, she retains the language of possession.
The visionary visitant of later poems takes many forms, but he is
always masculine, and he is threatening as well as inspiring, dangerous as well as beloved.[10] He is threatening more because, being
external, he can withdraw her poetic powers at will than because of
any dangerous content in the visions he brings. Her ambivalence
toward these figures produces an unstable relationship with them.
The poet early succeeds in exerting a measure of control over this
figure, but this control succeeds not in harnessing the visitant's
power but only counterproductively in suppressing it, and later the
visitant's power returns in a sinister form.

A poem of 1840 invokes a visitation from 'thee', using the
language of romantic love augmented by devotional speech:

My worn heart throbs so wildly
'Twill break for thee.
. . . .
Will not mine angel comfort?
Mine idol hear?
(P 138, A 11)

The first three stanzas place the speaker at the mercy of this figure,
but the last appears to fulfil its own wishes: 'O I shall surely win
thee, / Beloved, again!' 'Mine angel' here is at least fictively external
to the poet, but subsequent poems trace the internalisation of this
figure. The next poem, addressed to 'O Dream', records the passing
of a Wordsworthian gleam at the end of childhood. Though this
figure has entity enough to have an 'angel brow', the darkening
vision is the result of dissociating the dream from external lights.
Depriving this figure of its illusory otherness decreases its powers:

> The sun-beam and the storm,
> The summer-eve divine,
> The silent night of solemn calm,
> The full moon's cloudless shine,
>
> Were once entwined with thee,
> But now with weary pain,
> Lost vision! 'tis enough for me –
> Thou canst not shine again.
>   (P 86, A 12)

Whereas the discovery that this figure was not external but a function of the self might be expected to increase the poet's feeling of her own power, she experiences only loss. Turning from the light vanishing 'from off thine angel brow' to the loss of 'every joy that lit my brow', the next poem presents a further stage in this internalisation that merely contracts the vision to a relic of his former power and makes the self a mortuary without any compensatory gain in power.

> The barren mountain-side lies bare;
> And sunshine and awaking morn
> Paint no more golden visions there.
>
> Yet, ever in my grateful breast,
> Thy darling shade shall cherished be;
> For God alone doth know how blest
> My early years have been in thee!
>   (P 135, A 13)

She internalises this visionary faculty only as it diminishes because, like Dorothy Wordsworth, she cannot believe that any poetic power could be at once internal and powerful.

The issue of visionary power is closed for four years and the next eight poems in the copybook take up different themes. The next poem on this subject, 'My Comforter' (P 168, A 22), addresses a revived but very differently characterised figure. Having accepted the discovery of earlier poems that if visionary power is internal it must be weak, the poet now embraces rather than lamenting its triviality. Condescending to her comforter, she tells it that it has 'not taught / A feeling strange or new; / Thou hast but roused a latent thought', and she guards from it the secret of the occasion for which she is being soothed: 'What my soul bore my soul alone / Within itself may tell.' The speaker's hollow gain is that she is in the position of power now in this relationship, and she reduces her 'idol' to a 'sweet thing' that calms but could not comprehend. The next two poems, though separated in composition by a year, are paired in the manuscript because they both involve a figure named 'Fancy' who is, like this comforter, clearly a subordinate. The subject of the poem is the 'Dark world' of actuality, and the speaker simply conjures a substitutive dream through the agency of this servile 'Fancy ... my Fairy love!' A fantasy of perfect and happy worlds in heaven is introduced by a fiat: 'And this shall be my dream to-night – / I'll think ...' (P 157, A23). Acknowledged as a fantasy, this easy day-dream is hardly efficacious in any way. In assuming the powers of the figure she once pleadingly invoked and worshipped, she finds that its powers vanish. Its powers resided in its defiance and in her desire. Like Dorothy in 'Holiday at Gwerndwffnant', 'Irregular Verses', and the Cottage poems, she identifies her own poetry with fancy while readily admitting to its inferiority. As before, she does not conceive of a poetic power that would be both her own and powerful. The titling of the next poem in the notebook sequence, 'To Imagination' (P 174, A 25), represents an effort to ennoble this faculty by association with the term that Coleridge reserved for the mind's highest powers. Indeed, it is here not quite so servile as before: it is a 'benignant power' with a 'kind voice', a 'solacer of human cares', and 'my true friend'. But the poem still turns on a simplistic opposition between the hopeless 'world without' that includes 'Nature's sad reality' and 'Truth', and the escapist 'world within', comprising dreams and Fancy, which is the province of what she calls 'Imagination'. If not the fancy itself, it purveys a fanciful 'phantom bliss' that the speaker mistrusts even while she welcomes it. What is significant here is that the poet recognises that the moments of greatest power occur when this imagination voids the distinction between the 'world within' and the 'world without' to refer to a real but also desirable world elsewhere. She makes a continuity between fantasy and possibility:

> But thou art ever there to bring
> The hovering visions back and breathe
> New glories o'er the blighted spring
> And call a lovelier life from death,
> And whisper with a voice divine
> Of real worlds as bright as thine.

She increases the power of her imagination by associating it with 'real worlds', but the cost of that gain in power is that voice returns to a source outside the self.

The poem transcribed next, written six weeks later, returns to a suspiciously harsh opposition between real worlds and reason, which must be renounced, and a 'God of Visions', who, unlike her imagination, seems to require complete devotion. She calls it a 'radiant angel', an honorific term that has dropped out of her vocabulary since the early poems. Shunning 'the common paths that others run', she

> gave my spirit to adore
> Thee, ever present, phantom thing –
> My slave, my comrade, and my King!
> (P 176, A 26)

The next two verses explicate the last line. This passage is the main source for the myth of possession, as it is for comparisons between Brontë and Dickinson, who also addresses a power that is at once master and slave. Her accounts of 'slave' and 'comrade', though told with greater energy than before, are familiar, but when she turns to 'my King' she is scarcely convincing:

> And yet, a king – though prudence well
> Have taught thy subject to rebel.

> And am I wrong to worship where
> Faith cannot doubt nor Hope despair
> Since my own soul can grant my prayer?

There is no apparent reason for inflating this figure into a king, since at the same time she so overtly makes it a part of herself and easily governable. Her insistence on intimacy must be concealing some unexplained alienation, of which the term 'king' is the trace.

The account of the speaker's turn from reason to visions in this poem is framed by two opening stanzas and two closing lines that set the poem in a court of law. The poem's occasion is the speaker's invocation to her 'radiant angel' to come to her defence against 'Stern Reason's' judgement. Reason 'is mocking at my overthrow', as if the speaker had suffered or gone mad because of her preference. Her invocation is desperate:

> O thy sweet tongue must plead for me
> And tell why I have chosen thee!

> Stern Reason is to judgement come
> Arrayed in all her forms of gloom:

> Wilt thou my advocate be dumb?
> No, radiant angel, speak and say
> Why I did cast the world away.

The subsequent stanzas seem to do what the speaker is asking her God of Visions to do, in that they explain her choice, but that she closes with the same invocation with which she began indicates that this defence has been inadequate:

> Speak, God of Visions, plead for me
> And tell why I have chosen thee!

That implied inadequacy expresses powerlessness or subjugation far more vividly than does her guarded declaration that he is her king. If 'my own soul can grant my prayer', the poem logically ought not to end with the implication that her God of Visions has not spoken and will not speak for her. The God is a tongue or a voice, and an advocate is one who speaks for someone else. That the speaker thus displaces her powers of speech indicates that language is alien to her. Her soul may be synonymous with her God of Visions, but without certainty of her power over language visions are of no use for poetry and she is alienated from her own poethood. That language is an alien power may account for the reduction of visionary power from 'mine idol' to 'sweet thing', coincident with its internalisation. Mastering and containing the power undoes it, and yet to see it again as external threatens the poet's existence as a poet.

The next poem, 'Enough of Thought, Philosopher', carries the implications of the danger of the externality of poetic power one step further by considering the possibility that there is not much difference between a sought-after 'Spirit' (another imaginary visitant) and oblivious death. The Spirit represents a power to unify warring factions within human personality and to make their combined strength 'far more fair / Than the divided sources were' (P 181, A 27). But the 'lifeless rest' the speaker seeks when she abandons her futile search for this Spirit performs much the same function, if ingloriously:

> O let me die, that power and will
> Their cruel strife may close,
> And vanquished Good, victorious Ill
> Be lost in one repose.

This verse and the one preceding it were substituted for an original conclusion that characterises death simply as 'eternal sleep' rather than as the closure of strife, so that the parallel between death and the imaginative Spirit is not accidental, but the product of purposeful revision. That death mimics the Spirit here undermines imaginative efficacy. The speaker has imagined this Spirit and has created a compelling visual image of his powers of unification (the Spirit supervises the confluence of three rivers and kindles the 'inky sea' where they meet 'with sudden blaze' so that 'the glad deep sparkled wide and bright – / White as the sun'). But only its mimicker and antagonist, ironically, can fulfill the Spirit's promise.

'Enough of Thought, Philosopher', dated 3 February 1845, is the last of the poems in the non-Gondal notebook to consider as overt subject matter the topic of imaginative power. The poet does return to this subject, but as part of the Gondal sequence, suggesting that although the poet no longer wished to treat this difficult subject, and perhaps repressed it, it must have been an unfinished issue of considerable importance to have found another way to surface out of place. Rather than resolving the problem of her mastery over her God of Visions, this poem allows her to express her fears more freely because more indirectly. The poem in question is the one that begins 'Silent is the House – all are laid asleep', dated 9 October 1845. The passage on imagination is the first three stanzas, which exist in an uneasy relation to the rest of the poem, a narrative. Both Emily and Charlotte Brontë recognised this uneasiness, as the poem is printed only in excerpts in both the 1846 *Poems* and the group of poems published by Charlotte in her 1850 edition of *Wuthering Heights*. Emily selected parts of the narrative for the 1846 edition, and Charlotte printed just the three stanzas about imagination, with a two stanza conclusion of her own, under the title of 'The Visionary'. The 'I' in the first three stanzas of the original poem is apparently the same as the 'I' of the poems on imagination in the non-Gondal notebook, while in the rest of the poem the speaker is a dramatic character named Julian.

> Silent is the House – all are laid asleep;
> One, alone, looks out o'er the snow wreaths deep;
> Watching every cloud, dreading every breeze
> That whirls the 'wildering drifts and bends the groaning trees.
>
> Cheerful is the hearth, soft the matted floor;
> Not one shivering gust creeps through pane or door;
> The little lamp burns straight, its rays shoot strong and far;
> I trim it well to be the Wanderer's guiding-star.

Frown, my haughty sire; chide, my angry dame;
Set your slaves to spy, threaten me with shame:
But neither sire nor dame, nor prying serf shall know
What angel nightly tracks that waste of winter snow.

In the dungeon crypts idly did I stray,
Reckless of the lives wasting there away;
'Draw the ponderous bars; open, Warder stern!'
He dare not say me nay – the hinges harshly turn.

(P 190)

It is possible that the poet is identifying that Wanderer by moving, without indicating any transition, into an imaginative tale, as if the discovery of a topic for verse signalled the Wanderer's arrival. The 'I' idly straying in dungeon crypts would be the mind searching for an adventure to recount, taking on the persona of Julian only in the next line.[11]

Once his friend, Rochelle is now Julian's 'conquered foe', incarcerated in his dungeons. Julian visits the prison 'reckless of the lives wasting there away', and finds Rochelle beautiful and sanctified by her hope for liberty through a quick death. Falling instantly in love, he decides to free her, but not until after some deliberations that confirm the implicit obnoxiousness of his idle stroll through his own dungeons. Having forgotten that he must have incarcerated her for a reason, he worries that if he frees her she will not return his love, whereas if he keeps her in prison she will remain subject to him. Though he calls it 'selfish love' and makes his decision 'short strife', that he must elaborate his decision at all is appalling in a dramatic hero, given the romantic terms of the tale. Having freed her, he takes her home and nurses her back to health, self-righteously accruing a greater heroism by his devotion to her and his sacrifice of the opportunity to go to war, for which he is much scorned by his kin. Rochelle drops out of the tale once she has been rescued, so that it is quite startling when Julian thinks to refer to her at the end, even though she is now merely the object of his self-serving sacrifice and the ground for his self-praise.

Another hand than mine my rightful banner held
And gathered my renown on Freedom's crimson field;
Yet I had no desire the glorious prize to gain –
It needed braver nerve to face the world's disdain.

And by the patient strength that could that world defy,
By suffering, with calm mind, contempt and calumny;

By never-doubting love, unswerving constancy,
Rochelle, I earned at last an equal love from thee!

This self-serving character who, unsought, frees Rochelle from her dungeon invites comparison with the liberator she does seek, who is described earlier in the poem. 'A messenger of Hope', she tells Julian scornfully, visits her at twilight, and when he comes, 'visions rise and change which kill me with desire'. She describes the advent of these visions as if they were visions of poetic inspiration. First 'a soundless calm descends' in which she seems to forget her imprisonment,

'– unuttered harmony
That I could never dream till earth was lost to me.

'Then dawns the Invisible, the Unseen its truth reveals;
My outward sense is gone, my inward essence feels –
Its wings are almost free, its home, its harbour found;
Measuring the gulf it stoops and dares the final bound!'

Her 'messenger of Hope' is a vision of death, but the vision is described with Wordsworth's language for imaginative experience: '... we are laid asleep / In body, and become a living soul.' This allusion equates imaginative experience with death. There is no room in the narrative for finding this equation faulty, since the life Julian offers is so unappealing and so distastefully achieved. Rochelle's vision includes a soaring bird as the traditional image of the soul's escape; Julian uses a bird as his metaphor for capturing her. He fears that she will fly away, in the passage on his decision between 'ruth and selfish love:'

Then like a tender child whose hand did just enfold,
Safe in its eager grasp, a bird it wept to hold,
When pierced with one wild glance from the
     troubled hazel eye,

It gushes into tears and lets its treasure fly, ...

When she does not fly away upon release, it is because she is a 'wounded dove'. During her recovery, 'Death gazed greedily / And only Hope remained a faithful friend to me'. This possessive 'to me' opposes Rochelle's claim to a different hope, who came 'every night to me'.

That Rochelle's vision of death is valued more highly than her human liberator, and that it appears to be so similar to imaginative experience, would seem to make that vision analogous to the Wanderer of the first three stanzas. Both the messenger of hope and the Wanderer are imaginary visitants. Rochelle's 'My outward sense is gone, my inward essence feels' is quite like the poet's situation:

> Silent is the House – all are laid asleep;
> One, alone, looks out o'er the snow wreaths deep.

Rochelle's loss of self-consciousness is curiously paralleled by the use of 'one' instead of 'I' here, and by the trance of quietness in the poet's room. Furthermore, Julian, himself unimaginative, is associated with loss of voice. Rochelle seems delighted when the jailor's departure makes it possible for Julian to free her, but for this knowledge we are dependent on Julian's own untrustworthy reading of her expression, because she never speaks again after finishing her inspired description of the vision of death. Life with Julian is to be mute, but the vision of death inspires speech. Many commentators, reading Rochelle's vision as an extreme expression of mystical experience, identify that mystical experience as having been Brontë's own, and locate the passage as the culmination of a sequence of poems including those on imagination discussed above, thereby tacitly identifying mystical and imaginative experience.[12]

But the analogy between Rochelle's vision and the Wanderer cannot be made into an identity, because the poet is trying to avoid her suspicion that the Wanderer, as a muse-like bringer of poetry, is also a messenger of death. It cannot be that only the expectation of death is inspiring. Rochelle is entirely passive, and her desire fails, while the first three stanzas present an active self whose wish is efficacious: the Wanderer arrives. And what he brings is in itself efficacious. By relegating the fear of death, and passivity in relation to the control of voice, to the narrated story, the poet can exorcise these difficulties from the contemplation of her own imagination. Displacement fosters the belief that they are not her own. Still, the poet does not dispel her own intimation that imagination is the intuition and expectation of death. By setting the scene in winter the poet balances two possibilities. The snowy scene may exist to demonstrate the Wanderer's dependence on her: without the brightness and steadiness of her lamp's rays, the Wanderer would be lost in the snow, as Lockwood is lost in the snow at the beginning of *Wuthering Heights*. The poet makes that 'wildering' and threatening landscape safe and intelligible, so that whatever the Wanderer brings – the story – depends on the poet's primary powers of clarification. But because he crosses a 'waste of winter snow' the Wanderer may come from regions of death, like the messenger of hope. The room is warm and still because 'not one shivering gust creeps through pane or door', suggesting a resistance to the visitor's entrance as well as a welcome.

The third stanza, though part of the prefatory material on the poet's own experience, disrupts the tone that the first two verses establish. Their apparent calm and confidence is broken by its defensive anger:

> Frown, my haughty sire; chide, my angry dame;
> Set your slaves to spy, threaten me with shame:
> But neither sire nor dame, nor prying serf shall know
> What angel nightly tracks that waste of winter snow.

The source of this sudden defensiveness is uncertain. Nothing in the first two stanzas seems to provoke it, yet suddenly the poet's world is populated by suspicious and ill-intentioned people. The line 'Silent is the house – all are laid asleep' may refer to these people, whose silence would now be revealed to have been the result of suppression. The defence is against the inference that the Wanderer is a human lover, whether sire and dame are the house's inhabitants or the poem's readers. The poet may be disturbed at the unintentionally erotic implications of her myth. However, neither of these interpretations accounts for the abruptness of the tonal shift and for the energy of the poet's distress. There must be a quantity of pent-up anxiety that finds partial expression in these lines, as if redirected from its original goal. If the rest of the poem exhibits any potential source of anxiety, it is the association of the imagination with death, and it may be that the delusion of persecution in stanza three is a redirection of the poet's fears of her own imaginative experience. Those fears may have chosen this particular course with a certain design. Even though the poet's intention seems to be to discourage the view that the Wanderer is a human lover, it is she who first plants the suggestion in the reader's mind. It may be that she raises the erotic possibility as a screen to hide an even more threatening fatality. By invoking the presence of sire, dame, and serfs, no matter how nasty they are, she wakes the dead. 'Laid asleep', they represented the proximity of death and imaginative experience; frowning and chiding, they sever that connection.

The Wanderer does not actually bring death in the same way that Rochelle's messenger promises. It is because he may choose to give or withhold language that he is associated with death, because the withholding of language is death to the poetic vocation. The plea to 'speak for me' in the poem addressed to the God of Visions (P 176, A 26) betrays the dangers of alien control of language. That plea reappears in the messenger's envoicing of Rochelle, in Julian's domineering way of speaking for her, and in the Wanderer's provision of a story to the hitherto silent poet. Feminine figures rely on masculine figures for their speech, and the poet herself defers first to the Wanderer and then to Julian as his chosen speaker. The poet has no rebuttal for Julian's deceptively cheerful interpretation of the final state of events. The poem never returns to her, as if she had set in motion a self-sufficient machine.

There are several earlier poems from the non-Gondal notebook that touch, as does 'Silent is the House', on the matter of imaginative power without specifically addressing a personified dream or a God of Visions. Where the poet is not overtly myth-making, she can more easily find expression for anxieties and fears. As in 'Silent is the House', the mind resists the sources of its own inspiration, and this resistance is in direct contrast to roughly contemporary poems about the imagination that simply plead for the return of a dream (A 11, 1840) or lament its departure (A 12, 1838; or A 13, 1840). In 'Aye, there it is! It wakes to-night' (P 148, A 9), dated July 1841, the speaker describes the onset of a natural wind that acts as a supernatural influx into the mind of the poem's 'thou', who is never named. The speaker mentions 'thine altered cheek' and 'thy kindled gaze' as evidence of 'How wildly fancy plays'. The 'glorious wind / Has swept the world aside, / Has dashed its memory from thy mind', so that the experience described resembles Rochelle's 'My outward sense is gone, my inward essence feels'.

> And thou art now a spirit pouring
> Thy presence into all –
> The essence of the Tempest's roaring
> And of the Tempest's fall –
>
> A universal influence
> From Thine own influence free;
> A principle of life, intense,
> Lost to mortality.

One critic is prompted by tradition to read these verses as an address to the wind, because an influence or influx ought to be a wind, and because the lines resemble part of Shelley's 'Ode to the West Wind'.[13] But there is no indication that the speaker has turned from one interlocutor to another. The wind may initially have induced this outpouring of spirit, but the interlocutor's powers of influx are fully as great as the wind's. It is not that the interlocutor has assumed the wind's function, but that they have merged. Both wind and mind are spirit; both pour their presence into all; the mind has joined the wind in becoming a universal principle. Wind and woman are undifferentiated, and the vanishing of barriers between subject and object leads to an indifference to distinctions between life and death: 'lost to mortality'.

This exaltation is brought abruptly back to earth by the next and final stanza:

> Thus truly when that breast is cold
> Thy prisoned soul shall rise,
> The dungeon mingle with the mould –
> The captive with the skies.

There is apparently nothing in the poem to provoke this thought of death; on the contrary, the rest of the poem seems to be about an accelerating vitality. That this stanza might be an interpretation of the rest of the poem, as 'thus truly' signals, is nonsense. There is no rational cause to call the soul that has previously been described as an ecstatic spirit a 'prisoned soul'. A 'principle of life' that transcends distinctions between animate and inanimate can hardly be identified as a 'captive' whose release must wait for death. Like the defensive third stanza of 'Silent is the House', this stanza is dislocated from the rest by something that is not accounted for by the poem's ostensible plotting. The idea of death can only be a reaction to the foregoing ecstasies. The fusion of wind and mind in spirit is as threatening as it is exhilarating, because it necessitates the annihilation of individuality, perhaps even of individual life. 'Lost to mortality' suggests 'lost to life' as much as 'lost to death'. The narrative arrangement, with the speaker at once describing and addressing the poem's subject, indicates an aspect of that danger. In the poems on imagination there is normally a solitary inspired 'I'. Whether there are two distinct figures in this poem or two parts of one self, there has to be a watcher here because the one who is being described is incapable of speech. One of the signs of the

wind's influx is 'the words thou scarce dost speak'. Her mode of expression becomes that of the wind; the 'Tempest's roaring' is her
roaring too. Ecstatic mergence with spirit or wind takes place at the
price of language and perhaps of life.

That the speaker is not annihilated and the power of articulation
is kept separate from the ecstatic spirit is the poet's signal that the
'thou' 's experience, like Rochelle's vision of death, is not to be
identified as a parable of the poetic imagination. 'The Night-Wind',
a poem of ten months earlier than 'Aye, there it is', exhibits a
similar association between death, loss of language, and mergence,
but again outside the explicit discussion of the poetic imagination.
The poem is about the night-wind's efforts to seduce the speaker,
who is here a single consciousness. His seductions are all invitations
to death, though not explicitly so, since the images of darkness and
loss of self that he proffers are entirely lovely and beguiling.

> But still it whispered lowly,
> 'How dark the woods will be!
>
> 'The thick leaves in my murmur
> Are rustling like a dream,
> And all their myriad voices
> Instinct with spirit seem.'
> (P 140, A 7)

The night wind claims an inexorable power that belies his apparent
gentleness:

> The wanderer would not leave* me;   *or heed
> Its kiss grew warmer still –
> 'O come', it sighed so sweetly,
> 'I'll win thee 'gainst thy will.'

The speaker resists all these efforts because she understands what
they mean. The poem ends, like 'Aye, there it is', with a suddenly
hard and explicit image of death:

> 'And when thy heart is laid at rest
> Beneath the church-yard stone
> I shall have time enough to mourn
> And thou to be alone.'

Barbara Hardy takes this 'final darkness' to be 'what the wind has
always been uttering', and the explanation for its lures and for the
speaker's resistance.[14]

However convincing, this reading does not account for the wind's projected lamentation of his beloved's death, as if his project required her vitality. It may not be her death that he wants, primarily; the state evoked is very like that in Wordsworth's Lucy poems, in which Lucy's death is incidental to her incorporation into nature. Part of the speaker's defence here is her insistence on maintaining a distinction between heaven and earth, human and natural. The wind wants to obliterate this distinction and in doing so to steal her linguistic powers, which derive from difference. Reading and perhaps seeing herself in the Lucy poems may have detracted from Dorothy's sense of identity as a poet, and the Lucy situation here threatens to have the same effect on this poem's speaker. The poem begins with an open window and a verbal opening toward nature, in that nature is described:

> A cloudless moon shone through
> Our open parlour window
> And rosetrees wet with dew.

When the wind, softly waving the speaker's hair, speaks of a continuity between heaven and earth, however, the speaker recoils from it.

> It told me Heaven was glorious,
> And sleeping Earth was fair.
>
> I needed not its breathing
> To bring such thoughts to me, ...

Her recoil is against the wind's presumption in telling her her own thoughts, not against the thought itself; either way there is an undesired interpenetration of domains. The wind says that the voices are 'instinct with spirit'. She resists that interpenetration by countering with hierarchical thinking, speaking as if nature were low or childlike compared to the human mind. Addressing the wind, she says:

> 'Thy wooing voice is kind,
> But do not think its music
> Has power to reach my mind.
>
> 'Play with the scented flower,
> The young tree's supple bough,
> And leave my human feelings
> In their own course to flow.'

It is not entirely certain that the interpenetration she defends herself against is death – or, if death is its final form, the immediate threat is the possible collapse of language. When the speaker recoils from the wind's telling her her own thoughts, part of her fear is that nature may pre-empt human speech. In the verse that follows, the wind's self-description is spoken from the point of view of the human listener, not the natural speaker:

> 'The thick leaves in my murmur
> Are rustling like a dream,
> And all their myriad voices
> Instinct with spirit seem.'

Only substituting 'your' for 'my', this is the kind of speech that the human being should be making, full of metaphors and an outsider's uncertainty about appearances. The wind speaks for her. At least part of what disturbs her about the wind's seductions must be the threat that human language will cease. Her fears are justified by the wind's disregard of her verbal protests. For the wind, word and kiss are one. In his appeal to her nostalgia for childhood he almost images a reciprocal love:

> 'Have I not loved thee long?
> As long as thou hast loved the night
> Whose silence wakes my song.'

He reminds the speaker that she is a lover of the images of death – silence and the night – as if answering her objections to being herself silenced. In the image of death that the wind proffers as his last persuasion, the dead one is 'alone' and therefore beyond communication, while the wind will go on speaking: 'I shall have time enough to mourn'. Language depends on keeping the human and other aspects of nature separate; for the wind to speak in human terms violates intelligibility. If the wind's seductions are to death, then it would have to mourn its own deed, but 'silence wakes my song', and the wind is intent on eradicating difference, which wakes human song.

In 'Shall Earth no more inspire thee' (P 147, A 6) the wind has so successfully pre-empted human voice that he is the only speaker; there is no human voice at all. He chastises 'thee' for rejecting the earth's inspiration in favour of mental abstraction, 'regions dark to thee', and asks this 'lonely dreamer' to 'come back and dwell with me'. In the manner of the wind in 'The Night-Wind' the speaker blurs the distinction between heaven and earth:

> ... none would ask a Heaven
> More like this Earth than thine.

The earth uses for himself the terms that the poet elsewhere uses for imaginative power:

> I've seen thy spirit bending
> In fond idolatry.

The first line of the last verse, 'Then let my winds caress thee', recalls Wordsworth's address to Dorothy at the end of 'Tintern Abbey': '... let the misty mountain-winds be free / To blow against thee'. The speaker of 'Tintern Abbey' is for Brontë the type of the poet of the imagination, who dominates the woman he addresses by his privileged discourse with nature, by the maturity of his imagination, and also by his masculinity. By having the earth speak with his words, Brontë identifies the earth's powers with both imaginative power and with sexual dominance.

The repeated identification of a masculine wind with the pre-emption of language clearly refers to the tradition of the Word as the spirit or breath of God, or wind blowing from God. The poet's fear that she neither originates nor controls her own speech, a fear that she presents as a fear of death, arises from her being a woman writing in a masculine tradition. Coleridge's 'The Eolian Harp' images the mind as both passive and feminine, made to 'tremble into thought' by the passage of the 'intellectual breeze' that is identified with (an unorthodox) God. 'That simplest Lute' is 'by the desultory breeze caress'd, / Like some coy maid half yielding to her lover'. For Coleridge himself, the alignment of the sexes in this metaphor is not conducive to the highest imaginative power. Instead of experiencing sublimity, 'many idle flitting phantasies, / Traverse my indolent and passive brain'. And the mind thus imaged gives way later in the poem to an absurd orthodoxy. When Coleridge seeks an image of true imaginative power, the mind is no longer feminine or subject to the whims of the breeze, but the source of that breeze itself: 'The primary IMAGINATION I hold to be ... a repetition in the finite mind of the eternal act of creation in the infinite I AM.' Whereas the image of the mind as feminine and passive is not definitive for Coleridge, it intrudes itself into Brontë's serious formulations about her identity as a poet, as when Dorothy Wordsworth consciously aligns her poetic voice with Coleridge's definition of fancy. Unable to identify with the masculine Word or breath of God, Brontë portrays herself as its passive object in 'The Night-Wind' and in 'Shall Earth no more inspire thee' (A 7 and A 6). Where in 'Aye, there it is' (A 9) a female figure is united with an intellectual breeze, her assumption promotes thoughts of death, not of power.

From Margaret Homans, *Women Writers and Poetic Identity: Dorothy Wordsworth, Emily Brontë, and Emily Dickinson* (Princeton, NJ, 1980), pp. 104–29.

NOTES

['Emily Brontë' is extracted from the long chapter of that name in Margaret Homans's pathbreaking study. The opening of Homans's discussion develops the conclusions she has drawn earlier in her study about Dorothy Wordsworth's 'textual femininity as a response to the Romantic tradition'. Throughout this extract, Homans explores Brontë's complex poetic negotiations of male-identified Romantic subjectivity. Homans's work counts among the first Anglo-American studies to draw on areas of French feminist theory and aspects of deconstructive thought to articulate issues of sexual difference and poetic figuration in the work of nineteenth-century women writers. These methodological considerations are outlined in her opening chapter, 'The Masculine Tradition', which concentrates on 'two major ways in which women readers must have found woman's otherness enforced: her association with nature and her exclusion from a traditional identification of the speaking subject as male'.

Homans's exploration of how psychoanalytic theory, especially that developed from Lacanian paradigms, can illuminate our understanding of the struggles with female identification that we find in many nineteenth-century literary works by women is continued in *Bearing the Word: Language and Female Experience in Nineteenth-Century Women's Writing* (Chicago, 1986), and in '"Syllables of Velvet": Dickinson, Rossetti, and the Rhetorics of Sexuality', *Feminist Studies*, 11 (1985), 569–93. Ed.]

1. Quoted in Elizabeth Gaskell, *The Life of Charlotte Brontë* ([1857] Harmondsworth, 1975), p. 230.

2. From Charlotte Brontë, 'Biographical Notice of Ellis and Acton Bell', written for her 1850 edition of *Wuthering Heights* and *Agnes Grey*. All quotations from *Wuthering Heights* and Charlotte's prefatory material are from *Wuthering Heights*, ed. William M. Sale (New York, 1963), cited hereafter as *WH* with page numbers.

s of Charlotte's misunderstanding of her sister's work, and
rm it may have done, see Philip Henderson's introduction to
ontë, *Poems Selected with an Introduction* (London, 1947),
xii; and Robin Grove, '"It Would Not Do": Emily Brontë as
in Anne Smith (ed.), *The Art of Emily Brontë* (London, 1976),
,4–9.

4. Carol Ohmann discusses the way critics trivialised *Wuthering Heights* once its author's identity had been revealed, in 'Emily Brontë in the Hands of Male Critics', *College English*, 32 (1971), 906–13.

5. C. Day Lewis argues, on the biographical level, that Brontë was unconsciously frustrated at not being a man, and that her dissatisfaction with the world was a projection of this frustration. See 'The Poetry of Emily Brontë', *Brontë Society Transactions, 13* (1957), 94–7.

6. All quotations from Brontë's poetry are from *The Complete Poems of Emily Jane Brontë*, ed. C.W. Hatfield (New York, 1941), cited as P followed by the poem number assigned by Hatfield. In this edition, each of the poems in the non-Gondal notebooks bears a number according to its position in the notebook (A 1–A 31); these numbers, where applicable, will be cited as well as Hatfield's numbers, which are assigned chronologically.

7. Fannie E. Ratchford, *The Brontës' Web of Childhood* (New York, 1941), p. 12.

8. Grove, in Smith (ed.), *The Art of Emily Brontë*, pp. 42–6. Rosalind Miles, in an essay in the same collection, 'A Baby God: The Creative Dynamism of Emily Brontë's Poetry', pp. 68–73, searching for autobiographical information, laments the absence of an authorial self.

9. A number of readers have noted the Byronic themes and stances in Brontë's poetry, for example Helen Brown, 'The Influence of Byron on Emily Brontë', *Modern Language Review,* 34 (1939), 374–81; Dorothy J. Cooper, 'The Romantics and Emily Brontë', *Brontë Society Transactions,* 12 (1952), 106–12; Alan Loxterman, '*Wuthering Heights* as Romantic Poem and Victorian Novel', in Frieda E. Penninger (ed.), *A Festschrift for Professor Marguerite Roberts* (Richmond, VA, 1976), pp. 91–2. Cooper also cites parallels between Brontë's poetry and gothic novels.

10. J. Hillis Miller discusses her ambivalent relation to her imagination in *The Disappearance of God: Five Nineteenth-Century Writers* (Cambridge, MA, 1963), pp. 158–9; Charles Morgan also sketches a theory of ambiguously received possession, in *Reflections in a Mirror* (London, 1944), pp. 142–5. My purpose is to expand and elaborate these suggestions.

11. Jonathan Wordsworth has suggested that the 'I' is Julian throughout, and that the first three stanzas are the present-time frame for a

recollection. If the figure at the window is Julian, then the Wanderer would be his beloved, Rochelle, in human or ghostly form. This reading would account for the erotic implications of the third stanza, but the voice in the first three stanzas differs too much from the voice we learn to recognise as Julian's from this reading to make sense. See 'Wordsworth and the Poetry of Emily Brontë', *Brontë Society Transactions*, 16 (1972), 85–100.

12. See, among others: Margaret Willy, 'Emily Brontë: Poet and Mystic', *English*, 6 (1946), 117–22; Muriel A. Dobson, 'Was Emily Brontë A Mystic?', *Brontë Society Transactions*, 11 (1948), 166–75; Jacques Blondel, *Emily Brontë: Expérience spirituelle et création poétique* (Paris, 1955), pp. 192–218.

13. Winifred Gérin, *Emily Brontë: A Biography* (London, 1971), p. 154.

14. Barbara Hardy, 'The Lyricism of Emily Brontë', in Smith (ed.), *The Art of Emily Brontë*, pp. 105–6.

4

'Art's A Service': Social Wound, Sexual Politics, and *Aurora Leigh*

DEIRDRE DAVID

I

Elizabeth Barrett Browning's *Aurora Leigh* has become a key text for feminist critics concerned with nineteenth-century women writers. For some, *Aurora Leigh* is a revolutionary poem, a passionate indictment of patriarchy that speaks the resentment of the Victorian woman poet through a language of eroticised female imagery. For others, the poem is less explosive, and Barrett Browning's liberal feminism is seen as compromised by Aurora Leigh's eventual dedication to a life governed by traditionally male directives. In my view, however, *Aurora Leigh* is neither revolutionary nor compromised: rather, it is a coherent expression of Barrett Browning's conservative sexual politics, and I shall argue that female imagery is employed to show that the 'art' of the woman poet performs a 'service' for a patriarchal vision of the apocalypse. In *Aurora Leigh* woman's art is made the servitor of a male ideal.

Locating Barrett Browning in the tradition of nineteenth-century women writers and analysing 'the centrality of female experience' in *Aurora Leigh*, Cora Kaplan reads the poem as a revolutionary text: 'In spite of its conventional happy ending, it is possible to see it as contributing to a feminist theory of art which argues that women's language, precisely because it has been suppressed by patriarchal societies, re-enters discourse with a shattering revolutionary force, speaking all that is repressed and forbidden in human experience.'[1]

To be sure, the bold vitality of Barrett Browning's language and imagery in *Aurora Leigh* is undeniable; and the governing ideology of the poem is, indeed, revolutionary. However, revolutionary does not necessarily mean feminist in Barrett Browning's sexual politics: her novel-poem is an integrated expression of essentialist and ultimately non-feminist views of sex and gender, despite sharp attacks on sexual hypocrisy and devastating satire of women's education. Kaplan argues that because 'the woman as speaker-poet' replaces 'all male prophets' and 'dominates the symbolic language of the poem', *Aurora Leigh* dynamically confronts patriarchal attitudes.[2] *Aurora Leigh* is certainly confrontational: its antagonist, however, is more the middle-class materialism which found a convenient ally in Victorian patriarchal formations than it is patriarchy itself. As I shall show, in assuming a mission to transcend materialist ideology, Aurora Leigh joyfully assumes a role inscribed in and by male-dominated culture and society.

As an essentialist in sexual politics, Barrett Browning unequivocally sanctioned the concepts of 'masculine' and 'feminine' intelligence: after the death of Margaret Fuller, she evaluated the bulk of her writings as 'quite inferior to what might have been expected from so masculine an intellect'.[3] To speak of a masculine intellect evidently presupposes a feminine one, and as far as one can judge from Barrett Browning's letters and poetry, the feminine is inferior. Harriet Martineau is consistently praised by Barrett Browning for the 'male' qualities of her mind, and the following remarks about her fellow-invalid – addressed to Mrs Martin in 1844 – betray Barrett Browning's sanction of the Victorian allocation of men and women into categories of strong and weak thinkers: 'No case of a weak-minded woman and a nervous affection; but of the most manlike woman in the three kingdoms – in the best sense of man – a woman gifted with admirable fortitude, as well as exercised in high logic, a woman of sensibility and of imagination certainly, but apt to carry her reason unbent wherever she sets her foot; given to utilitarian philosophy and the habit of logical analysis.'[4] The model for intellectual superiority is the conventionally male one: Martineau is not nervous, possesses fortitude, and exercises the power of logical reasoning. When Barrett Browning wrote to H.S. Boyd that Martineau is 'the most logical intellect of the age, for a woman' she believed – with her contemporaries – that it was unusual for a woman to be logical (*L.EBB* 1, 225). In the Victorian discourse of sex and gender, logic is a male property, just as nurturance is a female one; and it is essential that Barrett Browning's employment of imagery associated with women's experience be located within the context of her entire sexual politics. To dislocate the imagery for celebratory purposes runs the risk of elaborating the same sexist, dualistic models of thought which governed the dominant Victorian understanding of intellect, sex, and gender.

Barrett Browning believed woman the intellectual inferior of man. She emphatically announced herself not a 'very strong partisan on the Rights-of-Woman-side of the argument ... I believe that, considering men and women in the mass, there IS *an inequality* of intellect, and that it is proved by the very state of things of which gifted women complain, – and more than proved by the manner in which their complaint is received by their own sisterhood.'[5] In this tautological denigration of female mind, women are proved inferior by their record, which implies that if they *were* intellectually powerful, then feminists would have nothing to complain of. The manner in which feminists complain confirms woman's intellectual inferiority. The actual constraints placed upon the lives of Victorian women, the necessity of fitting female desire for intellectual autonomy to the shapes of male cultural authority, tend to be evaded or ignored in Barrett Browning's sexual politics. For example, the need for women to be educated in which women like Harriet Martineau so strongly believed is of little interest to her: she confided to Robert Browning that women have 'minds of quicker movement, but less power and depth' than men: 'there is a natural inferiority of mind in women – of the – intellect ... the history of art and of genius testifies to this fact openly.' She made no secret of her dislike of everything to do with 'Women and their Mission' (her terms) and, as she confessed to Browning, early in her career she relinquished whatever interest she may have had in 'the Martineaudoctrines of equality'.[6]

Before her marriage to Robert Browning, Elizabeth Barrett made it clear that she shared his ambiguous assessment of women's intellectual and artistic capabilities: in a complex strategy of praise and criticism, Robert Browning deemed women too good to be in Parliament, implicitly too delicate for participation in the privileged rough and tumble of Westminster. In later June of 1846, he wrote to Elizabeth Barrett that it would be 'exquisitely absurd ... essentially retrograde a measure' for Harriet Martineau's call for female members of Parliament to become reality: 'Parliament seems no place for originating, creative minds – but for the second-rate minds influenced by and bent on working out the results of these – and the most efficient qualities for such a purpose are confessedly found oftener with men than with women' (*L.RB/EBB* 2, 280). This is one form of the insidious praise of women that constitutes Victorian deification and degradation of the 'softer sex'. Parliamentary practice calls for 'second-rate minds', practical rather than 'originating, creative' ones: men are more likely to possess these practical second-rate minds than women. This opinion seems to score one for the female side, but such praise also implies that women are inadequate to sustained, administrative work. Elizabeth Barrett replied to Browning's views of women and Parliament by declaring that not only do women lack the physical strength for such work (which Browning had also suggested), but they 'have not instruction, capacity, wholeness of intellect enough' to be in Parliament. Admittedly, this is a woman writing to the man she would marry in less than three months, and her letters in this period of their correspondence are more concerned with the joys and difficulties of their romance than with sexual politics: but the statement that women lack the 'instruction, capacity, wholeness of intellect' to participate in the political life of their country is not the statement of a woman on her way to confronting patriarchy, nor is it pregnant with the promise of 'speaking all that is repressed and forbidden in human experience', which is how Kaplan reads *Aurora Leigh*.

A poem that begins with the admonition from Ecclesiastes, 'Of writing many books there is no end', *Aurora Leigh* is pervaded by metaphors of writing, the most notable being that employed by Aurora in likening man's soul to a multiply-inscribed text. Refuting Enlightenment beliefs in the soul as 'clear white paper', she imagines it as:

> A palimpsest, a prophet's holograph,
> Defiled, erased and covered by a monk's –
> The apocalypse, by a Longus! poring on
> Which obscene text, we may discern perhaps
> Some fair, fine trace of what was written once,
> Some upstroke of an alpha and omega
> Expressing the old scripture.[7]

Richly invested with Barrett Browning's philosophical and political values, the lines signalise her recurrent preoccupation with the traditional Christian myth of lost unity. Man's soul is likened to a scripture which once possessed its own perfect form and its own in-

ternal coherence: as Christ declares in Revelation 1:8, 'I am Alpha
and Omega, the beginning and the ending', so man, in an ideal correspondence to this unity, once possessed a unified soul/text. But the
soul/text which once resembled the holograph inscribed by a prophet,
who was, in his turn, inspired by the original inscriber of all things,
has been defiled by later writers: man's original soul/text has been
debased from its primary, revelatory meaning and transformed from
oracular revelation to pastoral romance (the apocalypse inscribed by
a Longus). Implicitly proclaiming herself as God's new prophet and
as God's new inscriber of the ideal world which will replace that sun-
dered by a social 'cleft', Barrett Browning, through Aurora Leigh, instructs man in discovering traces of the original text in the degenerate
palimpsest. Aurora Leigh must perform the ideal mission which
Barrett Browning described in her Preface to 'A Vision of Poets', a
lengthy homage to poets of the far and recent past and included in
Poems (1844). She declares that the Victorian poet 'wears better
broad-cloth, but speaks no more oracles ... the evil of this social in-
crustation over a great idea is eating deeper and more fatally into our
literature than either readers or writers may apprehend fully' (2.147).
Acting as cultural agent between a troubled society and transcendent
values, the ideal poet performs an oracular function: if soul, text, and
form have been debased through inscribed interpretation, erasure,
and deformation, so, too, the alpha and omega of Victorian life have
become obscured by the inscriptions of materialism and socialist politics. Empowered through vocation to reveal the organic connections
between God, man, culture, and society which have been obscured in
a secular world, the ideal poet is made a woman poet in *Aurora
Leigh*. And the language of imagery derived from female experience
is employed by that woman poet in an alignment of two powerful
myths: the traditional myth of poet as witness to a transcendent
order is aligned with the traditional myth of woman as moral
servitor.

II

The *Westminster Review* in 1857 praised the mind that produced
Aurora Leigh as one remarkable for 'its abundant treasure of well-
digested learning, its acute observation of life, its yearning sympathy with multiform human sorrow, its store of personal, domestic
love and joy'. This was a rare moment in an avalanche of negative

criticism (including the rest of the *Westminster*'s review) which roundly condemned Barrett Browning's prolixity, extravagant metaphors, eccentric rhymes, riotous metre, and, most significantly and pervasively, her use of 'unfeminine' poetic language and her choice of poetic subject. She is labelled an 'unchaste poet'. Accused of depicting female types the critics seemed to prefer *not* depicted by a 'poetess' beloved as much for her refined seclusion as she was for the delicacy of her verse, she had dared to parade before her astonished readers a lascivious aristocrat, a raped working-class girl, and an intellectually independent heroine. Charge with writing in a 'high fever', of taking the literary field like Britomartis, an assertive, mythological maiden who escaped the sexual advances of Minos by leaping from a rock, Barrett Browning may be said to have leapt from her 'respectable' rock, not, however, as frantic escape from male pursuit, but to immerse herself in the representation of subjects more usually treated by the novel: utopian politics, female sexuality, rape, urban misery, and woman's struggle for professional recognition.

She is accused of indelicately affecting 'masculine' language, of becoming 'coarse' in her desire not to be squeamish. *Blackwood's Magazine* adopted a thoroughly offended male stance, finding 'the extreme independence' of Aurora detracting from the paucity of 'feminine' charm she might possess and marring all interest that the reader might have in 'so intellectual a heroine'. If there is one critical thread that holds the negative reviews of the poem together, it is an accusation of coarseness of language and of theme. Propriety and good taste are particularly called into question in discussion of what *The Spectator* called 'the "Clarissa Harlowe" calamity': 'The bar of the Old Bailey is the only place where we wish to hear of such things!'[8]

The plot of *Aurora Leigh* traces the development of its heroine from her Florentine childhood to eventual marriage to her cousin Romney. The child of an English father and Italian mother, she is sent to England to live with her aunt on the death of her parents at the age of thirteen. The aunt trains her in the conventional accomplishments of English young ladies and for marriage to her cousin. At the age of twenty Aurora refuses his proposal, inherits a small income on the death of her aunt, and moves to London determined to become a poet. Some ten years later (having achieved modest recognition of her work), she learns that the Christian socialism favoured by Romney which she had scorned as insufficient to remedy social evil, has taken the form of intended marriage to a working-class girl, Marian Erle. In a stunningly visual depiction that calls to mind Hogarthian London, rich and poor meet at St James's Church where Romney vainly awaits his bride. Marian never arrives, having been persuaded to leave for Australia by Lady Waldemar, the woman who wants Romney for herself. Duped by the maid of this voluptuous aristocrat, and drugged in a French brothel, Marian is raped. Aurora learns her story two years after 'the Clarissa Harlowe calamity' when she spots Marian, now the mother of a baby boy, in a Paris flower market. Aurora takes mother and child to Italy where they live happily together in the countryside of Aurora's childhood. Believing Romney to have married Lady Waldemar, Aurora is astonished to see him arrive on her porch one summer evening. The last two books of the poem are devoted to an extended dialogue between Romney and Aurora about the need to unify spiritual and material remedies for social ills. The poem ends with an apocalyptic vision of the New Jerusalem, Aurora having at last realised that Romney has been blinded by an injury received in the fire that destroys his utopian socialist community. The poem is punctuated by Aurora's lengthy meditations upon art; it contains an arresting amount of violent imagery; and by the time of Barrett Browning's death in 1861 it had gone through five editions.

Vigorously employing blank verse and multiple images of degradation and exploitation, Barrett Browning vividly places Marian's rape before the reader, if not in its details then in its absence. Social and literary decorum dictate that Marian's story remain unsaid, yet its marginal status intensifies its volatile content:

> We wretches cannot tell out all our wrong
> Without offence to decent happy folk.
> I know that we must scrupulously hint
> With half-words, delicate reserves, the thing
> Which no one scrupled we should feel in full.
> (6.1220–4)

Aurora becomes a mother to Marian, making those 'half-words' whole, giving utterance to a character who has no social right of narrative, repairing as much as she is able the injury she has suffered, and in the way of all mothers described by Aurora in evoking her own Italian childhood, 'kisses full sense' into what Marian cannot say.[9] In giving voice and protection to Marian, Aurora combats a social evil consistently attacked by Barrett Browning: the sexual hypocrisy of sexually respectable women. If there is one place where *Aurora Leigh* takes an unequivocal feminist stand, it is in its refusal to be silent about sexuality.

In 1861 Thackeray rejected one of Barrett Browning's poems, 'Lord Walter's Wife' for the *Cornhill* on the grounds that 'there are things my squeamish public will not hear', hastening to assure her that the wife of Browning and the mother of Pen was sacred to English readers. Barrett Browning's response was to the sexist point: 'It is exactly because pure and prosperous women choose to *ignore* vice, that miserable women suffer wrong by it everywhere' (*L.EBB* 2, 244–5). Moreover, Barrett Browning had long held such pronounced views: twenty years earlier, in writing to Mary Russell Mitford, she berated respectable women who will 'shrink from breathing the same air with a betrayed woman', yet will gracefully sit down to dinner with male adulterers (*L.EBB/M* 1, 295). 'Lord Walter's Wife' figures a quite different woman, one who makes a spirited attack on the prevailing sexual double standard. An engaged man declares to his friend's wife that he finds her 'too fair'. Deliberately encouraging his attentions, the woman, Lord Walter's wife, instructs him in the unhappy social truth that men treat all women as sexual commodities to be used and discarded. Had she succumbed to his advances he would no longer find her so desirable: 'Too fair? – not unless you misuse us! and surely if, once in a while, / You attain to it, straight way you call / Us no longer too fair, but too vile' (6:31–4). The poem is vitalised by the woman's anger, felt not only by the aristocratic wife but on behalf of all women who are either deified or degraded by men.

During the Crimean War, Barrett Browning wrote to a friend from her girlhood years at Hope End, Mrs Martin, that 'there are worse plagues, deeper griefs, dreader wounds than the physical. What of the forty thousand wretched women in this city? The silent writhing of them is to me more appalling than the roar of the cannons' (*L.EBB* 2, 213). In *Aurora Leigh* the wounds are both physical and symbolic: Marian is violently wounded by rape, and in a hellish scene of diseased bodies swelling the aisles of the church where Romney and Marian are to be married, all is an oozing 'peccant social wound'. The image of the wound is crucial not only to the poem, but also to Barrett Browning's work as a woman poet. In refusing to ignore the injuries suffered by prostitutes, in compelling society to look at the 'offal' it makes of 'fallen' women and of the poor, and in symbolising social evil as social wound, she creates herself as a ministering healer to an infected world. If society has been cleft in two by a symbolic knife, if women are cleft by rapacious men, then Barrett Browning will, through her poetry, dress the wounds, address the means of cure. An imagery of wounding cuts into *Aurora Leigh* as powerfully as an imagery of maternal nurturance may be said to unify it.

When establishing the presence of 'women's language' in *Aurora Leigh*, most feminist critics point to the poem's almost obsessive attention to suckling and its eroticised fascination with breasts: Aurora is symbolically suckled by the hills of her Italian childhood; she exhorts her fellow poets to 'Never flinch, / But still unscrupulously epic, catch / Upon the burning lava of a song / The full-veined, heaving, double-breasted Age' (5.214–17); Romney feeds the great carnivorous mouth of the poor through his Christian socialism.[10] This mammocentric imagery, however, is ambiguous: the image of proper poetic practice invoked by Aurora implies conventionally male rather than female meanings, and maternal nurturance is invested with strangely unsettling qualities. Aurora, the woman poet, rather peculiarly figures the poet's task in conventionally male terms – as unflinching, aggressive work – and she makes the subject of the poem almost primordially female – full-veined, heaving, double-breasted. The poet must make a swiftly moving song out of an age which seems to be immutably stable in its connection with mother earth. As further complication of the breast imagery, Marian's nurturance of her baby is invested with an almost malevolent quality: as she suckles him, she seems to consume him greedily in an image of appropriation, 'drinking him as wine'.

Moreover, Lady Waldemar's breasts both attract and repel. They are an unspoiled source of life and an image of demonic eroticism: the paradox suggests that contradiction between the deification and degradation of women which Barrett Browning attacks in her poem, 'Lord Walter's Wife'. Lady Waldemar offers a dazzling display of ripe female sexuality:

> ... How they told,
> Those alabaster shoulders and bare breasts,
> On which the pearls, drowned out of sight in milk,
> Were lost, excepting for the ruby clasp!
> They split the amaranth velvet-bodice down
> To the waist or nearly, with the audacious press

Of full-breathed beauty. If the heart within
Were half as white! – but, if it were, perhaps
The breast were closer covered and the sight
Less aspectable by half, too.
                                                    (5.618–28)

Proceeding through a sequence of false appearances and concealed truth, the description shows that 'aspectable' things are not what they seem. Nature herself (in the seductive shape of milky breasts) seems to drown out female ornamentation (the pearl necklace), yet the visible ruby clasp indicates Lady Waldemar's embellished sexuality. A single grey hair in her luxuriant bronze tresses contrasts ironically with the symbolism of her amaranth-velvet bodice (the purple colour of a mythical flower which never fades). The display of vibrant sexuality implies its own degeneration and in terms of what Lady Waldemar does to Marian, the radiant whiteness of her breasts conceals the dark heart within. Lady Waldemar is what her name implies – the 'weal' which 'marrs' all she touches.

The depiction of women in *Aurora Leigh* is framed by Barrett Browning's employment of three interwoven colour images: green, red, and white. The first symbolises the serenity Aurora enjoys in the time she is freed from her aunt's instruction in English womanhood; the other two tend to express, even when employed by Aurora herself, the prevailing nineteenth-century fragmentation of woman into a creature fractured by seemingly irreconcilable, and therefore dangerous, attributes. Such fragmentation is figured most prominently in the portrait of Aurora's mother, painted with white face and red dress, and appearing as 'Ghost, fiend, and angel, fairy, witch and sprite' to her daughter. Sometimes speaking this imagery of fragmentation, Aurora moves from the green, calm (but stultifying) time of her young womanhood to her mature, vibrant, fiery part in building the New Jerusalem:

I had a little chamber in the house,
As green as any privet-hedge a bird
Might choose to build in, though the nest itself
Could show but dead-brown sticks and straws; the walls
Were green, the carpet was pure green, the straight
Small bed was curtained greenly, and the folds
Hung green about the window which let in
The out-door world with all its greenery.
                                                    (1.567–74)

In the serene, cool space of the English countryside, employing the bird imagery that is everywhere in the poem, Aurora describes herself placidly nesting in her green chamber/privet hedge.

The first significant employment of the red/white imagery occurs in Aurora's description of her mother's portrait which was executed after her death. The face, throat and hands possess a 'swan-like supernatural white life', yet the body wears a red brocade dress; and to the child Aurora the face is 'by turns' that paradoxical female face of so much Victorian art – the angelic sprite who winds her hair around the neck of a knight in Waterhouse's 'La Belle Dame Sans Merci', the fiendish, contorted figure of Hunt's 'The Lady of Shallot', Rossetti's 'Lady Lilith' whose massive neck and powerful jaw signalise an awful female mystery.[11] When Aurora hears of Marian's flight from London, she relies upon the traditional symbolism of purity and whiteness to reassure Romney: his lost bride will stay as pure as 'snow that's drifted from the garden-bank / To the open road'. In Marian's own powerful evocation of her despair, however, the colour imagery becomes more complicated. She describes herself, pregnant and destitute, wandering the roads in France:

> And there I sat, one evening, by the road,
> I, Marian Erle, myself, alone, undone,
> Facing a sunset low upon the flats
> As if it were the finish of all time,
> The great red stone upon my sepulchre,
> Which angels were too weak to roll away.
> (6.1269–74)

The raped woman, spoiled yet innocent, soon to give birth to a joyful child from brutal rape, reddened by the blood of defloration which literally and symbolically is 'engraved' upon her white body, likens the setting sun to a red stone upon her sepulchre. In Marian's language, the red imagery links the dying day, the exhausted woman, and the weakened angels in a paradoxically fiery decline, suggesting a significant contrast to Aurora in her green chamber on her twentieth birthday. A radiant, vital and virginal Aurora, fresh from her vernal nest in the morning, foreshadows a depleted, violated Marian at sunset. On Aurora's morning, she is dressed in white, hopefully self-wreathed in ivy as symbol of the poetic power to come: 'The June was in me, with its multitudes / Of nightingales all singing in the dark, / And rosebuds reddening where the calyx split' (2.10–12). The green calyx splits to reveal the ripening rose and suggests the departure of a maturing Aurora from the green enclosure of her room.

If Marian suffers a symbolical fiery ordeal as she feels the weight of 'a great red stone' upon her grave, then Romney suffers a literal one when he is blinded in the fire set by local peasants, incensed by the 'drabs and thieves' he has housed in his Phalanstery. He describes himself as 'A mere bare blind stone in the blaze of day', a comparison which connects with Marian's evocation of a 'great red stone' upon her sepulchre. Aligning the traditional myth of poet as witness to a transcendent order with the traditional myth of woman as moral servitor, Aurora repairs the injuries suffered by Marian and Romney.

The informing structure of wounding and healing in the poem is emphatically etched by imagery of knifing. 'There, ended childhood' declares Aurora on the death of her father. Her life becomes 'Smooth endless days, notched here and there with knives, / A weary, wormy darkness, spurred i' the flank / With flame, that it should eat and end itself / Like some tormented scorpion' (1.219–22). Barrett Browning sustains the imagery of knifing throughout the poem. Aurora describes her aunt's discipline as a 'sharp sword set against my life', her aunt's gaze as 'two grey-steel naked-bladed eyes' searching through her face, a young man at a dinner party as possessing 'A sharp face, like a knife in a cleft stick' (1.691, 328; 5.629). Moreover, Aurora's sense of injured self is sometimes surprisingly gruesome: 'So I lived', she says, 'A Roman died so; smeared with honey, teased / By insects, stared to torture by the moon' (2.890–1); in London she likens the city sun to the 'fiery brass' of cages used in Druidic sacrifice 'from which the blood of wretches pent inside / Seems oozing forth to incarnadine the air' (3.172–5); and in justifying her refusal of Romney, she suspects that 'He might cut / My body into coins to give away / Among his other paupers' (2.790–1).

Knifing and bleeding are prominent symbols in the severe condemnation of female sentimentality which Romney, somewhat imprudently for a suitor, issues to Aurora, and which quite plausibly consolidates her refusal to marry him:

> ... Your quick-breathed hearts,
> So sympathetic to the personal pang,
> Close on each separate knife-stroke, yielding up

> A whole life at each wound, incapable
> Of deepening, widening a large lap of life
> To hold the world-full woe. The human race
> To you means, such a child, or such a man,
> You saw one morning waiting in the cold,
> Beside that gate, perhaps. You gather up
> A few such cases, and when strong sometimes
> Will write of factories and of slaves, as if
> Your father were a negro, and your son
> A spinner in the mills. All's yours and you,
> All, coloured with your blood, or otherwise
> Just nothing to you.
>
> (2.184–98)

From Romney's perspective of patriarchal socialism, women lack the male faculty of abstraction from personal experience to a general theory of society: wounded women give up their entire beings at one emotional 'knife-stroke', leaving no room in their maternal laps for the woes of the world. Through Romney's sexist sermon, Barrett Browning seems slyly to respond to those critics who derided the poems *she* wrote about factories and slaves, and also to a powerful Victorian myth about women writers: if women can only write about what is 'coloured' with their blood, can only think in terms of 'yours and you', as Romney scornfully announces, then their intellectual lives must be symbolically stained by the somatic signs of their womanhood. In the success of *Aurora Leigh* and in her own career, Barrett Browning defies the ugly implication that the intellectual lives of women must be marred by biological destiny.

In proposing to Marian, the cutting edge, as it were, of Romney's imagery is deflected from disdain for women's sentimentality to a passionate plea for the class unity that will be realised through their marriage:

> ... though the tyrannous sword,
> Which pierced Christ's heart, has cleft the world in twain
> 'Twixt class and class, opposing rich to poor,
> Shall *we* keep parted? Not so. Let us lean
> And strain together rather, each to each,
> Compress the red lips of this gaping wound
> As far as two souls can ...
>
> (4.122–8)

Assimilating Christian and socialist doctrine, Romney aligns the origin of class antagonism with the fall from unity which originated

in the piercing of Christ's body. Despite the eventual insufficiency
of Romney's materialistic remedy for social evil, Barrett Browning,
through deploying this imagery, expresses that yearning for reinte-
gration of the mythical bond between man and his world which
she, in common with many of her Victorian contemporaries, believed had been stretched to its most 'gaping' extent in the nineteenth century. Romney acknowledges that fallen, class-conscious
man can do little more than 'compress' the wound, and from the
manner in which Barrett Browning imagines the Church scene
where rich and poor come to witness this 'compressing' marriage, it
would seem there *can* be no successful healing. The social body is
deeply infected. Employing a language of violence and pestilence
which reminds us of the suffering scorpion burnt by flame, the
Roman eaten by insects, and the Druidic human sacrifices, Barrett
Browning paints a Brueghelesque picture.

The vision is infernal. How could a woman who had been se-
cluded from society until the age of forty, and after that who had
resided in Italy under the adoring protection of her husband, a
woman who was a mother, who had written heart-rending poems
about the untimely death of children and of female self-sacrifice
such as 'Isobel's Child' and 'Bertha in the Lane' – how could this
revered example of female virtue and delicacy describe that half of
the wedding party which comes from 'Saint Giles' in the following
language?

> ...Faces? ... phew,
> We'll call them vices, festering to despairs,
> Or sorrows, petrifying to vices: not
> A finger-touch of God left whole on them,
> All ruined, lost – the countenance worn out
> As the garment, the will dissolute as the act,
> The passions loose and draggling in the dirt
> To trip a foot up at the first free step!
> Those, faces? 'twas as if you had stirred up hell
> To heave its lowest dreg-fiends uppermost
> In fiery swirls of slime, ...
>   (4.579–89)

As far as one can judge from reading her letters, the closest
Barrett Browning ever got to such hellish faces was on a rare cab
trip to Shoreditch in search of Flush, dog-napped from Wimpole
Street. However, she was very close to such scenes of fiendish
misery through her daily reading of newspapers, periodicals and

novels of social realism, particularly of Sue, Hugo, and Balzac. Moreover, all readers of the London *Times* in the eighteen-forties would have read uncensored reports of testimony before the various Parliamentary committees investigating conditions in the factories, mines, and slum areas of the poor. The reports reveal a hellish world of stench, squalor, and disease, of open privies, of prostitutes and beggars living in dens which resembled animal lairs rather than human dwellings: it is a world consistently rendered in the language of the inferno where bodies tumble together in crowded hovels, dunghills dominate the landscape, and all is festering and pestilential.

In February 1843 Barrett Browning read the entire Report of the Royal Commission on the Employment of Children and Young Persons in Mines and Manufactories (one of its Assistant Commissioners was her close correspondent, R.H. Horne): as a consequence of that reading, she was compelled to write her first poem of social protest, 'The Cry of the Children' (a poem of the 'factory' species despised by Romney) which appeared in *Blackwood's Magazine* in August of that year. As an avid reader of virtually every kind of Victorian text, she was no stranger to representation of working-class suffering, and this, of course, is really the point – those faces 'festering to despairs' come from her extensive reading. In itself, the informing relationship between reading and writing in a poet's life is hardly remarkable, but by virtue of the limitations of Barrett Browning's experience, her work was undoubtedly more structured by text than it was by direct observation and it seems as if these sections of *Aurora Leigh* are the hellish distillation of her readings in the Victorian discourse of the poor.

Romney's plans for his marriage have a carnivalesque aspect: rich and poor are to transgress convention by meeting in a Mayfair church and by enjoying a marriage feast together on Hampstead Heath:

> Of course, the people came in uncompelled,
> Lame, blind, and worse – sick, sorrowful, and worse –
> The humours of the peccant social wound
> All pressed out, poured down upon Pimlico,
> Exasperating the unaccustomed air
> With a hideous interfusion. You'd suppose
> A finished generation, dead of plague,
> Swept outward from their graves into the sun,
> The moil of death upon them.
>
> (4.542–50)

The metaphor of the 'social cleft' is both repeated and literalised as the symbolic wound in the social body literally stinks, presses out its suppurating matter. The people clog the streets, ooze into the church 'In a dark, slow stream, like blood', and Barrett Browning pushes her infernal imagery to a hideous conclusion as the movement of the crowd is likened to that of bruised snakes crawling and hissing out of a hole 'with shuddering involution'. As the stinking poor makes its serpentine procession, the upper classes sit with handkerchiefs to their noses, and Barrett Browning aligns her pestilential imagery with her poetics of healing by having one of the aristocrats observe that the present spectacle, 'this dismembering of society', resembles the tearing apart of Damien's body by horses. The social wound, the ruptured body, the bloody procession, all seem to congeal in a dreadful vision of the dismembered body/social state. Aurora Leigh as woman poet is destined to work alongside Romney, curing her wounded social body, enacting Barrett Browning's ideal form of sexual politics.

III

As an intelligent girl confined to the provincial upper-middle class, Aurora Leigh has foisted upon her an education which is hardly apt apprenticeship for building the New Jerusalem. In a satiric feminist interrogation of the subjects thought suitable for women's minds, Barrett Browning shows Aurora acquiring a jumble of useless information and social skills designed to make her a desirable commodity in the marriage market. She learns the 'collects and the catechism', a 'complement of classic French', 'a little Algebra', the 'internal laws of the Burmese empire'. And she is educated in the conventional male views of female intellectual ability: 'I read a score of books on womanhood / To prove, if women do not think at all, / They may teach thinking' (1.428–30). In terms of my argument for the ultimately non-feminist nature of Barrett Browning's sexual politics, however, it is significant that in the angry arguments between Aurora and Romney about woman's contribution to remedying social evil and her potential for producing great art, the principal object of Aurora's contempt is less the male cultural authority which denigrates woman's mind, than it is male inability to feel. The angry woman utters a sentimental attack on male insensitivity. It is not Romney's politics that Aurora really objects to when she refuses his proposal, not his desire to fit women into the convenient social slots of wife, nurse, and helper, but rather that he is emotionally barren, as figuratively blind to Aurora's feelings as he is literally blind to her face at the end of the poem. To a sexually vibrant Aurora on her twentieth birthday morning, Romney is a cold fish.

In London ten years later, a successful Aurora muses on her solitary state. Praised by all the periodicals but bereft of physical love, she sits unhappily alone praying to God the Father / God the Artist, who understands her dilemma as woman poet. Despite a certain daring intimation of ungratified female sexual desire in these lines, they are, in my view, deeply conventional in the heartfelt praise of a patriarchal deity. This may be 'women's language' that Aurora speaks but it can hardly be said to contribute to what Cora Kaplan sees as a 'feminist theory of art which argues that women's language [speaks] all that is repressed and forbidden in human experience'.

> O my God, my God,
> O supreme Artist, who as sole return
> For all the cosmic wonder of Thy Work
> Demandest of us just a word ... a name,
> 'My father!' thou hast knowledge, only thou,
> How dreary 'tis for women to sit still,
> On winter nights by solitary fires,
> And hear the nations praising them far off,
> Too far! ay, praising our quick sense of love,
> Our very heart of passionate womanhood,
> Which could not beat so in the verse without
> Being present also in the unkissed lips
> And eyes undried because there's none to ask
> The reason they grew moist.
>   (5.435–47)

With a play upon the passionate beat of a woman's heart and the metre of her verse, Aurora implies that the creation of verse is unfulfilling to the woman poet unless she is sexually loved, kissed upon the lips. The making of poetry and the making of love are associated to show that woman's poetry is created from her sexuality, indeed that poetry and sexuality are part of the 'cosmic wonder' that is God's 'work'. Having heard Marian's story, Aurora assumes that Romney has married Lady Waldemar. She regrets her own refusal of him, for in so doing she had refused God's gift of the power to make poetry through love, and love through poetry: 'Now, if I had been a woman, such / As God made women, to save men by love, – / By just my love I might have saved this man, / And made a nobler poem for the world / Than all I have failed in' (7.184–8). Questioning her womanhood, her failure to 'save' Romney through sexual love, she denigrates her literary achievement by believing that to have 'written' Romney in marriage she would have produced a 'noble' text far superior to any she has composed. She then concludes that he is lost, 'And, by my own fault, his empty house / Sucks in, at this same hour, a wind from hell / To keep his heart cold, make his casements creak / For ever to the tune of plague and sin' (7.190–3). Unmade into a 'noble' poem by the 'good' Aurora, that is to say not sexually loved by her, Romney's body is as an empty house, sucking in an evil wind. She has figured herself as passionately warm, her heart and verse beating with desire: Romney, also alone, is made cold by the dissonant 'tune' hissed by the 'evil' Lady Waldemar; hers is a cold sexuality manifested in those marble breasts designed for display, not warm nurturance.

Having evoked her own mature emotional life in rosy, vibrant, terms and that of Romney through cold, white imagery, Aurora suggests that women possess a quality which permits them to transcend the symbolised dualism: they can undo their own iconised fragmentation through a legendary female ability to relinquish identity to the more powerful sex. While explicitly praising woman's ability to transcend ugly, aggressive self, Aurora actually perpetuates the unfortunate myth that woman lacks a strong sense of individual identity: we women, Aurora says, 'yearn to lose ourselves / And melt like white pearls in another's wine'; man 'seeks to double himself by what he loves, / And makes his drink more costly by our pearls' (5.1078–81). At the end of the poem Aurora dismantles the dualism of red and white imagery by melting the purity of her art and sexuality (the whiter pearls) into Romney's vision (the wine), and Romney, in his turn, ceases to appropriate women's feelings to his male politics. The rosy Florentine dawn that concludes the poem anticipates the forthcoming expression of Aurora's sexuality in marriage with Romney and a dissolution of his emotional anaesthesia through that union.

The closing lines of *Aurora Leigh* constitute a densely allusive hymn to work, sexual love, and the vision of a new city built from the consummation of man and woman, intellect and feeling, blindness and vision. Romney praises 'the love of wedded souls', which in the earthly counterpart of God's love:

> Sweet shadow rose, upon the water of life,
> Of such a mystic substance, Sharon gave
> A name to! human, vital, fructuous rose,
> Whose calyx holds the multitude of leaves,
> Loves filial, loves fraternal, neighbour-loves
> And civic – all fair petals, all good scents,
> All reddened, sweetened from one central Heart.
>   (9.884–90)

Political and social action will originate in and be sweetened from their marriage, from the rose of sexual love which is consummated and celebrated in the Song of Solomon: Judaic wedding song, Christian doctrine, social action, all centre in the rose image which evokes the vibrant twenty-year-old Aurora who feels the June within her, 'rosebuds reddening where the calyx split', and the present, mature Aurora, a ripe and blooming flower. And Aurora is also the radiant light of the morning star, destined for tutelage by the darkened, weary, blind Romney in her contribution to their joint work. In terms which express Barrett Browning's vision of woman's art as servitor of patriarchy, Aurora is instructed by Romney to become the witnessing poet of Barrett Browning's aesthetic discourse:

> ... Art's a service, – mark:
> A silver key is given to thy clasp,
> And thou shalt stand, unwearied, night and day,
> And fix it in the hard, slow-turning wards,
> To open, so, that intermediate door
> Betwixt the different planes of sensuous form
> And form insensuous, that inferior men
> May learn to feel on still through these to those,
> And bless thy ministration. The world waits
> For help.
>   (9.915–24)

The artist labours to unlock doors of perception, to mediate between material and spiritual 'planes', and the term 'wards' implies not only the mechanisms of a lock, but also places of confinement of the individual to the stifling materialistic ideologies which Barrett Browning despised. The poet's function, and it is a hard function, is to recover the original text of man's soul debased by deforming interpretation, to trace the first writing of that 'old scripture'.

Aurora is exhorted by Romney 'to press the clarion on thy woman's lips ... And blow all class-walls level as Jericho's'. Sandra Gilbert and Susan Gubar read these closing lines as a revolutionary fantasy too dangerous to be articulated by Aurora, and they suggest Romney's sanctification of revolution through marriage is a severe compromise of Barrett Browning's own politics: the 'millenarian programme Romney outlines is not, of course, his own; it is the revolutionary fantasy of his author – and of her heroine, his wife-to-be, discreetly transferred from female to male lips'. That the programme is revolutionary is undeniable, and Gilbert and Gubar are clearly correct in noting that all must be made new, even though 'a divine patriarch, aided by a human patriarch and his helpmeet' are doing the renovation.[12] Yet what is to be made new, and the means of making it new, are figured in highly traditional, even reactionary terms which, if placed in the context of Barrett Browning's sexual politics, make the ending of *Aurora Leigh* less a compromise than a fulfilment of her 'revolutionary fantasy'. It is important to examine the lines which follow Romney's call for Aurora to level class barriers: she must do so in order that all men and all women may be flattened to an equality of subjugation to God's will so they might ascend to an 'unsexing' of their incarnate state. To be sure, this is revolutionary, but not, it seems to me, in any way that suggests an adjustment of Barrett Browning's beliefs: men's souls 'here assembled on earth's flats' must 'get them to some purer eminence':

> ... The world's old,
> But the old world waits the time to be renewed,
> Toward which, new hearts in individual growth
> Must quicken and increase to multitude
> In new dynasties of the race of men;
> Developed whence, shall grow spontaneously
> New churches, new oeconomies, new laws,
> Admitting freedom, new societies
> Excluding falsehood: He shall make all new.
> (9.941–9)

New churches precede new economic systems and new laws in this taxonomy of Christian revolution: after all Romney has already decreed that there must be 'fewer programmes ... fewer systems': 'Less mapping out of masses to be saved, / By nations or by sexes! Fourier's void, / And Comte absurd, – and Cabet puerile' (9.867–9). This is Romney's *and* Aurora's *and* Barrett Browning's vision – coherent with her sexual politics and inspired first and always by a patriarchal God who demands hard work from his woman poets. Work is a 'key' word at the end of *Aurora Leigh* – the literal key which will enable the poet to unlock the symbolic wards which restrain man from seeing connections between 'sensuous' and 'insensuous' worlds. The woman poet labours in service to God, mankind, and man.

'I have *worked* at poetry – it has not been with me revery, but art. As the physician and lawyer work at their several professions, so have I, and so do I, apply to mine.' Writing to Horne in 1844, Barrett Browning insists upon her professional status as working poet.[13] In one of the 1844 Poems, 'A Fourfold Aspect', the speaker traces a child's fearful understanding of its mortality, gleaned from reading of the death of heroes. So awful are these stories that the child wakes shrieking in the night and spends its day mournfully preoccupied with the dead. The poem turns upon a lesson the child must learn: death leads to Heaven and in the mortal meantime man must pray, think, learn, and work: 'Work: make clear the forest-tangles / Of the wildest stranger-land' (3.119–20). This imperative originates in the Victorian preoccupation with clearing the wilderness, that renovation of the wasteland imagined, for example, in 'The Coming of Arthur', the first of Tennyson's *Idylls of the King* and figured in these lines, 'And so there grew great tracts of wilderness, / Wherein the beast was ever more and more, / But man was less and less, till Arthur came.'[14] And when Arthur does come, he drives out the 'heathen', slays the beasts, fells the forest 'letting in the sun'. Tennyson's Camelot is one version of the Victorian New Jerusalem, the city built from barbarism, darkness, and despair. Indignantly refusing Romney's offer of marriage and partnership in practice of his despised social theory, Aurora declares 'I too have my vocation, – work to do ... Most serious work, most necessary work / As any of the economists' (2.455–60).

'Blessed is he who has found his work; let him ask no other blessedness', thunders Carlyle in *Past and Present*; he who works, makes 'instead of pestilential swamp, a green fruitful meadow with its clear flowing stream'.[15] Barrett Browning's enduring insistence on the cultural function of the poet *in* the political world originates in this imperative to work: the poet clears a symbolical part, unlocks a symbolical door, dissolves the encrustations of debasing materialism which cover man's soul. Carlyle's Gospel of Work is the good news elaborated by Aurora and Romney at the end of the poem: men, women, creatures all, must work: 'Let us be content, in work', is repeated with slight variation in a hymn of praise sung throughout the night as Aurora and Romney await the new day. Aurora describes Romney crying out the litany which has united them:

> And then calm, equal, smooth with weights of joy,
> His voice rose, as some chief musician's song
> Amid the old Jewish temple's Selah-pause,
> And bade me mark how we two met at last
> Upon this moon-bathed promontory of earth,
> To give up much on each side, then take all.
> 'Beloved!' it sang, 'we must be here to work;
> And men who work can only work for men,
> And, not to work in vain, must comprehend
> Humanity and so work humanly,
> And raise men's bodies, still by raising souls,
> As God did first.'
>
> (9.843–54)

The poem ends as the dawn signals a new beginning and chastened lovers dedicate themselves to clearing the wilderness and to liberating man (and woman) from materialistic values. As Aurora is married to Romney and female art wedded to male socialist politics, the novel-poem *Aurora Leigh* becomes a form-giving epithalamium for Barrett Browning's essentialist sexual politics. In this poem we hear a woman's voice speaking patriarchal discourse – boldly, passionately, and without rancour.

From *Browning Institute Studies*, 13 (1985), 113–36.

NOTES

[Deirdre David's polemical essay shatters some of the assumptions on which earlier feminist criticism of *Aurora Leigh* had been built. By focusing on the significant role played by dominant discourses of class and sexual difference in Barrett Browning's verse-novel, David explains how and why it is misleading to think that this extraordinary poem is necessarily so very radical in the claims it may at times seem to be making about the specificity of women's experience. In this way, David's discussion drives against the grain of Cora Kaplan's introduction to her edition of *Aurora Leigh* (London, 1978), pp. 5–36, and Sandra M. Gilbert's essay, 'From *Patria* to *Matria*: Elizabeth Barrett Browning's Risorgimento', reprinted in this volume (pp. 132–66). The redoubtable strength of David's analysis lies in the manner in which she refuses to excuse those moments in Barrett Browning's poem that appear completely compromised by social expectations about the proper sphere of femininity, even if many sections of *Aurora Leigh* may seem to have a 'revolutionary' view on such matters. David's observations here should be compared with the larger argument of her study, *Intellectual Women and Victorian Patriarchy* (Basingstoke, 1987), which places the writings of Harriet Martineau and George Eliot, as well as those of Barrett Browning, under similar scrutiny. Ed.]

1. Cora Kaplan, Introduction to *Aurora Leigh with Other Poems* (London, 1978), p. 11. The first important feminist analysis of *Aurora Leigh* is to be found in Ellen Moers, *Literary Women* (New York, 1976).

2. Kaplan, Introduction to *Aurora Leigh*, p. 35.

3. Elizabeth Barrett Browning, *Elizabeth Barrett Browning's Letters to Mrs David Ogilvy 1849–1861, with Recollections by Mrs Ogilvy*, ed. Peter N. Heydon and Philip Kelley (New York, 1973), p. 32.

4. Barrett Browning, *The Letters of Elizabeth Barrett Browning*, ed. Frederic G. Kenyon, 2 vols (London, 1897), 1, pp. 196–7; hereafter abbreviated in the text as *L: EBB*: further page references appear in parentheses.

5. Barrett Browning, *The Letters of Elizabeth Barrett Browning to Mary Russell Mitford, 1836–1854*, ed. Meredith B. Raymond and Mary Rose Sullivan, 3 vols (Winstone, KS, 1983), III, p. 81; hereafter abbreviated in the text as *L:EBB.M*: further page references appear in parentheses.

6. *The Letters of Robert Browning and Elizabeth Barrett Browning* 1845–1846, 2 vols (New York, 1899), 1, pp. 116, 373, 357; hereafter d in the text as *L:RB/EBB*: further page references appear in

7. Barrett Browning, *Aurora Leigh*, in *The Complete Works of Elizabeth Barrett Browning*, ed. Charlotte Porter and Helen A. Clarke, 6 vols (New York, 1901), Book I, ll.826–32. All references in the text to the work of Barrett Browning are to this edition: citations are by volume and page number, except in the case of *Aurora Leigh* where citations are by book and line number(s).

8. *Westminster Review*, 68 (1857), 399–415; *Blackwood's Magazine*, 81 (1857), 23–41; *The Spectator*, 29 (1856), 1239–40. The following reviews of *Aurora Leigh* are also of particular interest: *Saturday Review*, 2 (1856), 776–8; *Dublin University Magazine*, 49 (1857), 460–70; *National Quarterly Review*, 5 (1862), 134–48.

9. In her sensitive reading of Marian Erle's relationship to mothers and the meaning of Marian's own motherhood, Sandra Gilbert makes the

point that Marian bears a likeness 'not only to the fallen woman Mary Magdalen but also the blessed Virgin Mary, whose immaculate conception was the sin of a divine annunciation': 'From *Patria* to *Matria*: Elizabeth Barrett Browning's Risorgimento', *PMLA*, 99 (1984), 194–211. [Reprinted in this volume, pp. 132–66. Ed.]

10. Sandra Donaldson, Barbara Charlesworth Gelpi, and Virginia V. Steinmetz offer closely related interpretations of the imagery of motherhood and suckling in *Aurora Leigh*. Donaldson links Barrett Browning's own motherhood and a more powerful poetry than that she had produced in her childless days: by the time of *Aurora Leigh* she uses the 'metaphor of breasts boldly as a symbol of activity and vitality': 'Motherhood's Advent in Power: Elizabeth Barrett Browning's Poems about Motherhood', *Victorian Poetry*, 18 (1980), 51–60. Focusing upon Aurora's ambivalent attitude towards her mother's portrait, Gelpi argues that Aurora finally trusts her own womanhood by the end of the poem: '*Aurora Leigh*: The Vocation of the Woman Poet', *Victorian Poetry*, 19 (1981), 35–48. Steinmetz's reading discusses the maternal images less positively and more psycho-analytically, and sees them as 'negative symbols reinforcing the theme of deprivation and representing the poet's needs to bring obsessive infantile desires into light where they could serve rather than dominate her': 'Images of "Mother-Want" in Elizabeth Barrett Browning's *Aurora Leigh*', *Victorian Poetry*, 21 (1983), 351–67.

11. Sandra Gilbert and Susan Gubar see these forms/faces in the portrait as 'melodramatic, gothic, the moral extremes of angel and monster characteristic of male defined masks and costumes': *The Madwoman in the Attic: The Woman Writer and the Nineteenth-Century Literary Imagination* (New Haven, 1979), p. 19. Dolores Rosenblum argues that when Aurora sees Marian's face in Paris, she *re*-sees the iconised female face of nineteenth-century poetry, and is thereby liberated to a full expression of her art: 'Face to Face: Elizabeth Barrett Browning's *Aurora Leigh* and Nineteenth-Century Poetry', *Victorian Studies*, 26 (1983), 321–38. Nina Auerbach splendidly dissects the contradictory 'faces' of Victorian woman in *Woman and the Demon: The Life of a Victorian Myth* (Cambridge, MA, 1983).

12. Gilbert and Gubar, *The Madwoman in the Attic*, pp. 579–80.

13. Barrett Browning, *Letters of Elizabeth Barrett Browning to Richard Hengist Horne*, with Preface and Memoir by Richard Henry Stoddard (New York, 1889), p. 263.

14. See John D. Rosenberg's *The Fall of Camelot: A Study of Tennyson's 'The Idylls of the King'* (Cambridge, MA, 1973) for a reading of the poem as apocalyptic vision and for examination of the *Idylls'* contribution to the Victorian literary concern with clearing the wasteland.

15. Thomas Carlyle, *Past and Present*, ed. Richard D. Altick (Boston, 1965), p. 197.

5

From *Patria* to *Matria*: Elizabeth Barrett Browning's Risorgimento

SANDRA M. GILBERT

> Then Lady Reason ... said, 'Get up, daughter! Without waiting any longer, let us go to the Field of Letters. There the City of Ladies will be founded on a flat and fertile plain ...'
> (Christine de Pizan, *The Book of the City of Ladies)*[1]

> Our lives are Swiss –
> So still – so Cool –
> Till some odd afternoon
> The Alps neglect their Curtains
> And we look farther on!
>
> *Italy* stands the other side!
> While like a guard between –
> The solemn Alps –
> The siren Alps
> Forever intervene!
> (Emily Dickinson, no. 80)[2]

> Our insight into this early, pre-Oedipus phase in the little girl's development comes to us as a surprise, comparable in another field with the discovery of the Minoan-Mycenaean civilisation behind that of Greece.
>
> (Sigmund Freud, 'Female Sexuality')[3]

> And now I come, my Italy,
> My own hills! Are you 'ware of me, my hills,

How I burn toward you? do you feel to-night
The urgency and yearning of my soul,
As sleeping mothers feel the sucking babe
And smile?
                    (*Aurora Leigh* 5.1266–71)[4]

I

When in 1860 Elizabeth Barrett Browning published *Poems before Congress*, a frankly political collection of verses that was the culmination of her long commitment to Italy's arduous struggle for reunification, English critics excoriated her as unfeminine, even insane. 'To bless and not to curse is woman's function', wrote one reviewer, 'and if Mrs Browning, in her calmer moments, will but contrast the spirit which has prompted her to such melancholy aberrations with that which animated Florence Nightingale, she can hardly fail to derive a profitable lesson for the future'.[5] Interestingly, however, the very first poem in the volume depicts Italy as a friendless, powerless, invalid woman, asking if it is 'true, – may it be spoken, – ' that she is finally alive

> ... who has lain so still,
> With a wound in her breast,
> And a flower in her hand,
> And a grave-stone under her head,
>   While every nation at will
> Beside her has dared to stand,
> And flout her with pity and scorn.
>   ('Napoleon III in Italy')[6]

Creating an ostensibly 'unfeminine' political polemic, Barrett Browning consciously or unconsciously seems to adopt the persona of a nurse at the bedside of an imperilled relative, almost as if she *were* a sort of literary-political Florence Nightingale. Putting aside all questions about the inherent femininity or unfemininity of political poetry, I will argue that this English expatriate's visions of *Italia Riuníta* had more to do with both her femaleness and her feminism than is usually supposed. In fact, where so magisterial a reader as Henry James believed that Barrett Browning's commitment to 'the cause of Italy' represented a letting down of 'her inspiration and her poetic pitch',[7] I believe instead that, as Flavia Alaya has also observed, Italy became for a complex of reasons both the embodiment of this woman poet's inspiration and the most vivid strain in her 'poetic pitch'.[8]

Specifically, I will suggest that through her involvement with the revolutionary struggle for political identity that marked Italy's famous risorgimento, Barrett Browning enacted and re-enacted her own personal and artistic struggle for identity, a risorgimento that was, like Italy's, both an insurrection and a resurrection. In addition, I will suggest that, by using metaphors of the healing and making whole of a wounded woman/land to articulate both the reality and fantasy of her own female/poetic revitalisation, Barrett Browning figuratively located herself in a re-creative female poetic tradition that descends from Sappho and Christine de Pizan through the Brontës, Christina Rossetti, Margaret Fuller, and Emily Dickinson to Renée Vivien, Charlotte Perkins Gilman, H.D., and Adrienne Rich. Infusing supposedly asexual poetics with the dreams and desires of a distinctively sexual politics, these women imagined nothing less than the transformation of *patria* into *matria* and thus the risorgimento of the lost community of women that Rossetti called the 'mother country' – the shadowy land, perhaps, that Freud identified with the mysterious 'Minoan-Mycenaean civilisation behind that of Greece'. In resurrecting the *matria*, moreover, these women fantasised resurrecting and restoring both the *madre*, the forgotten impossible dead mother, and the *matrice*, the originary womb or matrix, the mother-matter whose very memory, says Freud, is 'lost in a past so dim ... so hard to resuscitate that it [seems to have] undergone some specially inexorable repression'.[9]

Not surprisingly, then, Barrett Browning begins her covertly political 1857 *Kunstlerroman, Aurora Leigh*, with a meditation on this lost mother, using imagery that dramatically foreshadows the figure with which the poet opens her overtly political *Poems before Congress*. Gazing at a portrait of her mother that was (significantly) painted after the woman's death, young Aurora sees the maternal image as embodying in turn all the patriarchal myths of femaleness – muse, Psyche, Medusa, Lamia; 'Ghost, fiend, and angel, fairy, witch, and sprite' (1.154). But most heartrendingly she sees her as 'Our Lady of the Passion, stabbed with swords / Where the Babe sucked' (1.160–1): the only *maternal* image of the lost mother dissolves into the destroyed woman/country from *Poems before Congress*, 'who has lain so still, / With a wound in her breast' while 'every nation' has flouted her 'with pity and scorn'.[10]

II

Among eighteenth-, nineteenth-, and early twentieth-century English and American writers, tropes of Italy proliferated like flowers in Fiesole, so much so that the country, as its nationalist leaders feared, would seem to have had no reality except as a metaphor. As far back as the sixteenth but especially in the late eighteenth century, English romancers had exploited what Kenneth Churchill calls 'the violence-incest-murder-prison paradigm of Gothic Italy'.[11] More seriously, from Gibbon to Byron and Shelley to John Ruskin, George Eliot, Henry James, Edith Wharton, and D.H. Lawrence, English-speaking poets and novelists read the sunny, ruin-haunted Italian landscape as a symbolic text, a hieroglyph, or, perhaps more accurately, a palimpsest of Western history, whose warring traces seemed to them to solidify in the stones of Venice and the bones of Rome. Shelley, for instance, reflecting on the ancient city where Keats died seeking health, sees it both as 'that high Capital, where kingly Death / Keeps his pale court in beauty and decay' and as 'the Paradise, / The grave, the city, and the wilderness' ('Adonais' ll.55–6, 433–4) – a place whose ruins, building on and contradicting one another, suggest the paradoxical simultaneity of the originary moment (paradise) and the fall from that moment (the grave), the invention of culture (the city) and the supervention of nature (the wilderness). In 'St Mark's Place', Samuel Rogers is less metaphysical, but he too elaborates a vision of Italy as text, asserting that 'Not a stone / In the broad pavement, but to him who has / An eye, an ear for the Inanimate World, / Tells of past ages',[12] and George Eliot develops a similar perception when she writes in *Middlemarch* of 'the gigantic broken revelations' of Rome (bk. 2, ch. 15). Finally, emphasising the dialectic between culture and nature that, as Shelley also saw, underlies all such statements, Edith Wharton summarises the point most simply: Italy, she writes, is 'that sophisticated landscape where the face of nature seems moulded by the passions and imaginings of man'.[13]

Interestingly, however, as post-Renaissance Italy sank ever further into physical decay and political disarray, lapsing inexorably away from the grandeur that was imperial Rome and the glory that was fourteenth-century Florence, both native and tourist poets increasingly began to depict 'her' as a sort of fallen woman. In Byron's famous translation, for example, the seventeenth-century Florentine patriot Vincenzo da Filijaca imagines 'Italia' as a helpless naked seductress, while Byron himself writes of Venice as 'a sea Cybele' and Rome as the 'Lone mother of dead Empires', 'The Niobe of nations!' (*Childe Harold's Pilgrimage*, canto 4, sts 2, 78, 79).[14] Similarly, Ruskin, who sees Venice as 'the Paradise of cities', the positive of Shelley's more equivocal Rome, hints that 'her' charm lies in her seductive femininity,[15] and the expatriate novelist Ouida writes of her adopted city that 'in Florence [the past is] like the gold from the sepulchres of the Aetruscan kings that shines on the breast of some fair living woman'.[16] The trope of Italy or of one of 'her' city-states as a living, palpable, and often abandoned woman had become almost ubiquitous by the time Barrett Browning began to write her poems about the risorgimento, and of course it derived from a traditional grammatical convention that tends, at least in most Indo-European languages, to impute metaphorical femaleness to such diverse phenomena as countries, ships, and hurricanes. As applied to Italy, however, this metaphor of gender was often so intensely felt that, most notably for women writers, it frequently evolved from figure to fantasy, from specula-tion to hallucination. Thus Italy as art object 'moulded by the pas-sions and imaginings of man' becomes Italy as Galatea and, worse still, a Galatea seduced and betrayed by her creator,[17] while Italy as destroyed motherland becomes Italy as wounded mother, Madonna of the sorrows whose restored milk and honey might nourish errant children, and especially daughters, of all nations. Ultimately, then, such women writers as Christina Rossetti and Elizabeth Barrett Browning revise and revitalise the dead metaphor of gender that is their literary and linguistic inheritance, using it to transform Italy from a political state to a female state of mind, from a problematic country in Europe to the problem condition of femaleness. Redeeming and redeemed by Italy, they imagine redeeming and being redeemed by themselves.

More specifically, as artists like Rossetti and Barrett Browning (and Emily Dickinson after them) struggle to revive both the dead land of Italy and the dead metaphor of 'her' femaleness, they explore five increasingly complex but always interrelated definitions of this lost, fragmented woman-country: (1) Italy as a nurturing mother – a land that feeds, (2) Italy as an impassioned sister – a land that feels, (3) Italy as a home of art – a land that creates, (4) Italy as a magic paradise – a land that transforms or integrates, and (5) Italy as a dead, denied, and denying woman – a land that has been rejected or is rejecting.

Christina Rossetti's ostensibly religious lyric 'Mother Country' is the most visionary statement of the first definition, for in it this poet who was (paradoxically enough) fully Italian only on her father's side, mourns her exclusion from a dreamlike, distinctively female Mediterranean queendom:

> Not mine own country
> But dearer far to me?
> Yet mine own country,
> If I may one day see
> Its spices and cedars
> Its gold and ivory.[18]

Glamorous, rich, and giving, such a maternal paradise is opposed to *this* (implicitly patriarchal) country, in which 'All starve together, / All dwarfed and poor',[19] and the metaphorical climates of the two locales strongly suggest that the luxurious mother country is Italy while the impoverished fatherland – 'here' – is England. As if to support such an interpretation with matter-of-fact reportage, Elizabeth Barrett Browning writes countless letters from Pisa and Florence, praising the nurturing maternal land to which she has eloped with Robert Browning after her perilous escape from the gloomily patriarchal household at 50 Wimpole Street. Food, in particular, seems almost eerily ubiquitous. Barrett Browning never tires of describing great glowing oranges and luscious bunches of grapes; the Italian landscape itself appears largely edible, the scenery deliciously beautiful. As for 'real' meals, they continually materialise at her table as if by magic. In Florence, she reports that 'Dinner, "unordered", comes through the streets and spreads itself on our table, as hot as if we had smelt cutlets hours before', while more generally, in another letter, she observes that 'No little orphan on a house step but seems to inherit naturally his slice of watermelon and bunch of purple grapes'.[20]

This land that feeds is also a land that feels. As both a mother country and, again in Rossetti's words, a 'sister-land of Paradise',[21] female Italy neither contains nor condones the superegoistic repressions that characterise patriarchal England. Literary visions of Italy had always emphasised the passion and sensuality of 'her' people, but where Renaissance playwrights and Gothic romancers had dramatised the stagey strangeness of violent Italians, women writers like Barrett Browning, Rossetti, and later Dickinson wistfully set the natural emotiveness of this mother country against the icy artifice of the Victorian culture in which they had been brought up. Indeed, from Barrett Browning's Bianca in 'Bianca among the Nightingales', who freely expresses her fiery rage at the cold Englishwoman who has stolen her lover away,[22] to Rossetti's Enrica, who 'chill[s]' Englishwomen with 'her liberal glow' and 'dwarf[s]' them 'by her ampler scale',[23] the women who represent Italy in women's writing increasingly seem like ennobled versions of *Jane Eyre's* Bertha Mason Rochester: large, heated, dark, passionate foreigners who are wholly at ease – even at one – with the Vesuvius of female sexual creativity that Dickinson was later to find *un*easily 'at home' in her breast (no. 1705).

Together, in fact, such heroines as Barrett Browning's Bianca, her Laura Savio of 'Mother and Poet',[24] and Rossetti's Enrica seem almost to propose an ontology of female power as it might be if all girls were not, in Rossetti's words, 'minted in the selfsame [English] mould'.[25] That most of these women are in one way or another associated with a violent uprising against the authoritarian rule of Austria and the patriarchal law of the pope, with Enrica (according to William Michael Rossetti) based on a woman who knew both Mazzini and Garibaldi, further cements their connection with Brontë's rebellious Bertha, but with a Bertha revised and transformed so that she, the alien, is free, and English Jane is trapped. As if to demonstrate this point, Christina Rossetti was 'en route' to Italy ('Italy, Io Ti Saluto') when she imagined herself as 'an "immurata" sister' helplessly complaining that

> Men work and think, but women feel,
>   And so (for I'm a woman, I)
>   And so I should be glad to die,
> And cease from impotence of zeal.[26]

For, as Barrett Browning (and Charlotte Brontë) also knew, that 'Italian' speech of feeling was only 'half familiar' and almost wholly inaccessible to Englishwomen.

What made the inaccessibility of such speech especially poignant for poets like Rossetti and Barrett Browning, besides Italy's role as a feeding, feeling mother-sister, was 'her' special status as the home, even the womb, of European art; this mother-sister became a muse whose shapes and sounds seemed to constitute a kind of primal aesthetic language from which no writer should allow herself to be separated. In Florence, Barrett Browning imagines that she is not only in a city that makes art, she is in a city that *is* art, so much so that, as in some Edenic dream, the solid real and the artful unreal merge uncannily: 'The river rushes through the midst of its palaces like a crystal arrow, and it is hard to tell ... whether those churches ... and people walking, in the water or out of the water, are the real ... people, and churches'.[27] That the art of Florence is almost entirely male – Michelangelo's monuments of unageing intellect, Ghiberti's doors – appears oddly irrelevant, for living in Florence Barrett Browning begins to believe, if only briefly, that she might live in, even inherit, this art; in so far as art is Italy's and Italy might be her lost and reclaimed self, art itself might at last be her own.

In allowing herself such a dream, the author of *Aurora Leigh* was tacitly acknowledging the influence of a foremother she greatly admired, Mme de Staël, whose *Corinne ou l'Italie* was 'an immortal book' that, said Barrett Browning, 'deserves to be read three score and ten times – that is, once every year in the age of man'.[28] For not only is *Corinne*, in the words of Ellen Moers, 'a guidebook to Italy', it is specifically a guidebook to an Italy that is the nurturing *matria* of a 'woman of genius', the enchanting *improvisatrice* Corinne, whose brilliant career provided a paradigm of female artistry for countless nineteenth-century literary women on both sides of the Atlantic.[29] Like Aurora Leigh, Staël's poetic heroine is the daughter of an Italian mother and an English father, and, like Barrett Browning herself, she transforms the Italy dominated by relics of such great men as Michelangelo and Ghiberti into a land of free women, a female aesthetic utopia. Corinne herself, writes Staël, is 'l'image de notre belle Italie'.[30] Triumphing as she improvises on the theme of Italy's glory, dances a dramatic tarantella, and translates *Romeo and Juliet* into 'sa langue maternelle',[31] Corinne becomes not only a symbol of redemptive Italy but also a redemptive emblem of the power of symbolisation itself, for, observes Staël, 'tout étoit langage pour elle'.[32] No wonder, then, that Barrett Browning, *Corinne*'s admirer, seems secretly to imagine an Italian heaven of invention whose speech constitutes a different, mystically potent language, a mother tongue: as if to balance Rossetti's remark that 'our [English] tongue grew sweeter in [Enrica's] mouth', she writes wistfully of the way in which 'the Tuscan musical / Vowels ... round themselves as if they planned / Eternities of separate sweetness' (*Casa Guidi Windows* 1.1188–90).

Such a sense that even Italian speech encompasses 'eternities of ... sweetness' inevitably translates itself into a larger vision of

Italy as earthly paradise, a vision that brings us back to the 'green golden strand' of Rossetti's mother country and the vehement '*Italy*' of Dickinson's 'Our lives are Swiss –'. In this fourth incarnation, however, Italy is not just a nurturing mother country, she is a utopian motherland whose glamour transforms all who cross her borders, empowering women, ennobling men, and – most significantly – annihilating national and sexual differences. Describing the hopeful celebration of Florentine freedom that miraculously took place on the Brownings' first wedding anniversary in 1847, Barrett Browning writes about a jubilant parade: 'class after class' took part, and 'Then too, came the foreigners, there was a place for them' (*Casa Guidi Windows* 66). She notes that 'the people were *embracing* for joy' (*Casa Guidi Windows* 66) and expressing 'the sort of gladness in which women may mingle and be glad too' (*Casa Guidi Windows* 67). In this setting, both sexes and all nationalities become part of the newer, higher nationality of Florence, so that expatriation turns, magically, into expatriotism. Less mystically and more amusingly, Virginia Woolf makes a similar point about Italy as utopia in *Flush*, her biography of the Brownings' dog. Arriving in Pisa, this pedigreed spaniel discovers that 'though dogs abounded, there were no ranks; all – could it be possible? – were mongrels'. At last inhabiting a classless society, he becomes 'daily more and more democratic ... All dogs were his brothers. He had no need of a chain in this new world' (pp. 75, 78–9).

Finally, however, as Rossetti's 'Mother Country', 'Enrica', and 'An "Immurata" Sister' suggest, women writers from Barrett Browning to Dickinson are forced to admit that the nurturing, utopian, artful, feelingful, female land of Italy is not their own. Bred in what Barrett Browning and, after her, Rossetti call 'the rigid North', such writers are forever spiritually if not physically excluded from 'the sweet South', forever alienated from Italy's utopian redemption, if only by symbolic windows like those of Casa Guidi, which mark Barrett Browning's estrangement from Florence's moment of regeneration even while they allow the poet to view the spectacle of that rebirth.[33] As the poets make this admission, maternal Italy, guarded by the intervention of the 'solemn Alps' and 'the bitter sea', lapses back into the negated and negating woman whose image opens both *Poems before Congress* and *Aurora Leigh*. Dead, she is denied and denying: as Aurora leaves for England, her mother country seems 'Like one in anger drawing back her skirts / Which suppliants catch at' (1.234 5), and Christina Rossetti, exclaiming

'Farewell, land of love, Italy, / Sister-land of Paradise', summarises
the mingled regret and reproach with which these English daughters
respond to the drastic loss such denial enforces:

> Wherefore art thou strange, and not my mother?
> Thou hast stolen my heart and broken it:
> Would that I might call thy sons 'My brother',
>   Call thy daughters 'Sister sweet':
> Lying in thy lap, not in another,
>   Dying at thy feet.[34]

For Rossetti, the despair these lines express becomes a characteristic
gesture of resignation; the mother country is not to be found, not in
this world at any rate, and so she immures herself in the convent of
her soul, for 'Why should I seek and never find / That something
which I have not had?[35] For Barrett Browning, however, the struggle to revive and re-approach, rather than reproach, the lost mother
country of Italy becomes the narrative project to which she devotes
her two major long poems, *Casa Guidi Windows* (1851) and
Aurora Leigh.

III

Though explicitly (and successfully) a political poem that meditates
on two carefully defined historical occasions, *Casa Guidi Windows*
is also a preliminary working through of important psychological
materials that had long haunted Barrett Browning; as such, it is a
crucial preface to the poet's more frankly confessional *Aurora
Leigh*. To be specific: even while Barrett Browning comments in
part 1 on the exuberant 1847 demonstration with which the Italian
and 'foreign' citizens of Florence thanked Duke Leopold II for
granting them the right to form a militia, and even while she mourns
in part 2 the temporary failure of the risorgimento when in 1849
the Austrians defeated the Italians at Novara, she tells a more
covert story – the story of Italy's and her own seduction and betrayal by the brutality, indifference, and greed of patriarchal
history. From this betrayal, this fall into the power of powers not
her own, Italy/Barrett Browning must regenerate herself, and she
can only do this, the poet's metaphors imply, through a strategic
deployment of female, especially maternal, energies. By delivering
her children both to death (as soldiers) and life (as heirs), she can
deliver herself into the community of nations where she belongs.

For Barrett Browning this plot had distinctively personal overtones. 'After what broke [her] heart at Torquay' – the drowning of her beloved alter ego, 'Bro' – she herself, as she later told her friend Mrs Martin, had lived for years 'on the outside of my own life ... as completely dead to hope ... as if I had my face against a grave'.[36] Immuring herself in her room at 50 Wimpole Street, she had entrusted her future entirely to the will and whim of her notoriously tyrannical father, so much so that, as she also told Mrs Martin, employing a strikingly political metaphor, 'God knows ... how utterly I had abdicated myself ... Even my poetry ... was a thing on the outside of me ... [a] desolate state it was, which I look back now to [as] one would look to one's graveclothes, if one had been clothed in them by mistake during a trance'.[37] Clearly, in some sense, the drowning of the younger brother who was Barrett Browning's only real reader in the family and for whose death she blamed herself, caused a self-alienation so deep that, like Emily Brontë's Catherine Earnshaw Linton mourning the absence of *her* male alter ego, Heathcliff, she felt the world turn to 'a mighty stranger'. Invalid and isolated, she herself became a figure like Italy in part 1 of *Casa Guidi Windows*, who

> Long trammeled with the purple of her youth
> Against her age's ripe activity,
>   Sits still upon her tombs, without death's ruth,
> But also without life's brave energy.
>   (l. 171–4)

Yet just as the Italy of *Casa Guidi Windows*, part 1, trusts 'fathers' like Leopold II and Pio Nono to deliver 'her' from her living death, Barrett Browning expected her father to care enough to cure her illness; and just as Italy is duped by 'her' faith in these patriarchs, Barrett Browning was deceived by her faith in her father, who refused to send her south (significantly, to Italy) for her health, so that she was 'wounded to the bottom of my heart – cast off when I was ready to cling to him'.[38] But the plot thickens as the poet quickens, for, again, just as in Barrett Browning's own life a risorgimento came both from another younger brother figure – Robert Browning – and from the female deliverance of motherhood, so, in *Casa Guidi Windows*, promises of resurrection are offered wounded Italy both by the hope of a sturdy male leader who will 'teach, lead, strike fire into the masses' and by the promise of 'young children lifted high on parent souls', children whose innocence, fostered by maternal grace, may unfold 'mighty meanings' (2.769, 741).

Given the personal politics embedded in this story, it is no wonder that Barrett Browning prefaces the first edition of *Casa Guidi Windows* with an 'advertisement' in which she takes especially intense 'shame upon herself that she believed, like a woman, some royal oaths'; that in part 2 she reproaches herself for her 'woman's fault / That ever [she] believed [Duke Leopold] was true' (2.64–5); and that she also asks 'what woman or child will count [Pio Nono] true?' (2.523). It is no wonder, either, that, in aligning herself with the revolutionary cause of Italy, Barrett Browning aligns herself against the strictures and structures of her fatherland, England, whose 'close, stifling, corrupt system', like her imprisoning room in Wimpole Street, 'gives no air nor scope for healthy ... organisation',[39] a country for which 'nothing will do ... but a good revolution'.[40] As magisterial and patriarchal as Edward Moulton Barrett, England has 'No help for women, sobbing out of sight / Because men made the laws' and 'no tender utterance ... For poor Italia, baffled by mischance' (*Casa Guidi Windows* 2.638–9, 649–51). What is more remarkable in *Casa Guidi Windows*, however, and what more directly foreshadows the Italian dream of *Aurora Leigh* is the way in which Barrett Browning, dreaming behind the mediation of her windows, imagines Italy ultimately redeemed by the voices and visions of mothers and children: part 1 begins, after all, with 'a little child ... who not long had been / By mother's finger steadied on his feet' (2.11–12), singing 'O bella libertá, O bella', and part 2 ends with the poet's 'own young Florentine, not two years old', her 'blue-eyed prophet', transforming society with a clear, unmediated gaze not unlike Wordsworth's 'eye among the blind'. In between these epiphanies, Miriam the prophetess appears, clashing her 'cymbals to surprise / The sun' (1.314–16), and Garibaldi's wife outfaces 'the whistling shot and hissing waves, / Until she [feels] her little babe unborn / Recoil within her' (2.679–83).

But what is finally perhaps most remarkable and, as Julia Markus points out, 'most daring' about *Casa Guidi Windows* is the way in which, as Barrett Browning meditates on the plight of wounded 'Italia', the poet finally presents herself, against the weight of all the literary history she dutifully recounts throughout the work, as 'the singer of the new day':

> And I, a singer also, from my youth,
> Prefer to sing with those who are awake,

> With birds, with babes, with men who will not fear
> The baptism of the holy morning dew ...
>
> . . . .
>
> Than join those old thin voices with my new ...
>
> (1.155–62)

Crossing the Anglo-Italian frontier represented by Casa Guidi windows, Barrett Browning gains her strongest voice in Italy and regains, as we shall see, a vision of her strengthened self from and as Italy, for the female artistic triumph that this passage describes points directly to the triumphant risorgimento of the woman poet that *Aurora Leigh* enacts.

IV

As its title indicates, *Aurora Leigh* is a mythic narrative about 'the baptism of the holy morning dew' that Barrett Browning proposed to sing in *Casa Guidi Windows*. But before she and her heroine can achieve such a sacrament or become true singers of 'the new day' and of the renewed *matria/matrice* that day implies, both must work through precisely the self-division that left 'Italia' (in *Casa Guidi Windows*) and Barrett Browning (in Wimpole Street) living 'on the outside' of their own lives. Significantly, therefore, the tale of the poet-heroine's risorgimento, which parallels the plot of the poet-author's own insurrection-resurrection, begins with a fragmentation of the self that is both symbolised and precipitated by a shattering of the nuclear family, a shattering that leads to a devastating analysis of that structure. Just as significantly, the story ends with a reconstitution of both self and family that provides a visionary new synthesis of the relationships among men, women, and children.

As if to emphasise the larger political issue involved in these emotional dissolutions and resolutions, the heroine's self and family are defined by two *paysages moralisés*, her mother country of Italy and her fatherland of England, between which (although at one point Aurora claims that 'a poet's heart / Can swell to a pair of nationalities, / However ill-lodged in a woman's breast' [6.50–2]) she must ultimately choose. Both in its theatrical, sometimes hectically melodramatic, plot, then, and in its intensely symbolic settings, *Aurora Leigh* continually reminds us that it is not only a versified *Kunstlerroman* which famously aims to specify the interaction between an artist and the particular 'full-veined, heaving, double-breasted Age' (5.217) that created her, it is also an 'unscrupulously epic' (5.215) allegory of a woman artist's journey from disease toward what Sylvia Plath once called 'a country far away as health'.[41]

Not surprisingly, given these geographical and dramatic imperatives, *Aurora Leigh* begins and ends in Italy, the lost redemptive land that must be redeemed in order for both poet-heroine and poet-author to achieve full selfhood. Here, in book 1, Aurora encounters and is symbolically rejected by her dead mother, 'a Florentine / Whose rare blue eyes were shut from seeing me / When scarcely I was four years old' (1.29–31), and here, even as she comes to terms with 'a mother-want about the world' (1.40), her father dies, leaving her suddenly awake 'To full life and life's needs' (1.208–10). While the mother seems irremediably gone, however, the father, 'an austere Englishman' (1.65), is quickly replaced by 'A stranger with authority' (1.224) who tears the child so abruptly from the land which has come to represent her mother that, watching 'my Italy, / Drawn backward from the shuddering steamer-deck,/ Like one in anger drawing back her skirts' (1.232–4), she is uncertain whether the mother country has been rejected ('drawn back') or is rejecting ('drawing back').

This violent, neo-Wordsworthian fall into division from the mother and into 'my father's England', home of alien language and orphanhood, is followed by a more subtle but equally violent fall into gender. Arriving in patriarchal England at the crucial age of thirteen, Aurora discovers that she is a *girl*, destined to be brought up in 'A sort of cage-bird life' (1.305) by a new and different 'mother' – her 'father's sister', who is her 'mother's hater' (1.359–60), for 'Italy / Is one thing, England one' (1.626–7); inexorably parted, the two nations are irrevocable emblems of separation. Hence, as many feminist critics have pointed out, the girl is coerced into (at least on the surface) accepting a typical Victorian education in 'femininity', reading 'a score of books on womanhood / To prove, if women do not think at all, / They may teach thinking' (1.427–9), learning 'cross-stitch', and so forth. That she has 'relations in the Unseen' and in Nature, which romantically persist and from which she draws 'elemental nutriment and heat ... as a babe sucks surely in the dark' (1.473–5), and that she darkly remembers 'My multitudinous mountains, sitting in / The magic circle, with the mutual touch / Electric ... waiting for / Communion and commission' (1.622–6) – another striking image of the mother's nurturing breasts – are the only signs that somewhere in the shadows of her own psyche her mother country endures, despite the pseudo-Oedipal wrenching she has undergone.

As Aurora grows into the fragmentation that seems to be (English) woman's lot, things go from bad to worse. Exiled from the undifferentiated unity of her mother country, the girl discovers that her parents have undergone an even more complicated set of metamorphoses than she at first realised, for not only has her true dead southern mother been replaced by a false and rigid northern stepmother – her 'father's sister' – but her true dead father, after being supplanted by 'a stranger with authority', has been replaced by a false and rigid northern stepfather, her cousin Romney Leigh, who, upon her father's death, has become the putative head of the family. To be sure, as Aurora's cousin, Romney has the potential for becoming a nurturing peer, an empowering 'Bro' rather than a debilitating patriarch. But certainly, when the narrative begins, he is a symbolic father whose self-satisfied right and reason represent the masculine 'head' that inexorably strives to humble the feminine 'heart'.

'I am not very fond of praising men by calling them *manly*; I hate and detest a masculine man', Barrett Browning told one correspondent,[42] and clearly by 'masculine' she did not mean 'virile' but 'authoritarian'. Yet such (implicitly patriarchal) authoritarianism is exactly what characterises Romney Leigh at the cousins' first meeting, for his, says Aurora, was 'The stranger's touch that took my father's place / Yet dared seem soft' (1.545–6), and she adds 'A godlike nature his' (1.553). That Aurora has evidently been destined to marry this man makes the point even more clearly. Drawn away from the natural lore and lure of the mother, she has been surrendered to what Lacan calls the law of the father, inscribed into a patrilineal kinship system where she is to be doubly named by the father, both as daughter-Leigh and as wife-Leigh, just as Elizabeth herself was originally named Elizabeth Barrett Barrett. That Romney refuses to read her poetry, claiming that her book has 'witchcraft in it' (2.77), clarifies the point still further. Her work is either 'mere' or 'magical' 'woman's work' (2.234) because she exists 'as the complement / Of his sex merely' (2.435–6), an (albeit precious) object of exchange in a network of marital transactions that must by definition deprive her not only of her autonomy but, more importantly, of her desire.

Nevertheless, Aurora insists on continuing to transcribe the texts of her desire, poems whose energy is significantly associated with her inner life, her 'relations in the Unseen', and her mother country. At the same time, because she has been exiled in her fatherland, she must inevitably write these works in her father tongue. Inevitably, therefore, because she is struggling to find a place in traditions created by that masculine (and masculinist) language, she must study her father's books. Creeping through the patriarchal attic 'Like some small nimble mouse between the ribs / Of a mastodon' (1.838–9), she finds a room 'Piled high with cases in my father's name' (1.835) and 'nibbles' fiercely but randomly at what amounts to a paradigmatic library of Western culture. Most inevitably, however, this furtive self-education, which both parallels and subverts her aunt's effort to educate her in 'femininity', leads to further self-division. She can and does reject both Romney's offer of marriage and the financial legacy he tries with magisterial generosity to bestow on her, but once she has internalised – nibbled, devoured – the texts that incarnate patriarchal history, she is helplessly implicated in that history, so that even her 'own' poetry is tainted, fragmented, impure.

How, then, is Aurora to rectify and clarify both her art and her self? Barrett Browning's 'unscrupulous' epic seeks to resolve this crucial issue, and, perhaps paradoxically, the author begins her curative task by examining the ways in which her other major characters are just as fragmented and self-alienated as her heroine. To start, for instance, she shows that, despite (or perhaps because of) his superegoistic calm, Romney too is self-divided. This 'head of the family', she quickly suggests, is no more than a 'head', abstractly and, as his abortive wedding to Marian Erle will prove, ineffectually espoused to 'social theory' (2.410). In fact, he is not just a false father because he has replaced Aurora's 'true' father, he is a false father because, as Barrett Browning decided after her long imprisonment in Wimpole Street, all fathers are in some sense false. Indeed, the very idea of fatherhood, with its implications of social hierarchy and psychic fragmentation ('man with the head, woman with the heart' [Tennyson, *The Princess* 5.439]), is dangerously divisive, not only for women but for men. As a brother like her own 'Bro', Romney might be able to 'read' (and thus symbolically unite with) the texts of female desire that transcribe Aurora's otherness, but as a father he is irremediably blind to them. As a brother, moreover, he might more literally unite himself to the social as well as sexual others from whom his birth and breeding separate him, but as a father or 'head', he is, again, hopelessly estranged from most members of the 'body' politic.

That Romney craves a union with both social and sexual others is, however, a sign that, like Aurora, he is half consciously struggling toward a psychic reunification which will constitute as much of a risorgimento for him as it will for her. His ill-fated and 'misconceived' proposal to Aurora suggests his intuition of his own need, even while the fact that she 'translates' him 'ill' emphasises the impossibility of communion or communication between them. In addition, his eagerness to go 'hand in hand' with her among 'the arena-heaps / Of headless bodies' (2.380–1) till, through her 'touch', the 'formless, nameless trunk of every man / Shall seem to wear a head with hair you know, / And every woman catch your mother's face' (2.388–90) implies that, at least metaphorically, he understands the self-division that afflicts both him and his cousin, even while Aurora's reply that since her mother's death she has not seen 'So much love ... / As answers even to make a marriage with / In this cold land of England' (2.398–400) once again outlines the geography of 'mother-want' in which both characters are situated. Similarly, his subsequent plan to 'take [a] wife / Directly from the people' (4.368–9) reveals once more his yearning to heal in his own person the wounds of the body politic, even while Aurora's recognition that his scheme is both artificial and divisive, 'built up as walls are, brick by brick' (4.353), predicts the project's failure. For Romney, who feels himself 'fallen on days' when marriages can be likened to 'galley-couplings' (4.334), redemption must come not from the outward ceremony of marriage but from an inward metamorphosis that will transform him from (false) father to (true) brother, from (false) 'god' to (true) groom.

Despite its misguided formulation, however, Romney's impulse to wed Marian Erle does begin the crucial process of metamorphosis, for this 'daughter of the people' (3.806), an 'Erle' elf of nature rather than an 'earl' of patriarchy, has a history that parallels his and Aurora's history of fragmentation at the same time that she is an essential part of the reunified family/being he and Aurora must become.[43] Ignored and emotionally abandoned by a drunken father who beat her and a bruised mother who tried to prostitute her to a local squire, this 'outcast child ... Learnt early to cry low, and walk alone' (3.874–7). Her proletarian education in alienation offers a darkly parodic version of Aurora's bourgeois education in femininity. Reading the 'wicked book' of patriarchal reality (3.952) with the same fervour that inspired Aurora's studies of her father's patriarchal texts, Marian imagines a 'skyey father and mother both in one' (3.899) just as Aurora imagines inscribing her desire for her motherland in her father's tongue. Finally, too, the shriek of pain Marian utters when her mother tries to sell her to the squire – 'God, free me from my mother ... / These mothers are too dreadful' (3.1063–4) – echoes and amplifies Aurora's impassioned protest against the 'Keeper's voice' (2.561) of the stepmother-aunt, who tells her that she has been 'promised' to her cousin Romney: 'I must help myself / And am alone from henceforth' (2.807–8). Repudiating the false mothers of patriarchal England, both these literally or figuratively orphaned daughters cry out, each in her own way, the intensity of the 'mother-want' that will eventually unite them, along with Romney and with Marian's child, in the motherland of Italy, where each will become a nurturing mother country to the other.

When Marian and Aurora first meet, however, both are stranded in the alienating cityscape of nineteenth-century London, where each lives in an attic that seems to symbolise her isolation from world and self alike. Though Aurora has ostensibly become a successful poet, her ambition continually reminds her of her failure, since it constantly confronts her with fragmented verses whose 'heart' is 'Just an embryo's heart / Which never yet had beat' (3.247–8), while Marian, though her 'heart ... swelled so big / It seemed to fill her body' (3.1083–5), lives up a 'long, steep, narrow stair, 'twixt broken rail / And mildewed wall' (3.791–2). Parts of a scattered self – the one heartless, the other too great-hearted – this pair of doubles must be unified like the distant and dissonant city-states of Italy, and ultimately, of course, the two are brought together by Romney's various though similar desires for them. To begin with, however, they are united by the visits of yet another potential wife of Romney's – Lady Waldemar – to their parallel attics.

Voluptuous and vicious, the figure of Lady Waldemar offers a further comment on nineteenth-century ideals of 'femininity'. In fact, as we shall see, she is the (false) wife/mother whose love the (false) father must reject if he is to convert himself into a (true) brother. At the same time, though, her beckoning sexuality both initiates and instigates the 'plot' proper of *Aurora Leigh*, emblematising a fall into heterosexual desire with which Aurora and Marian must variously struggle before they can become whole. Almost at once, Aurora perceives this fashionable aristocrat as a male-created, socially defined 'lady' – 'brilliant stuff, / And out of nature' (3.357–8) – a perception Lady Waldemar's name reinforces with its reminiscences of generations of Danish kings. But even while Aurora defines her as 'out of nature' in the sense that she is an anti-natural being, a cultural artifact, this 'fair fine' lady defines herself as being 'out of nature' in the sense that she is *from* nature, nature's emissary. For, confessing that she has 'caught' love 'in the vulgar way' (3.466), Lady Waldemar instructs the poet-heroine that 'you eat of love, / And do as vile a thing as if you ate / Of garlic' (3.450–2) since 'love's coarse, nature's coarse' (3.455). Two books later, when she reappears at a party Aurora attends, the very image of Lady Waldemar's body reiterates her 'natural' sexuality. Gorgeously seductive, 'the woman looked immortal' (5.618), her bare breasts splitting her 'amaranth velvet-bodice down / To the waist, or nearly, with the audacious press / Of full-breathed beauty' (5.622–4).

As emblems of nurturing maternity, breasts have obsessed both author and heroine throughout *Aurora Leigh*, but this is the first time their erotic potential is (quite literally) revealed, and tellingly the rev-elation is associated with Aurora's growing sense of artistic and sexual isolation: 'Must I work in vain, / Without the approbation of a man?' (5.62–3); with her confession of 'hunger ... for man's love' (5.498); and, most strikingly, with her feeling that her 'loose long hair [has begun] to burn and creep, / Alive to the very ends, about my knees' (5.1126–7). Furthermore, Lady Waldemar's eroticism is associated with – indeed, causes – Marian's betrayal into sexuality, a betrayal that leads to both a 'murder' and a rebirth, while Aurora's mingled fear of and fascination with Lady Waldemar's erotic pre-sence finally drive the poet back to her motherland of Italy, where she is ultimately to be reunited with both Marian and Romney. In fact, what have often been seen as the awkward or melodramatic turns of plot through which Barrett Browning brings these three characters back together in a sort of Florentine paradise are really important dramatic strategies by which the author herself was trying to work out (and out of) the 'problem' of female sexuality by first confronting the engendered world as it is and then re-engendering and reconstituting it as it should be.

Trusting the duplicitous Lady Waldemar, who 'wrapped' the girl in her arms and, ironically enough, let her 'dream a moment how it feels / To have a real mother' (6.1001–3), Marian is treacherously brought to France by the servant of this false 'mother', placed in a brothel where she is drugged and raped, and thereby sold into sexual slavery – a deed that, as Marian herself notes, was 'only what my mother would have done' (7.8–9). At the same time, Aurora – missing her 'woodland sister, sweet maid Marian' (5.109), and convinced that Romney is about to marry the 'Lamia-woman', Lady Waldemar (7.152) – finally decides to return to the Italy that she has long heard 'crying through my life, / [with the] piercing silence of ecstatic graves' (5.1193–4). Not coincidentally, she plans to finance her trip by selling the 'residue / Of my father's books' (5.1217–18), a crucial first step in what is to be a definitive renunciation of the power of the fatherland. Her journey to the mother country, however, is impelled as much by desire as by denial, for, in the passage I have used as an epigraph to this essay, she 'burns' toward her 'own hills' and imagines that they desirously reciprocate her 'yearning ... As sleeping mothers feel the sucking babe / And smile' (5.1268–71). Thus, when en route she encounters the lost Marian in a Paris flower market, she begins the process of reunification that will regenerate both these wounded daughters. For the 'fallen' Marian, whose face haunts Aurora like the face of a 'dead woman', has become a mother whose assertion of what J.J. Bachofen was later in the century to call 'mother right' – 'I claim my mother-dues / By law' – proposes an empowering alternative to 'the law which now is paramount', the 'common' patriarchal 'law, by which the poor and weak / Are trodden underfoot by vicious men, / And loathed for ever after by the good' (6.665–9). Becoming such a powerful figure, moreover, she has become a creative authority whose maternal eroticism speeds the two women toward the unfallen garden of female sexuality that they will plant in the richly flowering earth of Florence. There Marian's 'unfathered' child will 'not miss a ... father', since he will have 'two mothers' (7.124), there Aurora will set Marian like a 'saint' and 'burn the lights of love' before her pure maternity (7.128), and there, in a revision of her own eroticism, Aurora will exorcise the haunting vision of what she now comes to see as Lady Waldemar's distorted (Lamia-like) sexuality.

For when she returns to her motherland with Marian as her sister/self, Aurora returns transformed. No longer merely an arching outcast daughter crying her inchoate 'mother-want', she has become herself, symbolically at least, a mother, since she is one of the 'two mothers' of Marian's child. In addition, transformed into a hierophant of 'sweet holy Marian' (6.782), she has learned to devote herself to the specifically female theology of the Madonna, the Queen of Heaven whom the Florentine women worship and whose rituals facilitate Aurora's increasing self-knowledge. Finally, she has become a poet, an artist-heroine who can not only weep but word her desire, in a language that through her interaction with Marian she has begun to make into a mother tongue. In fact, as she learns some weeks after her arrival in Florence, people in England have finally begun to 'read' her. Her new book, writes her painter friend Vincent Carrington, 'Is eloquent as if you were not dumb' (7.553), and his fiancée, who has Aurora's verses 'by heart' more than she has her lover's words (7.603), has even insisted on having a portrait painted with 'Your last book folded in her dimpled hands/ Instead of my brown palette as I wished' (7.607–8).

That Marian's child is 'unfathered' contributes in yet another way to the regenerative maternity both women now experience, for, after all, the baby is only figuratively unfathered; literally, he was fathered by some nameless customer in a brothel. To call him 'unfathered', therefore, is to stress the likeness of his mother, Marian, not only to the fallen woman Mary Magdalen but also to the blessed Virgin Mary, whose immaculate conception was the sign of a divine annunciation. That Barrett Browning surrounds Marian's maternity with the rhetoric of Mariolatry implies the theological force she wants to impute to this 'maiden' mother's female energy. As opposed to the often sentimentally redemptive power ascribed to such Victorian 'mothers' boys' as Gaetano (in Browning's *The Ring and the Book*), Leonard (in Mrs Gaskell's *Ruth*), or Paul Dombey (in Dickens's *Dombey and Son*), Marian's son has an austerely religious significance. Nameless but beautiful, he is hardly ever characterised as a real child might be. Rather, when Marian explains that, in her despair after her rape, 'I lived for him, and so he lives, / And so I know, by this time, God lives too' (7.112–13), the ambiguity of her language – does she believe that he is the 'God' who 'lives' or does his survival mean that 'God lives'? – argues that he is in some sense a divine child, a baby god whose sacred birth attests to the divinity of his mother. Thus, even while she revises the story of the annunciation to question the brutality of a male God who uses women merely as vessels for his own ends, Barrett Browning suggests that the female creativity 'holy' Marian and reverent Aurora share can transform the most heinous act of male sexual brutality, a rape, into a redemption. At the same time, by demonstrating the self-sufficient strength of Marian and Aurora's mutual maternity, she interrogates the idea that there is anything more than a momentary biological need for fathers or fatherhood.

It is noteworthy, then, that when she returns to Italy Aurora keeps reminding herself that she has returned to the land where her father is buried, the land of her mother's birth and her father's tomb, her 'father's house / Without his presence'. Though both her parents are buried near Florence, it is, curiously enough, evidence of only her father's disappearance that Aurora seeks and finds; when she revisits 'the little mountain-house' where she had lived with him, she discovers that it has been effaced by female fertility symbols – 'lingots of ripe Indian corn / In tessellated order and device / Of golden patterns' (7.1124–6) – so that 'not a stone of wall' can be seen, and a black-eyed Tuscan girl sits plaiting straws in the doorway, as if forbidding entrance. While Aurora's mother lives on in the Italian motherland, her father is as irretrievably dead as Marian's child's father is non-existent.

But how are both Aurora and Barrett Browning to deal with the wished-for but unnerving fate of the dead father? Freud famously argued that anxiety about the murder of this mythic figure ultimately constituted a social order in which 'his' absent will was internalised as the superego, that creates the law.[44] Barrett Browning, however, as if responding in advance to Freud's hypothesis, implicitly suggests that man as father must be exorcised rather than internalised and that, in a risorgimento of matriarchal law, he must be replaced with man as brother or man as son. For, unlike such a precursor as Christine de Pizan (in *City of Ladies*) or such a descendant as Charlotte Perkins Gilman (in *Herland*), Aurora does not envision an all-female paradise. Rather, she longs for a mother country or 'sisterland to Paradise' in which women *and* men can live together free of the rigid interventions and interdictions of the father.

Thus, even when she and Marian and Marian's child have been securely established in 'a house at Florence on the hill / Of Bellosguardo' (7.515–16), from which, like goddesses surveying past and future, they can see sunrise and sunset, 'morn and eve ... magnified before us' (7.525–6) – a scene that recalls Marian's 'skyey father and mother both in one' – Aurora yearns obsessively for Romney. 'Like a tune that runs / I' the head' (7.960–1), the erotic longing for her cousin that was first signalled by the appearance of Lady Waldemar has made her, she admits at last, just what Lady Waldemar confessed herself – a 'slave to nature' (7.967). In addition, that longing reveals Aurora's radical sense of incompleteness, a feeling of self-division which suggests that, for Barrett Browning as for her heroine, a *matria* without men might become madly and maddeningly maenadic. As she sinks into a sort of sexual fever, Aurora notes that even her beloved Florence 'seems to seethe / In this Medæan boil-pot of the sun' (7.901–2) and ruefully confesses that, in the absence of the consort whom she desires because his presence would complete the new configuration of humanity toward which she aspires, even her old 'Tuscan pleasures' seem 'worn and spoiled' (7.1041).

In endowing a woman named *Aurora Leigh* with such erotic feeling for a cousin whom she wishes to remake in the image of a brother, however, Barrett Browning must at least half consciously have understood that her wish to provide her protagonist with a fraternally understanding and erotically egalitarian lover might oblige her to risk retracing the outlines of the nineteenth century's most notorious brother–sister incest plot: Byron's affair with his half-sister, *Augusta Leigh*. Unlike such 'realistically' depicted sister-brother pairs as Tom and Maggie Tulliver in *The Mill on the Floss*, but like Romney and Aurora, Byron and Augusta rarely met until they were young adults, when both couples discovered and resisted similar mutual attractions. To be sure, the socially illicit Byronic duo made a far weaker effort at resistance than Barrett Browning's socially 'legitimate' pair of cousins. Nevertheless, what Leslie Marchand says of Byron and Augusta is equally true of Romney and Aurora: 'in their formative years they had escaped the rough familiarity of the brother–sister relationship', so that 'consanguinity', with all the equality it might imply for peers of the same generation, was 'balanced by the charm of strangeness'.[45] But Barrett Browning, who as a girl had dreamed of dressing in boy's clothes and running away to be Lord Byron's page, grew up to become, if not as censorious as her friend Carlyle was toward the hero of Missolonghi, at least ambivalent toward him. Even while insisting that her 'tendency' was 'not to cast off my old loves', she wrote that Byron's poems 'discovered not a heart, but the wound of a heart; not humanity, but disease'.[46] In addition, she was close to both the 'wronged' Lady Byron's friend Anna Jameson and to Harriet Beecher Stowe, author of *Lady Byron Vindicated*, both of whom would have reminded her of the masculine exploitativeness involved in Byron's sexual exploits.

Simultaneously inspired and exasperated by the Byron story, therefore, Barrett Browning had to rewrite it to gain strength from it. Thus the seductive and anti-poetic Augusta Leigh becomes the pure poet Aurora Leigh, and the morally corrupt but sexually devastating and romantically self-dramatising Byron becomes the morally incorruptible but physically devastated and romantically diffident Romney. Furthermore, the sexual inequities implied by Byron's sordid secret affairs and by Romney's one-time authority as 'head' of the Leigh family are eradicated both by Aurora's purity and by her recently achieved matriarchal strength. Newly defined 'brother' and 'sister' can unite, and even unite erotically, because the Byron episode has been re-enacted on a 'higher' plane, purged of social disorder and sexual disease.

The humbled Romney's arrival in Florence does, then, complete both the reconfiguration of the family and the regeneration of the motherland that poet-author and poet-heroine have undertaken. Blinded in a fire that recalls yet another famous nineteenth-century plot – the denouement of *Jane Eyre* – this former patriarch seems to have endured the same punishment that Brontë's Bertha dealt Rochester, although in personality Romney is closer to Jane Eyre's austere cousin St John Rivers than to that heroine's extravagant 'master'. Significantly, however, Barrett Browning – who seems vigorously to have repressed her memory of the *Jane Eyre* episode, no doubt so she could more freely revise it[47] – swerved from Brontë in having Romney's injury inflicted not by a mad wife but by a bad father: William Erle, the tramp and poacher who began his career of destructiveness by bruising and abusing his daughter, Marian. Women do not need to destroy the fatherland, Barrett Browning implies by this revision, because it will self-destruct. Again, Barrett Browning swerves from Brontë in allowing her disinherited patriarch to rescue one item from the house of his fathers – a portrait of the lady from whom Aurora inherited her mouth and chin. A woman, she implies by this revision, may be an inheritor. In the end, therefore, as Romney describes 'the great charred circle' where his ancestral mansion once stood with its 'one stone stair, symbolic of my life, / Ascending, winding, leading up to nought' (8.1034–5), his saving of the picture suggests also that the power of the Leighs has not been destroyed but instead transferred to 'a fairy bride from Italy' (9.766), who has now become the true heir and 'head' of the family.

That Aurora has successfully become a 'head' of the family, the figure both Romney's father, *Vane* Leigh, and Romney himself only vainly strove to be, is made clearest by her blinded cousin's revelation that he has at last really read and recognised her work. Seeing through and because of his blindness, like wounded father figures from Oedipus and Gloucester to Rochester, Romney receives and perceives Aurora's prophetic message – 'in this last book, / You showed me something separate from yourself, / Beyond you, and I bore to take it in / And let it draw me' (8.605–8) – and that message, 'Presented by your voice and verse the way / To take them clearest' (8.612–13), elevates her to the 'dearest light of souls, / Which rul'st for evermore both day and night!' (9.831–2). Finally too, therefore, he has become, as both 'Bro' and Robert Browning were for Barrett Browning herself, a 'purely' attentive brother-reader who can at last comprehend the revisionary mother tongue in which the woman poet speaks and writes. It is no coincidence, surely, that Barrett Browning has Aurora, who never before associated Romney with the ocean, envision her lost lover as arising from beneath the bitter waters that had engulfed her lost brother and standing before her like a 'sea-king' while 'the sound of waters' echoes in her ears (8.59–60).[48] Deciphering the texts of Aurora's desire, Romney has accomplished his own transformation into an ex-patriarch who entrusts himself and his sister-bride to the 'one central Heart' (9.890) of love that may ultimately unify all humanity by eradicating the hierarchies and inequities of patriarchy. At the same time, emigrating from the rigid north of the Leighs to the warm south ruled by his 'Italy of women' (8.358), he has become both an expatriate and an ex-patriot, a dweller in the new matria where, in a visionary role reversal, the empowered Aurora will 'work for two' and he, her consort and cohort, 'for two, shall love' (9.911, 912).

Romney's violent metamorphosis reminds us of Barrett Browning's implicit belief that, as in *Casa Guidi Windows* (where the poet advocates the self-sacrifice of Italian men), only the devastation of the fatherland can enable the risorgimento of the mother country.[49] Both Marian and Aurora too, however, have experienced violent metamorphoses, Marian literally, in the rape she describes as a 'murder', and Aurora figuratively, in her passionate struggle to come to terms with the eroticism Lady Waldemar incarnates and with the murderous rage 'the Lamia-woman' evokes. Now, though, after all this violence, these characters are brought together in a symbolically reunified family of brother/husband and sister/wife and mother and son. Is Aurora the dawn in which Marian and Romney can be reborn? Is Marian the womb that gives new life to Aurora's and Romney's light? Is Romney the lover who can read their new roles rightly in the 'bittersweet' darkness of his visionary blindness? Is Marian's child the redemptive son whose coming signals a new day? There is certainly a temptation to define each member of this prophetic quartet allegorically. But even without stipulating meanings that the epic 'unscrupulously' leaves in shadow, it is clear that in its final wholeness this newly holy family integrates what the writer called 'Philosophical Thought' with what she called 'Poetical Thought' and unifies both with the powerful dyad of mother and child, womb and womb fruit.[50] Eastering in Italy, moreover, these four redeemed beings begin to make possible the 'new day' that their author imagined in, for, and through the country she chose as her *matria*. For among themselves they consti-tute – to go back to the qualities women writers have sought in Italy – a land that feels, that feeds, that makes art, and that unmakes hierarchies. In mythologising them as she does, Barrett Browning sets against the exhaustion of belatedness that she thought afflicted contemporary (male) poets 'who scorn to touch [our age] with a finger tip' a matriarchal future that she hoped would be sacramentally signalled by 'the holy baptism of the morning dew'.

V

In its ecstatic delineation of a female risorgimento, the redemption of Italy that Barrett Browning began to imagine in *Casa Guidi Windows* and fully figured in *Aurora Leigh* was both predictable and precarious. Given the long history of Italy as a literary topos, together with the country's personal association for this woman poet, it is not surprising that that embattled nation would come to incarnate both a mother's desire for *bella libertà* and a daughter's desire to resurrect the lost and wounded mother. Certainly Barrett Browning's American contemporary Margaret Fuller imagined the country in a similar way. 'Italy has been glorious to me', she wrote Emerson in 1847, explaining that her expatriate experience had given her 'the full benefit of [a] vision' of rebirth 'into a state where my young life should not be prematurely taxed'. In an 1848 dis-patch to the *Tribune*, she added that in Rome 'the sun and moon shine as if paradise were already re-established on earth. I go to one of the villas to dream it is so, beneath the pale light of the stars'.[51]

Part of this visionary passion no doubt arose from Fuller's revi-talising and egalitarian romance with Angelo Ossoli, in whom, as one observer put it, she loved 'an imagined possibility in the Italian character' much as Aurora, in loving Romney (and Elizabeth Barrett, in loving Robert Browning), loved 'an imagined possibility' in the English character.[52] At the same time, however, Fuller's dream of an Italian paradise was not just energised by her hope for a utopian future that the risorgimento might make possible; it was also shaped by her sense that behind Italy's 'official' history of popes and patriarchs lay another history, the record of a utopian, and specifically matriarchal, past. Visiting 'an Etrurian tomb' in 1847, she noted that 'the effect ... was beyond my expectations; in it were several female figures, very dignified and calm ... [whose] expression ... shows that the position of women in these states was noble'. Later, passing through Bologna, she remarked that 'a woman should love' that city 'for there has the spark of intellect in woman been cherished with reverent care', and she made similar points about Milan, as well as, more generally, about the Italian 'reverence to the Madonna and innumerable female saints, who, if like St Teresa, they had intellect as well as piety, became counsellors no less than comforters to the spirit of men'.[53]

But in particular Fuller's analysis of Etruscan tomb paintings, like the novelist Ouida's apparently casual likening of Florence's past to 'gold from the sepulchres of the Aetruscan kings ... on the breast of some fair living woman', should remind us that as early as the 1840s, in just the years when both Fuller and Barrett Browning were imagining the risorgimento of an Italian *matria*, the Swiss jurist J.J. Bachofen was visiting Etruscan tombs outside Rome, where his discovery of a painting depicting 'three mystery eggs' led him to speculate that in 'Dionysian religion ... the supreme law governing the transient world as a *fatum* [is] inherent in feminine matter' and that 'the phallic god striving toward the fertilisation of matter' stands merely 'as a son' to 'the maternal womb'.[54] This speculation, published only two years after *Aurora Leigh* in Bachofen's 1859 *Essay on Mortuary Symbolism*, led in turn to the even more radical hypotheses of his *Mother Right* (1861), in which he presented the first strong argument that matriarchy was the primordial form of social organisation.

In visiting, studying, and 'reading' Etruscan tombs (as Freud too would do some fifty years and D.H. Lawrence some eighty years later), Bachofen was in one sense 'reading' the palimpsest of Italy the way travellers like Shelley, Rogers, and Ruskin did in the archaeological metaphors I quoted earlier. Unlike them, however, and like both Fuller and Barrett Browning, he was 'reading' beyond or beneath the patriarchal history Western tourists had always expected to find among the ruins of Rome and the monuments of Florence and interpreting his reading as Freud did his reading of the 'Minoan-Mycenaean' age. Thus Bachofen too was preparing at least his female audience to resurrect the old lineaments of a 'new, near Day' (*Aurora Leigh* 9.956) just as the newly matriarchal Aurora does at the end of Barrett Browning's epic when, in a revisionary swerve from Shelley and Ruskin, Barrett Browning has her 'read' an Italian sunrise for Romney in the language of Apocalypse: 'Jasper first ... And second, sapphire; third, chalcedony; / The rest in order: – last, an amethyst' (9.962–4). Through such revisionary readings, moreover, both writers (along with Fuller) were preparing the way for such a descendant as H.D.: her *Tribute to Freud* ends with a reading of Goethe's 'Kennst du das Land', the German poet's vision of Italy as sister land to paradise, a vision that makes the American modernist think of 'the *Ca d'Oro*, the Golden House on the Grand Canal in Venice ... the *domus aurea* of the Laurentian litany'.[55] That it was Goethe who sought also to understand the *Ewige Weibliche* and whose injunction to 'go down to the Mothers' deeply influenced Bachofen (see *Faust* 2.1.6215–21) would have surely given extra richness to the regenerated Italy of his (and H.D.'s) 'Land wo die Zitronen blühn ...' Guarded by siren mountains and a bridge of clouds, as Emily Dickinson also believed, the regenerated *matria* of Italy stands 'on the other side' of patriarchal history.

Yet both Goethe's poem and H.D.'s *Tribute* end with Mignon's equivocal plea: 'o Vater, lass uns ziehn!' For both the female poet and her German precursor, the journey to the magic land can only be accomplished with the guidance of the father. If he permits, the *matria* will be revealed; if not, the Alps and clouds, emblems of despair as well as desire, must, in Dickinson's words, 'forever intervene'. Similarly, Barrett Browning's visions of female regeneration are subtly qualified, for even while the plots and characters of *Aurora Leigh* and *Casa Guidi Windows* propose matriarchal apocalypses, the poet acknowledges that such consummations, though devoutly wished, require (in this world) male cooperation – Romney's abdication, the sacrifices of Italian men and (in heaven) the grace of God the Father, who, with masculine wisdom, will build into 'blank interstices' (*Casa Guidi Windows* 2.776) and make all new (*AL* 9.949). By the time she wrote *Poems before*

Congress, Barrett Browning's quasi-feminist vision had darkened even further. In just the poem whose image of Italy as an invalid woman echoes and illuminates Aurora's vision of her dead mother as 'Our Lady of the Passion, stabbed with swords', the author imagines the redemption of her *matria* by, and only by, the grace of the French ruler Louis Napoleon, whose feats of male military bravery will make him 'Emperor/Evermore'. And, in fact, Italy's risorgimento was finally achieved only by the manoeuvres of traditionally masculine 'heroes' like Louis Napoleon, Mazzini, Garibaldi, Victor Emmanuel, Charles Albert, and – most of all – the Machiavellian statesman Cavour.[56] Thus the specifically matriarchal risorgimento of *Aurora Leigh* is ultimately almost as momentary and provisional as the brief hopeful revelation of the 'mercy Seat' behind the 'Vail' that ends *Casa Guidi Windows*. For inevitably the reality of patriarchal history, with its successes and successions, obliterated Barrett Browning's implicit but impossible dream of a *matria*.

Though Barrett Browning was disturbed by the unfavourable comparison one English reviewer made between her and Florence Nightingale, then, she might have sympathised with the view that unfairly stereotyped 'lady with the lamp' expressed in a book the author of *Aurora Leigh* probably never read. As if commenting on the marriage of true minds Barrett Browning's epic envisions at its close, Nightingale argued in *Cassandra* (written in 1852 and privately printed in 1860) that 'the true marriage – that noble union, by which a man and woman become together the one perfect being – probably does not exist at present upon earth' (p. 44). Indeed, this woman, whose Christian name – Florence – was intended to honour the very city in which Barrett Browning found a modicum of *bella libertà* and who hoped that the 'next Christ' might be, like the redemptive Aurora, a 'female Christ', used a specifically Italian metaphor to describe the enchained reality of nineteenth-century woman: 'She is like the Archangel Michael as he stands upon Saint Angelo at Rome. She has an immense provision of wings ... but when she tries to use them, she is petrified into stone' (p. 50).

Perhaps, given the power and pressure of history, a woman who is 'nobody in the somewhere of patriarchy' can only, as Susan Gubar has observed, be 'somebody in the nowhere of utopia',[57] for even a land like Italy, with all the metaphorical possibilities that give it strength as a matriarchal topos, is inextricably part of the larger topos of European time. As such, it is a text whose usefulness to women can be countered by masculinist rereadings that redeem it for both the father and the phallus. Even Bachofen, the theorist of matriarchy, was to argue that 'mother right' must historically be transformed and transcended by 'father right', and sixty years after Barrett Browning imagined Italy as a *matria*, D.H. Lawrence claimed the land as a metaphorical *patria*, asserting that 'To the Italian the phallus is the symbol of individual creative immortality, to each man his own Godhead'.[58] Even the word *matria*, moreover, which I have used throughout this essay to describe the visionary country sought by women like Fuller, Rossetti, Barrett Browning, and Dickinson, is non-existent. The real Italian word for 'mother-land' is *madrepatria*, a word whose literal meaning – 'mother-fatherland' – preserves an inexorably patriarchal etymology. In Italian linguistic reality, there is no matriarchal equivalent to patriarchal power: one can only imagine such an antithetical power in the 'nowhere' of a newly made vocabulary.

It is no wonder, then, that Barrett Browning appointed Louis Napoleon 'Emperor/Evermore' and that in the last poem she ever wrote, entitled 'The North and the South', she came full circle back to Aurora's self-divided beginnings, admitting the dependence of the matriarchal south on the patriarchal language of the rigid north. While the north sighs for the skies of the south 'that are softer and higher', the south sighs 'For a poet's tongue of baptismal flame, / To call the tree or the flower by its name!'.[59] Though she had enacted and examined a vision of female redemption far more radical than any Rossetti had allowed herself to explore, Barrett Browning would have conceded that, along with Rossetti, she was chained like Nightingale's angel to the rock of patriarchal Rome, and, along with Rossetti, she finally had to bid farewell to the Italy both had dreamed might be a sister land to paradise. As Christine de Pizan and Charlotte Perkins Gilman knew, in the world as it is, the City of Ladies can only be built on 'the Field of Letters'.

From *PMLA*, 99 (1984), 194–211.

NOTES

[Sandra M. Gilbert has, with Susan Gubar, co-authored four major studies of the place of the woman writer in the nineteenth and twentieth centuries. Their highly influential first joint work, *The Madwoman in the Attic: The Woman Writer and the Nineteenth-Century Literary Imagination* (1979), has done much to transform our understanding of the construction of

gender in Victorian and modern culture. Gilbert's critical approach is characterised by sedulous attention to textual details to explore the strategies
that women writers have undertaken to negotiate patriarchal structures of
power.

The work of Gilbert and Gubar, however, has been critiqued by other
feminists for its 'essentialist' assumptions about femininity. Two significant
interventions on this aspect of their writing are Mary Jacobus, Review of
The Madwoman in the Attic, *Signs*, 6:3 (1981), 517–23, and Toril Moi,
Sexual/Textual Politics: Feminist Literary Theory (London, 1985),
pp. 57–69. Ed.]

1. Christine de Pizan, *The Book of the City of Ladies*, trans. Earl Jeffrey
   Richards (New York, 1982), p. 16.

2. Emily Dickinson, *Complete Poems of Emily Dickinson*, ed. Thomas
   Johnson (Boston, 1960). All poems cited by number in the text.

3. Sigmund Freud, 'Female Sexuality', trans. Joan Riviere, in *Sexuality
   and the Psychology of Love*, ed. Philip Rieff (New York, 1963),
   p. 195.

4. All quotations from *Aurora Leigh* in this essay come from the edition
   introduced by Cora Kaplan (London, 1978). All references *to Casa
   Guidi Windows* are to the edition by Julia Markus (New York, 1977).
   Book and line numbers from each poem appear in the text.

   I am deeply grateful to Elliot Gilbert for critical insights that have
   been helpful throughout this essay. In addition, I am grateful to Susan
   Gubar and Dorothy Mermin for useful comments and suggestions.
   Finally, I want to thank my mother, Angela Mortola, for inspiring me
   to think about Italy. This paper is dedicated to her, with love.

5. [Anon.], 'Poetic Aberrations', *Blackwood's*, 87 (1860), 494.

6. Barrett Browning, 'Napoleon III in Italy', *Poems before Congress*, in
   The Poetical Works of Elizabeth Barrett Browning, ed. Harriet Waters
   Preston (1900), reprinted with an introduction by Ruth M. Adams
   (Boston, 1974), p. 412.

7. Quoted by Markus, in her edition of *Casa Guidi Windows*,
   pp. xvi–xvii.

8. In a brilliant essay on the Brownings and Italian politics, Flavia Alaya
   notes the connections among the regeneration of Aurora Leigh, the
   reunification of Italy, and Elizabeth Barrett Browning's personal sense
   of rebirth after her flight with Browning from England to Italy. But
   Alaya's study emphasises the literary dialectic between two major
   poets who were, as she puts it, 'quite literally political bedfellows', for
   she shows through a close reading of *The Ring and the Book* how
   Browning's Pompilia constitutes a re-vision of both Elizabeth and
   Italy, so that the husband's complex set of dramatic monologues is in

some sense a response to his wife's earlier, apparently more naïve and personal epic of a heroine's risorgimento. In addition, through close readings of Barrett Browning's letters and some of her poems, Alaya vigorously defines and defends this woman poet's often misunderstood (and frequently scorned) political stance: 'The Ring, the Rescue, and the Risorgimento: Reunifying the Brownings' Italy', *Browning Institute Studies*, 6 (1978), 1–41.

9. Freud, 'Female Sexuality', p. 195.

10. For a discussion of Aurora's vision of her mother's portrait, see Gilbert and Gubar, *The Madwoman in the Attic: The Woman Writer and the Nineteenth-Century Literary Imagination* (New Haven, 1979), pp. 18–20.

11. Kenneth Churchill, *Italy and English Literature 1764–1930* (London, 1980), p. 66.

12. Samuel Rogers, *The Complete Poetical Works of Samuel Rogers*, ed. Epes Sargent (Boston, 1854), p. 301.

13. Edith Wharton, 'An Alpine Posting Inn', in *Italian Backgrounds* (New York, 1905), p. 3.

14. Alaya also discusses this pervasive trope of Italy as a tragic woman and the political function of the image in the risorgimento ('The Ring, the Rescue, and the Risorgimento', pp. 14–16).

15. John Ruskin, *The Diaries of John Ruskin*, ed. J. Evans and J.H. Whitehouse (Oxford, 1956), I, p. 183, and *Ruskin's Letters from Venice 1851–1852*, ed. J.L. Bradey (New Haven, 1955), p. 128. Significantly, Ruskin describes the way the pillars of the porches of San Marco 'half-refuse and half yield to the sunshine, Cleopatra-like, "their bluest veins to kiss" ...': *Ruskin's Letters from Venice*, p. 128.

16. Ouida, *Pascarel*, quoted in Churchill, *Italy and English Literature 1764–1930*, p. 163.

17. For a discussion of woman as Galatea, see Gilbert and Gubar, *The Madwoman in the Attic*, pp. 12–13.

18. Christina Georgina Rossetti, *The Poetical Works of Christina Georgina Rossetti*, ed. William Michael Rossetti (London, 1928), p. 245.

19. Ibid.

20. Barrett Browning, *The Letters of Elizabeth Barrett Browning*, ed. Frederic G. Kenyon, 2 vols (New York, 1899), I, pp. 341, 342. Elsewhere, Barrett Browning remarks that '[we] can dine our favourite way ... with a miraculous cheapness ... the prophet Elijah or the lilies of the field took as little thought for their dining, which exactly suits us': *Letters*, I, p. 303.

21. Rossetti, *Poetical Works*, p. 377.

22. Ibid., pp. 428–30.

23. Ibid., pp. 377–8.

24. Barrett Browning, *Poetical Works*, pp. 446–8.

25. Rossetti, *Poetical Works*, p. 377.

26. Ibid., p. 380.

27. Barrett Browning, *Letters*, I, p. 332.

28. Barrett Browning, *Elizabeth Barrett to Mr Boyd*, ed. Barbara McCarthy (New Haven, 1955), p. 176.

29. For an extraordinarily useful analysis of *Corinne*'s significance to nineteenth-century women writers, and especially to Elizabeth Barrett Browning, see Ellen Moers, *Literary Women* (New York, 1976), pp. 173–210. On *Corinne*'s Italy as a 'land of women', see Madelyn Gutwirth, *Madame de Staël, Novelist: The Emergence of the Artist as Woman* (Urbana, IL, 1978), pp. 208–15, and Ellen Peel, 'Both Ends of the Candle: Feminist Narrative Structures in Novels by Staël, Lessing, and Le Guin', Dissertation, Yale University, 1982. I am grateful to Ellen Peel for sharing this material with me.

30. Mme de Staël, *Corinne ou l'Italie* (1807), ed. Claudine Herman (Paris, 1979), p. 50.

31. Ibid., p. 183.

32. Ibid., p. 141.

33. For the 'rigid North', see 'Enrica' and *Casa Guidi Windows*, I. 1173; it is possible, even likely, that Rossetti borrowed from Barrett Browning. For 'the sweet South', see Rossetti's 'Italia, Io Ti Saluto', *Poetical Works*, pp. 378–9.

34. Rossetti, 'En Route', *Poetical Works*, p. 377.

35. Ibid., p. 380.

36. Barrett Browning, *Letters*, I, p. 288.

37. Ibid.

38. Ibid., I, p. 291.

39. Ibid., II, p. 190.

40. Ibid., II, p. 193.

41. Sylvia Plath, 'Tulips', *Ariel* (New York, 1965), p. 12. Until recently, few critics have dealt directly with *Aurora Leigh*; major modern writers on the subject include Virginia Woolf, '*Aurora Leigh*', in *The Second Common Reader* (New York, 1932), pp. 182–92; Ellen Moers,

Literary Women (New York, 1976), especially pp. 201–7; Helen Cooper, 'Working into Light: Elizabeth Barrett Browning', in Gilbert and Gubar (eds), *Shakespeare's Sisters: Feminist Essays on Women Poets* (Bloomington, IN, 1979), pp. 65–81; Cora Kaplan, Introduction to *Aurora Leigh and Other Poems* (London, 1978), pp. 5–36; Barbara Gelpi, '*Aurora Leigh*: The Vocation of the Woman Poet', *Victorian Poetry*, 19:1 (1981), 35–48; Virginia Steinmetz, 'Beyond the Sun: Patriarchal Images in *Aurora Leigh*', *Studies in Browning and his Circle*, 9:2 (1981), 18–41; and Dolores Rosenblum, 'Face to Face: Elizabeth Barrett Browning's *Aurora Leigh* and Nineteenth-Century Poetry', *Victorian Studies*, 26:3 (1983), 321–38.

42. Barrett Browning, *Letters*, I, p. 134.

43. The name Marian Erle evokes Goethe's 'Erlkönig', the uncanny and elfish forest spirit who is a manifestation of nature rather than of culture.

44. See Freud, *Totem and Taboo*, in *The Basic Writings of Sigmund Freud*, trans. and ed. A.A. Brill (New York, 1938), especially pp. 915–19.

45. Leslie Marchand, *Byron: A Biography*, 2 vols (New York, 1957), I, p. 396.

46. For Barrett Browning's ambivalent feelings toward Byron, see Gardner B. Taplin, *The Life of Elizabeth Barrett Browning* (New Haven, 1957), p. 103.

47. See Kaplan, Introduction to *Aurora Leigh and Other Poems*, pp. 23–4. Dorothy Mermin has pointed out to me the resemblances between Romney Leigh and St John Rivers, a likeness Taplin also takes up: *The Life of Elizabeth Barrett Browning*, pp. 316–17. Interestingly, as Romney becomes more like Rochester, he also becomes, in a sense, more Byronic; at the same time, however, his kinship to St John Rivers mutes (and thus makes acceptable) his Byronic qualities.

48. Immersed in Browning's very name is a wordplay on 'Bro's' fate: 'Browning' suggests a conflation of 'Bro' and 'drowning'.

49. See *Casa Guidi Windows*, 2.399–405:

> I love no peace which is not fellowship,
>   And which includes not mercy. I would have
> Rather, the raking of the guns across
>   The world, and shrieks against heaven's architrave;
> Rather the struggle in the slippery fosse
>   Of dying men and horses, and the wave
> Blood-bubbling ...

50. See Barrett Browning, 'A Thought on Thoughts', in *The Complete Works of Elizabeth Barrett Browning*, ed. Charlotte Porter and Helen

A. Clarke, 6 vols (New York, 1900 [facsimile edition, New York, 1973), VI, pp. 352–9.

51. Quoted in Bell Gale Chevigny, *The Woman and the Myth: Margaret Fuller's Life and Writings* (Old Westbury, NY, 1976), pp. 435, 453.

52. Chevigny ascribes this comment to W.H. Hurlbut, who thought Ossoli an 'underdeveloped and uninteresting Italian' (ibid., p. 375). In any case, the parallels between Barrett Browning and Fuller are interesting. Although Barrett Browning makes Romney older than Aurora, both Ossoli and Browning were considerably younger than their mates, as though Fuller and Barrett Browning had each half-consciously decided that in a utopian rearrangement of the relationship between the sexes men should be younger than their wives in order symbolically to free women from the bonds of daughterhood. In addition, both Fuller and Barrett Browning, quite late in life and rather unexpectedly, had children in Italy, and the private experience of maternity may well have reinforced their mutual hopes for a public experience of matriarchy.

53. Ibid., pp. 427–8. As Susan Gubar has pointed out to me, the conclusion of George Eliot's *Romola* (1863) imagines a kind of private matriarchy secretly existing behind the patriarchal facade of fifteenth-century Florence.

54. J.J. Bachofen, 'The Three Mystery Eggs', in *Myth, Religion, and Mother Right: Selected Writings of J.J. Bachofen*, trans. Ralph Manheim (Princeton, NJ, 1967), pp. 28–9.

55. H.D. [Hilda Doolittle], *Tribute to Freud: Writing on the Wall, Advent* (New York, 1975), p. 111.

56. As Chevigny notes, Fuller's experiences during the risorgimento were marked by similar – and more dramatically personal – ambiguities, for motherhood simultaneously empowered and weakened her. While Ossoli was fighting in Rome, she was in Rieti, absorbed in child care, and 'in their letters [during this period] they came near assuming conventional sex roles': *The Woman and the Myth*, p. 385.

57. Gubar, '*She* in *Herland*: Feminism as Fantasy', in George E. Slusser, Eric S. Rabkin, and Robert Scholes (eds), *Coordinates: Placing Science Fiction and Fantasy* (Carbondale, IL, 1983), pp. 139–49.

58. D.H. Lawrence, 'The Lemon Gardens', in *D.H. Lawrence and Italy* (New York, 1972), pp. 32–54.

59. Barrett Browning, *The Poetical Works of Elizabeth Barrett Browning*, p. 450.

6

The Religious Poetry of Christina Rossetti

JEROME J. McGANN

I

One of the difficulties which an explicitly Christian poetry or art presents for criticism is its appearance of thematic uniformity. Readers of such work (even critics of such work) frequently seem to think not merely that religious ideas are in themselves eternal truths which wake to perish never but that these ideas are traditionary, self-consistent, and unchanging – in brief that the ideas are transcendent rather than historically particular (whatever the scale of their historical particularity may be). Of course, one recognises that certain doctrinal positions may produce divergent religious emphases in different poets – as, for example, the ideological differences between the Christian poems of Donne, Herbert, Crashaw, and Dryden. But if the specifically controversial poems are set aside (like certain of the Holy Sonnets and *The Hind and the Panther*), the doctrinal variances, we often think, tend to disappear into a basically congruent economy of Christian thought. Christian poetry from the Middle Ages to the present thus comes to us as a body of work which, despite shifting emphases and interests, expresses a uniform world view or ideological focus.[1]

In one sense, of course, this general conception is quite correct: Christian poetry, whether sixteenth- or nineteenth-century, whether Calvinist or Catholic, Evangelical or Anglican, English or French, rests in a tradition of such length and continuity that all its divergent expressions trade in certain common shares of feeling and thought.[2] Nevertheless, if Christian poetry exhibits many common elements, the individual work of different poets is marked by distinctive qualities. Scholars will try to mark out these distinctive features by restoring the work of the religious poets to their special local habitations. If you map the verse of Donne or Herbert on the grids of a historical or biographical analysis, the peculiar features of their work are forced to yield themselves up. This result is especially important in the case of religious poetry read in a culture which maintains and (to a large extent) still propagates the ideological self-representations of such poetry. For in such a culture we are continually tempted to attribute some sort of inherent value to the content of religious verse.

But suppose for a moment you wanted to convince a non-Christian Japanese friend of the power of Christina Rossetti's poetry or – perhaps better – a humanist scholar from the Soviet Union – or simply any non-believer. What line would you take? What would you say?

Rossetti's poetry might be usefully approached in terms of such a problem. For Western scholars and readers like ourselves, who have been brought up within the ideological apparatuses of a Christian culture, such a study of Rossetti's poetry might be useful precisely because her poetry has been largely judged inferior, or at most only of incidental interest, by the chief twentieth-century spokesmen for cultural values. The enormous revival of interest in Christian and even Catholic poetry which began in the modern period and which flourished with the New Criticism did not take any serious account of Rossetti's work. Hopkins yes, Rossetti, no.[3]

Why this choice should have been made by those who celebrated the virtues of so many seventeenth-century religious poets is not a subject to be dealt with in a short essay such as this, for the topic involves the whole de-historicising programme of modernism and the New Criticism. But we must pause to consider the roots of this choice, if only in a brief way. Why is it that not a single critic associated with the New Critical movement ever wrote anything about Rossetti? And what does that disinterest mean?

II

Let me begin with a few commonplaces. The poetry of the English metaphysicals, particularly their religious poetry, was one of the touchstones by which the New Critics would measure a poet's value. This criterion was itself allied to a more general one which prized verse that exhibited a high degree of surface tension, ambiguity, and complexity. Such qualities were associated with the presence of a central conflict or paradox which seemed to define the very nature of the poet and poetry itself: a struggle to reconcile opposite and discordant qualities such as tradition and individual talent, reason and feeling, religion and the secular world. Furthermore, immediately behind the work of the New Critics lay the example of the early modern poets, who seemed to exhibit many of these qualities in their own verse. Most dramatically, the work of the early modern poets sought and found a way to break the spell and authority of Tennyson, Swinburne, and Pre-Raphaelitism, where the poetic surface tended to disguise or sublime all forms of disjunction and irregularity.

The cultural vantage of modernism and New Criticism, then, stood in a hostile relation to much of what the modern poets understood as 'the Victorian frame of mind', as manifested in a poetic medium. The model of Donne seemed more useful as a point of departure, for poet and critic alike, than the model of Tennyson. Yet the religious and moral critique of science and the secular modern world, so vigorously maintained (and in certain respects initiated) by the Victorians, was a cultural resource which was far from being abandoned or repudiated. What would greatly benefit the polemic of the New Criticism would be a Victorian religious poet who stood in some clear antithetical relation to his own age – whose verse seemed to stand closer to Donne or Dante than to John Keble's *Christian Year* and the Society for the Propagation of Christian Knowledge.[4]

From various points of view, therefore, Hopkins was just the sort of person whom 'the (new) age demanded'. He was Victorian, but he didn't sound like Tennyson or Swinburne; his verse displayed an extraordinarily high degree of surface tension (unusual rhythms, obscurity, disjointed syntaxes, startling images and conceits); and – not least of all – he was a religious poet who went virtually unrecognised in his own time. Hopkins was the very epitome of the sort of poet whom Eliot had set up as a model in his 1921 essay 'The Metaphysical Poets'. The fact that he was a Catholic poet writing in an age dominated by sentimental late-Protestant religious verse only underlined his significance. In Hopkins one discovered an example of resistance to that dissociation of sensibility which had been exerting such an evil effect upon poetry since the seventeenth century. In Hopkins one could discern, as it were, a proof case that the touchstone event of the Metaphysicals might arise at any time and anywhere – might arise as an obscure Jesuit writing agonised verse in what was widely regarded as the most bland and enervated period of English literary history.

If Hopkins had never existed, the New Criticism would have had to invent him (and, to the degree that they elevated him above the master poets of the late Victorian period, this is precisely what they did). It is highly significant that Hopkins only exploded onto the literary scene in 1930, with the publication of the second edition of his *Poems*. The first edition, published in 1918 in a print run of 750 copies, sold slowly over the next twelve years, though the critical notices were favourable and often written by significant critical figures. The first edition was compiled and introduced by Hopkins's friend Robert Bridges, the elegant, learned, and ageing poet laureate. Bridges died in 1929, however; so the second edition, when called for, had a new editor – the young Anglo-Catholic Charles Williams. It is with the publication of this second edition that Hopkins's reputation as a major poet begins.[5]

In many ways the early 1930s represent the watershed moment for the next forty years of literary and cultural criticism.[6] John Crowe Ransom's *God Without Thunder. An Unorthodox Defense of Orthodoxy* was published in 1930, Eliot's *Selected Essays* and *After Strange Gods* appeared in 1932 and 1934, and Tate's *Reactionary Essays* came out in 1936. The religious and anti-historical focus which was to dominate the New Criticism is rooted in this period. It is the period of Hopkins's astonishing academic ascendency; it is also the period which marks the virtual disappearance of Rossetti from our cultural consciousness.[7]

Why Rossetti, whom Hopkins admired to a fault, should have thus fallen out of fashion may seem at first rather odd – or at least it may seem odd that the Christian, Anglican and Anglo-Catholic polemicists should not have maintained her reputation. She was a Dantist, she was Anglican and severely orthodox in her public profession, she was impeccably conservative. Later critics who found a rich mine of ore in the drama of Hopkins's spiritual and psychic life were not interested in these aspects of Rossetti, whose personal life, like her poetry, remained virtually a closed book until the theme of sexual frustration offered itself to certain readers.[8]

But Rossetti's orthodoxy is not sufficiently 'unorthodox', at least by New Critical standards. When B. Ifor Evans says of her work that it 'is removed from the Elizabethan tradition by infrequency of conceit, and by an increased earnestness', he indicates three of the more apparent (and related) reasons for her lack of favour with the new apologists for poetry.[9] The style of her verse is simple, chaste, and severe, but it is also recognisably in a Victorian stylistic tradition, and in that respect it is 'orthodox' precisely where modern poets and New Critics looked for the 'unorthodox'. Her poetry does not get worked up at the surface.

More crucial, perhaps, is an ideological deviance between Rossetti and certain less explicit aspects of New Critical theory. Consider the conclusion to Ransom's influential *God Without Thunder*:

> With whatever religious institution a modern man may be connected, let him try to turn it back towards orthodoxy.
> Let him insist on a virile and concrete God, and accept no Principle as a substitute.
> Let him restore to God the thunder.
> Let him resist the usurpation of the Godhead by the soft modern version of the Christ, and try to keep the Christ for what he professed to be: the Demigod who came to do honor to the God.[10]

For Rossetti, some of this will do, but some of it will not do: and the final exhortation about Christ will never do. Worst of all, for a poet such as she, is the aggressive *maleness* of all this, in that Ransom simply takes his patriarchalism for granted. Serious issues are at stake for Ransom, and those issues, therefore, will be conceived in a patriarchal mode such as this. What Ransom has most in mind is the historical transformations which Christianity had been undergoing since the early nineteenth century: the persistent tendency toward Broad Church and liberal doctrinal positions with their correspondingly innovative interpretations of the Christian experience. Because religion for Ransom is an original matter, a God without thunder is seen as a latter-day perversion of Christianity, and a dangerous apparition. This is the burden of his attack upon the religious ideologies which spill out from various nineteenth-century forms of Protestant thought.[11]

Related to these issues of poetic style and religious idea is the conviction that the practice of poetry is a serious intellectual and moral event. Indeed, it is an event of such moment that it leaves no room for the sentiment of pathetic or (good) intentional fallacies. Its object is no less than the Truth, and its function is to seize and define the Truth in times of crisis (whether personal or cultural). Rossetti's poetry, even among those critics who profess to admire it, seems to lack the intellectual rigour which alone can sustain its (evident) moral seriousness. As Lionel Stevenson has put it: 'Christina Rossetti's poety comes closer to the pure lyric mode than that of any other Victorian, male or female, for the obvious reason that it contains a minimum of intellectual substance. Though she was equipped with a normally keen mind, it was firmly suppressed by several forces.'[12] One might argue with this passage on a number of counts. Here I want only to call attention to Stevenson's idea that Rossetti's poetry lacks 'intellectual substance'. As we shall see shortly, this idea is profoundly mistaken – *profoundly* not simply because it is not in fact true but because the error arises out of a lapse in historical awareness.[13]

Indeed, all of the reasons just given might count for little against Rossetti had the New Criticism not set out, deliberately, to 'revolt against historical scholarship'.[14] These words are Tate's own characterisation of the New Critical programme, and they go far to explain why and how Rossetti disappeared so long from our critical consciousness. The restoration of a historical perspective to the critical task will therefore help us to understand Rossetti not only in her own terms – from a historicist perspective – but in terms that are important for readers and educators of this later day.

III

To survey the line of commentary that has preserved the name of Rossetti in twentieth-century literary culture is to discover, first, that the New Criticism ignored her work and, second, that those who praised her did so in terms which were bound to prove largely ineffectual: she is a pure craftswoman, she is the best woman lyricist of the nineteenth century, she is an impassioned mystical poet, she is the poetess of the Tractarian movement; her verse is 'spontaneous', 'ascetic', 'unblemished', and 'sweet'.[15] There are a few important commentaries on Rossetti in the fifty or sixty years following her death, but they are – in contrast to the critical work on Hopkins – exceptional in every sense.

The consequence of this situation, it seems to me, is that Rossetti has reaped the benefits of what Trotsky once called 'the Privilege of Historic Backwardness'.[16] Those who gathered the strength of writers like Donne, Herbert, and Hopkins found Rossetti's work variously 'morbid', 'sterile', 'sweet' – in any case, from a Christian perspective, far inferior to the 'virile' work of those religious poets of our Great Tradition. This neglect of her verse kept her safe from the critical presuppositions and approaches of modernism and New Criticism. As a consequence, her work is once again being read seriously only in recent years, and her best readers now have nearly all been more or less strongly marked by other critical vantages and presuppositions, not the least of which are those we associate with feminist criticism and its natural ally, historical method.[17]

I want to argue, therefore, that to read Rossetti's religious poetry with understanding (and therefore with profit and appreciation) requires a more or less conscious investment in the *peculiarities* of its Christian orientation, in the social and historical particulars which feed and shape the distinctive features of her work. Because John O. Waller's relatively recent essay on Rossetti, 'Christ's Second Coming; Christina Rossetti and the Premillenarianist William Dodsworth', focuses on some of the most important of these particulars, it seems to me one of the most useful pieces of scholarship ever written on the poet. The essay locates the special ground of Rossetti's religious poetry in that peculiar Adventist and premillenarian context which flourished for about fifty years in mid-nineteenth-century culture. In point of historical fact – and it is a historical fact which has enormous significance for the aesthetic character of Rossetti's poetry – her religious verse is intimately meshed with a number of particular, even peculiar, religious ideas.[18] From the vantage of her strongest poetry, the most important of these ideas (along with the associated images and symbols they helped to generate) were allied to a once powerful religious movement which later – toward the end of the century – slipped to a marginal position in English culture.

> The whole question [of premillenarianism] was overshadowed first and last by the Tractarian Movement, Anglo-Catholicism, and the resulting Protestant reaction. And we can see in retrospect that all through the years [1820–1875] the theological future actually belonged to liberal, or Broad Church, principles. By the middle 1870s, apparently, [the issues raised through the premillenarian movement] were no longer very alive.[19]

In this context we may begin to understand the decline of Rossetti's reputation after the late nineteenth century, when she was still regarded as one of the most powerful and important contemporary English poets. Her reputation was established in the 1860s and 1870s, when Adventism reached the apogee of its brief but influential career. Thereafter, the availability of religious poetry was mediated either through the Broad Church line (which stretches from Coleridge and the Cambridge Apostles and Arnold, to figures like Trilling and Abrams in our own day) or through the High Church and Anglo-Catholic line (which was defined backwards from certain influential twentieth-century figures like Eliot to include the Noetics, Hopkins, and various seventeenth-century religious writers). The premillenarian and evangelist enthusiasm which supported Rossetti's religious poetry had been moved to the periphery of English culture when the canon of such verse began to take shape in the modern period.

To read Rossetti's religious poetry, then, we have to willingly suspend not only our disbelief in her convictions and ideas but also our *belief* in those expectations and presuppositions about religious poetry which we have inherited from those two dominant ideological lines – Broad Church and High Church and Anglo-Catholic. Waller has drawn our attention to the general premillenarian content of her work, and I should like to follow his lead by emphasising another crucial and even more particular doctrinal feature of her poetry.

IV

The well-known lyric 'Up-Hill' is a useful place to start. In certain obvious ways, this moving poem follows a traditional model, and its all but explicit forebears are two of Herbert's most familiar pieces, 'The Pilgrimage' and the last poem in *The Temple*, 'Love (III)'. When we set Rossetti's poem beside the two by Herbert we will perhaps be initially struck by the difference in tone: Rossetti's poem is melancholy (one might even say 'morbid') whereas Herbert's two lyrics discover and disclose their religious confidence in their respective conclusions:

> My hill was further; so I flung away,
> > Yet heard a crie,
> Just as I went, 'None goes that way
> And lives'. 'If that be all', said I,
> 'After so foul a journey death is fair,
> > And but a chair.'
> > > ('The Pilgrimage')

'You must sit down,' says Love, 'and taste my meat.'
   So I did sit and eat.

('Love (III)')

If Herbert's pilgrimage has been long and weary, and if his soul –
conscious that it is 'Guilty of dust and sin' – at first hesitates to
accept Love's invitation, in the end all comes to confidence, content,
and even joy. For at the end of his life, the Christian (this Christian)
comes to the feast of the blessed and a place in the house of God.

In Rossetti it is different, and the difference is signalled in the
startling last two lines of her poem 'Up-Hill'. The speaker questions
her divine interlocutor about the pilgrimage, but the answers she
gets are strange and mysteriously portentous through the first
twelve lines. Finally, however, Rossetti is told, in a disturbingly ambiguous phrase, that her laborious journey will be complete: 'Of
labour you shall find the sum.' The poem then concludes:

Will there be beds for me and all who seek?
   Yea, beds for all who come.[20]

Surely this seems a peculiar way to end a poem which seems to describe the pilgrimage of the Christian soul to its final reward. No
'feast' opens before her final eyes, nor does she seem to believe that
the dying Christian should expect to receive anything other than a
bed, presumably to sleep in. The image is almost grotesque in its
lowliness and not far from a parody of such exalted Christian ideas
that at death we go to our eternal rest or to sleep in the bosom of
God. Does Rossetti imagine that when we go to heaven we shall
sleep away our paradise, or is she simply a weak-minded poet,
sentimentally attached to certain traditional phrases and ideas
which she has not really thought through?

The conclusion of 'Up-Hill' would not have been written as it
was if Rossetti had not subscribed to, and thoroughly pondered the
artistic possibilities of, the peculiar millenarian and Anabaptist doctrine known popularly as 'Soul Sleep'.[21] This idea, in a richly dispersed and elaborated variety of poetic forms, pervades the work of
her greatest years as a poet, that is, the period from 1848 to 1875.
It takes its origin from the time of Luther (whose position on the
matter was unsettled), and it means to deal with the problem of the
so-called waiting time, that is, the period between a person's death
and the Great Advent (or Second Coming). The orthodox view distinguishes between the Particular Judgement, which the soul under-

goes at death, and the General Judgement, which takes place at the end of the world. According to traditional doctrine (epitomised in Episcopalian and Roman Catholic theology), the soul at death passes to its final reward (I leave aside here the possibility of a purgatorial period) and suffers no 'waiting time'. The body corrupts in the grave and is reunited with the emparadised soul on the Last Day. According to Adventist doctrine of Soul Sleep, however, death initiates the period during which the soul is placed in a state of 'sleeping' or suspension. Only at the Millennium, on the Last Day, is that sleep broken and the soul confronted with its final reward.

There is no question that Rossetti adhered to the doctrine of Soul Sleep, for it can be found at all levels of tenor and vehicle in her work. From her earliest to her latest poems – from works like 'Dream Land' composed in 1849 (and placed third in her first-published volume) to the famous culminant lyric 'Sleeping at Last', written in 1893 or early 1894 – this premillenarian concept is the single most important enabling principle in Rossetti's religious poetry. By this I mean that no other idea generated such a network of poetic possibilities for her verse, that no other idea contributed so much to the concrete and specific character of her work.

Most obviously, the doctrine provides a ground from which Rossetti can both understand and judge her sense of the insufficiency of a mortal existence. The pervasive theme of *vanitas vanitatum* is generated and maintained through the energy of an emotional weariness, through a sense that living in the world is scarcely worth the effort it requires, since what the world has to offer is, in any case, mere vanity, empty promises, betrayal. Soul Sleep is precisely what would appear to be the first and greatest need of the weary pilgrim under such circumstances; in a word, it answers to the most fundamental emotional demand which Rossetti's poetry sets forth. In addition, however, the doctrine validates Rossetti's peculiarly passive stance toward the world's evil. Rossetti's negative judgements of the world do not take the form of a resistance but of a withdrawal – a strategic withdrawal carried out under the premillenarian conciousness that any commitment to the world is suicidal. It is highly significant that one of the principal sections of her 1893 volume of devotional poems, *Verses*, should have been headed 'The World. Self-Destruction'.

From the doctrine of Soul Sleep also emerges Rossetti's special employment of the traditional topos of the dream vision. Several of Rossetti's poems set forth paradisal visions, and in each case these proceed from a condition in which the soul, laid asleep, as it were, in the body, is permitted to glimpse the millennial world. In fact, the logic of Rossetti's verse only allows her access to that world through the dream visions that are themselves only enabled by the concept (and the resultant poetic reality) of Soul Sleep. How that logic operates can be readily seen by studying the relations between a group of poems like 'Paradise' ('Once in a dream I saw the flowers'), 'Mother Country' ('Oh what is that country'). 'I Will Lift Up Mine Eyes Unto the Hills', 'Advent' ('This Advent moon shines cold and clear'), 'Sound Sleep' ('Some are laughing, some are weeping'), 'Rest' ('O Earth, lie heavily upon her eyes'), and even the exquisite 'Song' ('When I am dead, my dearest'). The sleeping soul is surrounded by a 'stillness that is *almost* Paradise' ('Rest', l.8; my italics), a condition of virtually complete stasis that is also (and paradoxically) premonitory: 'Until the morning of Eternity / Her rest shall not begin nor end, but be' ('Rest', ll.12–13). And in that sleep which is not death what dreams may come? Rossetti says that 'Night and morning, noon and even,/ Their sound fills her dreams with Heaven' ('Sound Sleep', ll.17–18). Soul Sleep permits the visions and dream glimpses of paradise which are the objects of those who desire a better country (compare the poem 'They Desire a Better Country').

> As I lie dreaming
>> It rises, that land:
> There rises before me,
>> Its green golden strand,
> With the bowing cedars
>> And the shining sand;
> It sparkles and flashes
>> Like a shaken brand.
> ('Mother Country', ll.9–16)

The initial rule in Rossetti's ideology is that only the dreams of Soul Sleep give one access to the real details of the Christian paradise (compare her poem 'I Will Lift Up Mine Eyes Unto the Hills'). The poetic imagination of what such dreams must be produces, in turn, the actual verse descriptions of paradise which we find in Rossetti's poetry. In all cases, however, the importance of the initial rule is emphasised by a secondary (operating) rule: that Rossetti's poetry will only venture upon a description of paradise through the rite of passage initially defined in the doctrine of Soul Sleep (with its accompanying poetic imagination of the 'dreams' and visions which must accompany such a state). So, in the poem 'Paradise' Rossetti gives a detailed description of the heaven she saw 'Once in a dream', a concrete representation which she draws from various traditionary Christian sources, not the least of which is the New Testament, and in particular the Book of Revelation. The catalogue of details which makes up her picture of heaven concludes in an 'o altitudo', however, which means to emphasise the secondary nature of the poetic representation. For the poem records, as it were, a dream of the sleeping soul's more final dream, and as such it stands at three removes from paradise. The dream *version* of the sleeping soul's *dream vision* is itself beyond any possibility of an accurate concrete rendering. The closest approximation one can arrive at in this world to the vision that can be expected after death in Soul Sleep is a description not of paradise itself but of the emotional effect which results from the actual desire for such a vision. Thus it is that the poem's description of paradise concludes (indeed, culminates) in the utter defeat of all concrete imaginative detail:

> Oh harps, oh crowns of plenteous stars,
>   Oh green palm branches many-leaved –
> Eye hath not seen, nor ear hath heard,
>   Nor heart conceived.
>   ('Paradise', ll.37–40)

The premonitory dreams of the sleeping soul take place in a region set far apart from the ordinary, 'self-destructive' world; and that world is thereby submitted to the negative judgement implicit in the invocation of such a visionary place.

But that is only one function of the machinery of Soul Sleep as used by Rossetti. Its other principal function is to provide Rossetti with a rationale capable of explaining, and even justifying, her existence in the late Victorian world of getting and spending, which she judged so severely. That is to say, Rossetti consistently used the grammar of the doctrine of Soul Sleep as an analogue for the condition of the contemporary Christian. Rossetti's poems take their model from the visions of Soul Sleep, and the latter state is itself used repeatedly as a model for the state of the Christian soul in the premillennial period of late Victorian England. By thus manipulating the machinery of the doctrine of Soul Sleep, Rossetti was able to produce such famous and beautiful poems as the 'Song' ('When I am dead, my dearest'), for in that and so many similar works she elaborated an analogy between the (physical) 'resting place' of the body and the (spiritual) place in which the sleeping soul was to be suspended.

This last result has a widespread and profound effect upon the character of Rossetti's poetry. In the first place, it tends to blur any clear distinction between her secular and her religious poetry, since almost all of her best work is generated through a poetic grammar that is fundamentally religious in origin and character. We must, of course, distinguish between her 'Devotional' and her non-devotional poetry, partly because *she* made such a distinction and partly because it is an important distinction *in fact*.[22] But if a large part of her work is not specifically *devotional*, it is virtually all 'religious' in its orientation.

In the second place, when we begin to see that a specific religious orientation has had a signal impact on all aspects of her verse, we are unexpectedly (and almost paradoxically) provided with a means for gathering the power of her work outside of its own religious self-representations. That is to say, we begin to see how the Christian and Adventist machinery in her work is a historically specific set of images which do not so much describe actual spiritual realities (like paradise and so forth) as they indicate, by poetic obliquity, how difficult it seemed to imagine, least of all actually to live, a fully human life in the real world of her place and time.

This non-religious, this *human*, view of her poetry is implicit in the following shrewd set of remarks made about Rossetti's work in 1895 by A.C. Benson in the *National Review*:

> Some writers have the power of creating a species of aerial land-scape in the minds of their readers, often vague and shadowy, not ob-truding itself strongly upon the consciousness, but forming a quiet background, like the scenery of portraits, in which the action of the lyric or the sonnet seems to lie. I am not now speaking of pictorial writing, which definitely aims at producing, with more or less vividness, a house, a park, a valley, but lyrics and poems of pure thought and feeling, which have none the less a haunting sense of locality in which the mood dreams itself out.
>
> Christina Rossetti's *mise-en-scène* is a place of gardens, orchards, wooded dingles, with a churchyard in the distance. The scene shifts a little, but the spirit never wanders far afield; and it is certainly singular that one who lived out almost the whole of her life in a city so majestic, sober, and inspiring as London, should never bring the consciousness of streets and thoroughfares and populous murmur into her writings. She, whose heart was so with birds and fruits, cornfields and farmyard

sounds, never even revolts against or despairs of the huge desolation, the laborious monotony of a great town. She does not sing of the caged bird, with exotic memories of freedom stirred by the flashing water, the hanging groundsel of her wired prison, but with a wild voice, with visions only limited by the rustic conventionalities of toil and tillage. The dewy English woodland, the sharp silences of winter, the gloom of low-hung clouds, and the sigh of weeping rains are her backgrounds.[23]

Benson has indeed located the primal scene, as it were, of all of Rossetti's poetry. First, it is a scene which stands in an antithetical relation to the life of Rossetti's immediate experience, to the life and 'the way we live now'. Second, this scene elaborates a set of images which are, as we have already noted, analogous to those which were generated through Rossetti's use of the doctrine of Soul Sleep. In each case, however, we may come to understand that such 'poetical' places and scenes constitute Rossetti's imaginative transpositions – poetic idealisations – of actual places and scenes which she either knew and recoiled from (the Babylon that she saw as the world of London) or that she recollected, dreamed of, and yearned toward. It is beyond question that the charming *mise-en-scène* to which Benson draws our attention is a fantasy delineation of the rural environs of Holmer Green in Buckinghamshire, where Rossetti's grandfather Gaetano Polidori had a cottage and small garden. Rossetti's child-hood visits to this place (they ended when she was nine years old) were later to become, by her own acknowledgement, the source of the ideal forms which she associated with the natural world.[24] As such, they allow us to reconceptualise her 'religious' idealisations, which are structurally congruent with the 'natural' idealisations. In each case we are dealing with symbol structures that express, and re-present, a network of socially and psychologically specific tensions and contradictions. In a word, Rossetti's poetry is not 'about' that fantasy scene pointed out by Benson, nor is it about the equally ab-stract 'religious' scenes offered to us at the surface of her poetry. Her poetry is an oblique glimpse into the heaven and the hell of late Victorian England as that world was mediated through the particular experiences of Christina Rossetti.

As I have noted elsewhere, Rossetti's heaven and hell are always conceptualised in terms of personal love relations: true and real love as opposed to the various illusions of happiness, pleasure, and fulfilment.[25] Indeed, hell for Rossetti is merely the culminant experi-ence of any life which has been lived in a 'worldly', which is to say in a self-destructive, way. Heaven, conversely, is the achievement of a complete and final escape from such an existence. The importance of the doctrine of Soul Sleep is that it postulates a condition or state which mediates between the finalities of heaven and hell. In that state, according to the doctrinal position adopted by Rossetti's poetry, one achieves an initial release from the wearying confusions of the world as well as one's first visionary glimpses of a paradisal (or non-worldly) existence.

Carried over into her verse, the doctrine of Soul Sleep provides Rossetti with an analogue for poetic vision itself – more specifically, for a poetic vision conceived in certain religious terms which are broadly grounded in the general ideology of Christian ideas. It is as if Rossetti were postulating a doctrinal foundation for Wordsworth's famous Romantic formulation of the state of poetic vision, when one is laid asleep in body to become a living soul, and when one may finally begin to 'see into the life of things'. This poetic employment of the doctrine of Soul Sleep provides Rossetti, as we have already seen, with the means for generating 'paradisal images' which answer to her emotional needs: images which at once sustain her deepest and most frustrate desires, and which also help to reveal the circumstances which are responsible for experiences of misery and betrayal.

The doctrine also helped Rossetti to develop a complex theory of dream vision which can be most graphically seen in poems like 'Sleep at Sea' and in particular the great 'From House to Home'. 'Sleep at Sea' narrates the voyage of a ship of fools who are called 'the sleepers' and whose ominous fate is specifically connected to the sleep in which they are caught up.[26] In this state they have certain dreams that recall the premonitory dreams of paradise we have already noted in the poems written out of the doctrine of Soul Sleep; but in this case the dreams are represented as perilous illusions, just as the sleep is only a parodic version of a true Soul Sleep.

> Oh soft the streams drop music
>   Between the hills,
> And musical the birds' nests
>   Beside those rills:
> The nests are types of home
>   Love-hidden from ills,
> The nests are types of spirits
>   Love music fills.
>
> So dream the sleepers,
>   Each man in his place:

> The lightening shows the smile
>   Upon each face:
> The ship is driving, driving,
>   It drives apace:
> And sleepers smile, and spirits
>   Bewail their case.
>   ('Sleep at Sea', ll.17–32)

The original manuscript title of the poem, 'Something Like Truth', indicates the purposefulness with which Rossetti constructed this demonic version of Soul Sleep and dream vision.[27] The doctrinal message of the poem is, of course, quite clear: that the Christian must be watchful on all occasions, that the structures and images of the spiritual life are themselves liable to an evil inversion. Particularly treacherous are the paradisal temptations which are generated out of the desire for rest, comfort, and the eternal life:

> No voice to call the sleepers,
>   No hand to raise:
> They sleep to death in dreaming
>   Of length of days.
> Vanity of vanities,
>   The Preacher says:
> Vanity is the end
>   Of all their ways.
>   (ll.81–8)

In 'From House to Home' the contrast between illusory dreams and paradisal vision is even more elaborately developed. The first seventy-five lines of the poem construct the dream of 'An earthly paradise supremely fair / That lured me from the goal' (ll.7–8). But the central love-object in that paradise eventually flees, and the speaker is left empty and devastated (see ll.77–104). The second part of the poem develops an alternative dream sequence in which the goal of a paradisal vision is associated with a nightmare rite of passage. The importance of this association, from a technical (rather than a doctrinal) point of view, is that it forces Rossetti to subject all aspects of her own poetical machinery to a critical examination at all points; and this in its turn frees her to exploit in unusual ways the imagistic, tonal, and symbolic materials which are generated out of that machinery. Specifically, any image, mood, or symbol is laid open to sudden and arbitrary inversions of their apparent poetic value. Indeed, it seems to me that the often-noted melancholia which pervades so much of Rossetti's poetry is a direct function of its openness to such arbitrary inversions – as if she were herself aware of the treacherousness of her own most cherished dreams and ideals, as if she were also aware that all that she might say might just as well have been unsaid, or been said rather differently, or might not even have been said at all. This is the burden that hangs about the touching and plangent lines of a song like 'When I am dead, my dearest', where the poetry is haunted by the vanity and inconsequence which it reveals and appears to triumph over, but by which it too is at least partially victimised.

V

Thus, the ultimate marginality of Rossetti's particular Christian stance was to become the source of its final strength, the privilege of its historical backwardness. The ideological triumph of Broad Church Christianity and Anglo-Catholicism in the early twentieth century – in the academy at any rate – drove Rossetti out of the Great Tradition and its attendant anthologies. To us, however, her work seems peculiarly alive, *as poetry*, to her age's cultural contradictions because it is able to reveal how those contradictions are replicated at the heart of her own deepest beliefs and commitments. Moreover, that those commitments should have been located within the tradition of Christianity proves to be the conclusive source of her poetry's importance and power. On the one hand, her poetry contains a forcible and persistent reminder that the themes of Christian poetry – even the greatest of such themes, like those of guilt and redemption, of resurrection, of incarnation – are time and place specific, that they have had a beginning, and a middle, and that they will finally have an end as well. To imagine otherwise is a vanity and an illusion, a peculiar blindness from which only those who recognise their own historical backwardness will be exempt. On the other hand, her poetry also demonstrates, through the self-destruction of its own special worldliness (that is, through the self-destruction of its own religious certainties), the true ground of poetic transcendence. Poetry does not triumph over its times by arriving at a 'vision' or idea of the Truth, whether religious or otherwise; it triumphs when it reveals, once again, the local and human origin of all particular and historical events. Hence it is that poetry only maintains its life in later ages and cultures when it preserves its integrity, when it confronts those later ages and cultures with a human world which is important to other human worlds precisely because it is different, local, limited. The survival of that which is specific and therefore obsolete – in particular, the survival of those things which are most conscious of their own limitedness – is the ground of all we can mean by 'transcendence'. It is the reciprocal, indeed, the dialectical gift which past and present give to each other in order to secure the future.

From *Critical Inquiry*, 10 (September 1983), 127–44.

NOTES

[Jerome J. McGann, a distinguished textual editor and critic, has written several studies of Romantic, Victorian, and modern writing that draw on developments within the New Historicism. Five of McGann's books belong to an extended engagement with devising a 'historical method for Euro-American literary studies which would be grounded in the practice of critical hermeneutics'. Beginning with *The Romantic Ideology* (Chicago, 1983), this project is continued in *A Critique of Modern Textual Criticism* (Chicago, 1984), *The Beauty of Inflections* (Oxford, 1985), *Social Values and Poetic Acts: The Historical Judgement of Literary Work* (Cambridge, MA, 1988), and *The Literature of Knowledge* (Oxford, 1989).

Emerging in the late 1970s, New Historicism seeks to place literary works in a variety of illuminating historical contexts. Its project, in many respects, is to counter the formalist emphasis of the influential New Critics (such as Cleanth Brooks), whose scrupulous methods of practical criticism had far-reaching effects on the study of literary representation from the time of the Second World War. The work of the New Critics often implied that the text was a complex artefact which first and foremost had to be understood independently from the cultural and political conditions of its production.

Unlike Marxist critics, whose attention to historical forces largely concerns issues of class struggle and state formation, New Historicists generally show by means of juxtaposition how poetry, drama, and fiction relate to other representational practices in specific periods. McGann's essay, 'The Religious Poetry of Christina Rossetti', is reprinted in *The Beauty of Inflections*, a volume which brings together several influential critical explorations of Byron and Tennyson, as well as Rossetti. This essay is the first serious re-evalaution of Rossetti's position as a writer employing a distinctive and unusual form of Anglican eschatology. Ed.]

1. Because the ideological arguments within Christianity were so central during the Renaissance, contemporary writers of various persuasions

tended to emphasise the differences between their doctrinal positions. During the Enlightenment a secular challenge began to be raised against Christianity in general, and the consequence of this was the emergence, within the various Christian sects, of a consolidating movement. Broad Church Protestantism gained its ascendancy during the nineteenth and twentieth centuries, a period in which we have also observed, particularly during the last fifty years, several strains of ecumenism. These developments within Christianity follow upon the challenge of humanism and secularism, and they can be seen quite clearly in the world of literary criticism and scholarship as well. M.H. Abrams's *Natural Supernaturalism* (New York, 1971) is an obvious instance, and the entire corpus of Northrop Frye's work is paradigmatic.

2. The root of the matter probably hinges upon that famous Pauline *sine qua non*: 'If Christ be not risen, then is our faith in vain' (1 Corinthians, 15: 13–14). This text contains essential features of the Christian economy in all its variant forms: of faith in Jesus as the saviour of mankind and of the nature of Christian hope in the individual's own salvation through resurrection. The other key features of Christianity involve the eucharistic feast and its practical/doctrinal concomitant, the ideal of Christian love (cf. especially the Gospel of John 15: 12–13 and Matthew 5: 43–4; the latter should be compared with what is said in Matthew 22: 36–40).

3. See R.W. Crump, *Christina Rossetti: A Reference Guide* (Boston, 1976), where the history of Rossetti's critical reception is schematically presented in a good annotated bibliography. The neglect of Rossetti is especially remarkable when one considers the (often noted) similarity between much of her verse and the work of George Herbert. The latter is, we know, one of the favourite subjects of New Critical and contemporary formalist exegesis.

4. I choose the second example because several of Rossetti's later books were published under the auspices of that society.

5. For a survey of Gerard Manley Hopkins's critical reception, see the first two chapters of Todd K. Bender, *Gerard Manley Hopkins: The Classical Background and Critical Reception of his Work* (Baltimore, 1966).

6. For a survey of some critical views of the New Criticism, see Murray Krieger, *The New Apologists for Poetry* (Minneapolis, 1956); Richard Foster, *The New Romantics: A Reappraisal of the New Criticism* (Bloomington, IN, 1962), and chs 2 and 5 of Gerald Graff, *Literature against Itself* (Chicago, 1979).

7. See Crump, *A Reference Guide*. A number of books about Rossetti appeared in the early 1930s, several quite good, but after that she virtually disappeared from the academic scene for almost three decades;

and even then she remained a marginal interest for another ten years or more.

8. This line is epitomised in Lona Mosk Packer, *Christina Rossetti* (Berkeley, CA, 1963).

9. B. Ifor Evans, *English Poetry in the Later Nineteenth Century*, revised edition (1933; reprinted New York, 1966), pp. 100–1.

10. John Crowe Ransom, *God without Thunder: An Unorthodox Defense of Orthodoxy* (New York, 1930), pp. 327–8.

11. See ibid., ch. 1. In literary/critical terms, Ransom sets his face against ideological models which were developed out of Romanticism and Victorianism, including their characteristic tendency to define volatile and problematic issues via historicist and symbolical methods. In England this tendency is epitomised in the work and programme initiated by Coleridge. Early twentieth-century reactionary criticism from Irving Babbitt to T.S. Eliot, Allen Tate, and Cleanth Brooks deplored this tendency and its methods. The well-known catchphrase 'split religion' accurately describes the double nature of their criticism of Romantic and post-Romantic poetry: that it represented equally a debasement of the proper objects of poetic discourse and the appropriate character of religious experience.

12. Lionel Stevenson, *The Pre-Raphaelite Poets* (Chapel Hill, NC, 1972), p. 88.

13. I should point out that Stevenson is a distinguished historical scholar. His failure, in this case, to grasp the historical issues at stake in reading Rossetti's poetry is not typical of his work, and least of all is it a function of any New Critical anti-historicism.

14. See 'The New Criticism', a discussion involving Tate and several others, *The American Scholar*, 20 (1951), 218–31.

15. These terms and ideas (as well as 'morbid' and 'sterile', cited below) tend to occur repeatedly in the critical literature on Rossetti.

16. Leon Trotsky, *The Russian Revolution: The Overthrow of Tzarism and the Triumph of the Soviets*, selections from *The History of the Russian Revolution*, ed. F.W. Duprée, trans. Max Eastman (Garden City, NY, 1959), p. 3.

17. For recent feminist and feminist-influenced essays on Rossetti, see Barbara Fass, 'Christina Rossetti and "St Agnes' Eve"', *Victorian Poetry*, 14 (1976), 33–46, and Nan Miller, 'Christina Rossetti and Sarah Woodruff: Two Remedies for a Divided Self', *Journal of Pre-Raphaelite Studies*, 3 (1982), 68–77. Significant historical scholarship has been produced in Crump's various works, including *The Complete Poems of Christina Rossetti*, 3 vols (Baton Rouge, LA, 1979–90), and the *Reference Guide* cited above; in Gwynneth Hatton, 'An Edition of

the Unpublished Poems of Christina Rossetti with a Critical Introduction and Interpretive Notes to All the Postumous Poems' (PhD dissertation, St Hilda's College, University of Oxford, 1955); and in essays like John O. Waller, 'Christ's Second Coming: Christina Rossetti and the Premillenarianist William Dodsworth', *Bulletin of the New York Public Library*, 73 (1969), 465–82, and Joe K. Law, 'William Dyce's *George Herbert at Bemerton*: Its Background and Meaning', *Journal of Pre-Raphaelite Studies*, 3 (1982), 45–55.

18. It is a commonplace of Rossetti criticism that her poetry is the best expression we have of the ideas and attitudes of Tractarianism. But this is a most misleading view (though not entirely wrong); one might rather turn to a work such as John Keble's *The Christian Year* (1827) for an epitome of Tractarian ideology. Rossetti's evanglical sympathies kept her Protestantism resolute, as one can readily see in her lifelong hostility to the revival of Marianism. Waller's observation is very much to the point: '[Rossetti's] spiritual adviser [i.e. William Dodsworth] during her impressionable adolescence [was an] improbable combination of High Church activist and premillenialist preacher that would mould the peculiar configuration of her religious sensibility' ('Christ's Second Coming', 466).

19. Waller, 'Christ's Second Coming', 477. For a general discussion of millenarianism in the early nineteenth century, see J.E. Harrison, *The Second Coming: Popular Millenarianism, 1780–1850* (London, 1979).

20. 'Up-Hill', *The Complete Poems of Christina Rossetti*, ed. Crump, ll.14–16; all subsequent line references to Rossetti's poetry are from this edition and will be included in the text.

21. The technical term for this doctrine is 'psychopannychism'; the *OED* defines 'psychopannychy' as 'the state in which (according to some) the soul sleeps between death and the day of judgement'. For further discussion, see O. Cullmann, *Immortality of the Soul; or, Resurrection of the Dead?* (New York, 1958), and two papers by J. Héring, 'Entre la mort et la résurrection', *Review of the History of Philosphy and Religion*, 40 (1960), 338–48, and 'Eschatologie biblique et idéalisme platonicien', in W.D. Davies and D. Daube (eds) *The Background of the New Testament and Its Eschatology* (Cambridge, 1956), pp. 443–63.

22. The distinction is marked in her volumes of poetry, where specifically 'devotional' poems are marked off in a separate section at the end. Her 1893 *Verses* is a volume exclusively containing devotional poems. While almost all of her poetry could be called 'religious', the 'devotional' poems are those which deal with specific liturgical topics and occasions. To a strict Sabbatarian like Rossetti (and many of her readers were Sabbatarians as well), only devotional verse would be suitable for perusal on Sunday. Moreover, the devotional verse is

always conceived with an audience in mind which understands and
actively practises devotional exercises of various kinds.

23. A.C. Benson, 'Christina Rossetti', *National Review*, 24 (1894), 753, as
quoted in Mackenzie Bell, *Christina Rossetti: A Biographical and
Critical Study*, fourth edition (London, 1898), pp. 330–1.

24. Bell, *Christina Rossetti*, pp. 9–11. See also 'Rossetti Family in Bucks',
Notes and Queries, 159 (1930), 176.

25. See my 'Christina Rossetti's Poems: A New Edition and a
Revaluation', *Victorian Studies*, 23 (1980), 237–54.

26. I do not know that critics have yet pointed out a signal aspect of this
poem: that it is in crucial ways a meditation on, and interpretation of,
Coleridge's 'Rime of the Ancient Mariner', and especially the (later)
parts of the poem which treat the dead mariners and the visiting
troupe of animating spirits.

27. See *The Complete Poems of Christina Rossetti*, p. 262.

7

Consumer Power and the Utopia of Desire: Christina Rossetti's 'Goblin Market'

ELIZABETH K. HELSINGER

The language of Christina Rossetti's best-known poem, 'Goblin Market', is remarkably mercantile. 'Come buy, come buy', the iterated cry of the 'merchant men' that punctuates the poem, has few parallels in English poetry in the nineteenth century. While buying and selling, markets and merchants and their customers, are a staple of nursery rhymes – 'To market, to market, jiggety jig' – most literary Victorian poetry, like the little pig, resolutely stays home from commercial encounters. 'Goblin Market' not only adopts the forms of the nursery rhyme but also carries the mercantile preoccupations of Mother Goose into a volume of serious poetry.[1] Much of the criticism of 'Goblin Market' treats its story of buying and selling, like its rhymes and goblins, as the figurative dress for a narrative of spiritual temptation, fall, and redemption.[2] But what happens if instead we read the figure as the subject: buying and selling, or more specifically, the relation of women to those markets of the nursery tales?

Rossetti's merchants are goblin men; their customers are maidens. When Lizzie and Laura step from home into the male marketplace of Rossetti's poem, they cross a fictive but strongly invested boundary separating not only serious poetry from nursery rhymes but also moral from economic space, private from public, 'natural' creativity from the alienated labour of capitalist production, and – underwriting and sustaining these distinctions –

female from male.[3] Victorian culture acknowledges only one figure who transgresses this boundary – the prostitute. The threat she inevitably poses to the security of these distinctions is contained when she is cast out from the company of moral women. Rossetti's poem is haunted by that shadowy figure. As in so many Victorian narratives of the fallen woman, Laura purchases pleasure only to discover that her own body is ultimately consumed. But Laura is not a prostitute; she is never excluded from the company of moral women by Lizzie or by her author. Rossetti avoids what might be thought the bolder move: she does not take the prostitute as a defining instance of all women's relation to buying and selling, thus negating the fiction of separate spheres. The poem stops short of identifying Laura with the prostitute, for reasons to which I shall return, but its fiction that Laura buys fruit (however magical), not sex, may make the same point more effectively. Rossetti's poem makes visible the contradictory assumptions that render women's relation to the most ordinary forms of consumption, in both the Victorian marketplace and texts about that marketplace, unique and peculiarly risky – both to themselves and to the fragile fictions that legitimise some activities as properly economic while refusing to recognise others. In 'Goblin Market' and a related group of Rossetti's poems, the domestic desires of women are examined as dramas of competitive buying and selling in which women are always at risk as objects to be purchased, yet also implicated as agents of consumption. Rossetti's poems do not acknowledge the fiction of separate spheres; the mercantile language of 'Goblin Market' is one sign of her persistent inclination to consider tales of female love and desire as caught up in the operations of a contemporary economics that extends to sex and marriage. A Victorian ideology of separate spheres returns (but with quite a different figuration) only as the utopian fiction that concludes 'Goblin Market'.

'Goblin Market', then, is a transgressive poem that denies (or at least defers) a series of linked distinctions constructed on the fiction of moral woman's difference from economic man, a fiction that much Victorian writing and thinking posited as normal and natural. The story of Lizzie and Laura represents a specifically female experience of Victorian political economy – one which is often occluded or erased from imaginative and analytic accounts of that economy's operations in the service of maintaining gendered distinctions. Rossetti's economics of sex and marriage is primarily an economics of consumption. A very brief look at some other texts on consumption may suggest how conceptions of gender difference have paradoxically erased women's different experience of consumption, even in the most critical accounts of capitalist relations.

At first glance women are far from absent from such accounts. A surprising number of texts, from the eighteenth through the twentieth centuries, specify that the consumer is female or feminised. For example, both novels in England and rococo art in France were condemned in the eighteenth century for encouraging a love of luxury and idleness by associating them with women.[4] Yet the real targets of these critiques of consumption were all those, from the working classes to the aristocracy, who did not share bourgeois values of hard work and careful saving. The taste for luxury and idleness attributed to women stood for similar tastes in the socially useless aristocrat or the lazy domestic servant. By attributing such dangerous consumption to women's appetites and influence, these criticisms acknowledged a power they intended to contain. Both then and later, the association of luxurious tastes with women outran the facts – women need not be the primary or exclusive buyers, authors, or patrons of novels or rococo art in order to activate denunciations of a consumption with which they were identified.[5]

The grounds for the strong associations between women and consumption probably lie in the fact that in eighteenth- and nineteenth-century monied society women were themselves a sign of luxury, indicating in their persons the power of their fathers, husbands, or lovers to consume. Where this power was feared, female consumption was criticised; where it was applauded, women were expected to buy and display the ornaments of a luxury and leisure that they also represented. In the rococo world of eighteenth-century France but also, much later, in the bourgeois world of mid-Victorian England, women displayed the conspicuous consumption that conferred social status on men. Their role as luxury objects of consumption, in other words, influenced their characterisation as agents of consumption, enabling them to stand for – and sometimes, deflect criticism from – those whose consuming passions they represented. The speaker of Dante Gabriel Rossetti's 'Jenny' only half grasps the evasions that shape his meditations on the prostitute who *is* the pleasure men consume while (he imagines) she herself shares – and can therefore embody – that morally suspect but consuming passion.[6]

Marx carefully points out the contradiction between the bourgeois asceticism expressed in critiques of consumption and capitalism's own dependence on consumers. But his argument, in the
'Economic and Philosophic Manuscripts' of 1844, employs the
same associations between consumption and the feminine, this
time to portray both capitalists and the consumers they dupe as
emasculated or feminised. The capitalist is an 'industrial eunuch'
who puts himself at the service of the consumer's most depraved
fancies, plays the pimp between him and his need, excites in him
morbid appetites, lies in wait for each of his weaknesses – all so
that he can then demand the cash for this service of love. The
capitalist-pimp seeks to compensate with money for his lack of
(masculine) power by preying on the 'weaknesses', the longings
for 'potency', of the consumer-other.[7] Like Christina Rossetti a
few years later, Marx uses the buying and selling of sexual pleasure to stand for all markets. But in his version of the exchange
of money for sex there is no place for women as either buyers
or sellers. Like money, women represent a power properly belonging to masculinity and are the objects, not the agents, of the
exchange.

Returning to the same subject a century later, Max Horkheimer
and Theodor Adorno bring their condemnation of mass culture to a
climax by repeating Marx's charge: the consumer under late capitalism is a man wrongly placed in the feminine position, deprived of
economic subjecthood and hence of the dignity of the father, like a
boy perpetually subjected to the symbolic castration of an initiation
rite:

> The possibility of becoming a subject in the economy, an entre-
> preneur or a proprietor, has been completely liquidated. Right down
> to the humblest shop, the independent enterprise, on the manage-
> ment and inheritance of which the bourgeois family and the position
> of its head had rested, became hopelessly dependent. Everybody
> became an employee; and in this civilisation of employees the dignity
> of the father (questionably anyhow) vanishes. .... The attitude into
> which everybody is forced in order to give repeated proof of his
> moral suitability for this society reminds one of the boys who, during
> tribal initiation, go round in a circle with a stereotyped smile on their
> faces while the priest strikes them. Life in the late capitalist era is a
> constant initiation rite. ... The eunuch-like voice of the crooner on
> the radio, the heiress's smooth suitor, who falls into the swimming
> pool in his dinner jacket, are models for those who must become
> whatever the system wants.[8]

Where the female consumer of eighteenth-century critiques of capitalism represented a threatening male power, from above or below, that critics were eager to contain, the feminised consumer of these Marxist accounts represents a male subject shamefully deprived of power. But some things do not change: not only can the feminine never represent a legitimate possessor of power, it can never represent itself. None of these accounts considers how or why the sexes may be differently related to consumption. Indeed, in most of them, women disappear. One could continue this history and argue, as Tania Modleski has recently, that when postmodernist writers like Jean Baudrillard or the novelist Manuel Puig appear to place a higher value on consumption (as against political activism, for example) and thereby to imply that such consumption is feminist, they are only reinscribing a time-honoured association between consumption and the feminine. The suppression of real gender differences in the power relations of the marketplace, Modleski concludes, can offer very little to a feminist politics.[9]

Against this history of texts in which women appear only to figure male power or powerlessness, Christina Rossetti's fable of female consumption stands out as an exception. Like many other Victorian writers, Rossetti is deeply suspicious of a world of unrestricted buying and selling associated primarily with men; unlike her contemporaries, however, she assumes that women are already implicated as both agents and objects in an economics of consumption – but differently from men.[10] In the utopian conclusion of her poem, the female protagonists undo the erasure with which a male market, like male texts on the market, threatens their existence. The poem becomes a fantasy of consumer power, where the empowered consumer is a woman.

Yet Lizzie and Laura triumph over the market only to withdraw from it. At the point when women seem most empowered, the poem reaches the limits of its ability to conceive their relations to the market. Rossetti's women must consume and be consumed, or declare an impossible independence of all economic relations. An analysis that looked more closely at women's relations to production (as Rossetti, for reasons I will suggest below, hesitates to do) might argue that women in the marketplace are also producers of the product with which they are identified – that femininity and female sexuality, like books, are cultural artifacts in the construction of which women participate, 'the masquerade of femininity'.[11] In this analysis the prostitute who produces herself for sale would figure not only all women's risky relation to consumption but also a (hidden) relation to production. The prostitute so understood threatens any distinction between public, male, spheres of labour shaped by market relations and private, female spheres where work remains unpaid and thus 'natural'. It is not surprising that the prostitute should be a figure of scandal – nor that women who wrote for a market, like Rossetti, should especially fear an association with prostitutes, whose trangressive appearance in the marketplace was not so different from their own.[12] 'Goblin Market' acknowledges no relation to production for Lizzie and Laura except one that is naturalised by its apparent independence from all markets – like butter-making (represented without reference to sale or exchange) or mothering. I will return to the question of the poem's ideological limits, but I want first to recover its critical potential as an account of Victorian women's relation to consumption.

I

Though the poems of a reclusive Victorian woman may seem an unlikely place to look for such an account, two aspects of Rossetti's biography may suggest why she has a particular interest in the gendering of market relations. First, as a number of critics have noted, she was a lay 'Sister' at a home for fallen women in the late 1850s and 60s.[13] Charitable institutions like St Mary Magdalene's Penitentiary, Highgate, run by the Diocese of London, were intended to redeem through spiritual reformation women who had strayed into a moral abyss. But they were also a means of keeping women off the market until they had something to sell other than their bodies – until they could return as domestic servants or needlewomen, not as prostitutes. Rossetti joined the 'self-devoted ladies' whose influence and instruction was to bring about a moral and economic reformation.[14] Though she did not, as an Associate, live at St Mary's, she evidently stayed there for occasional periods of several days or weeks over a decade, until ill health curtailed her activities in 1870. Her duties while in residence probably included reading aloud to the penitents while they worked at sewing. Her association may not have permitted much detailed knowledge of the lives of these women (they were enjoined to silence about their past, partly to protect the Sisters and partly, one suspects, as part of the process of remaking their identities). It did, however, keep vividly before Rossetti's eyes the consequences of a market in which women participated at great risk.

Rossetti also had complicated relations with another market where gender seemed to make a difference. Her interest in art sales and literary publication was elicited by both her own and her brothers' productions. Rossetti's attitudes suggest a combination of ambivalence and ironic awareness of her status as woman with respect to the aesthetic market. On the one hand, she allowed her writing to be produced, if not authored, almost entirely through the mediation of the male members of her family, particularly Dante Gabriel. Between 1847 and 1850, she wrote and published a number of poems, but her only volume was privately printed by her grandfather, and six of eight published poems appeared in *The Germ*, the Pre-Raphaelite journal organised by her brothers, under a pseudonym chosen for her by Dante Gabriel. He was active again in 1852–4 in soliciting (mostly unsuccessfully) publication on her behalf, and it was he who finally arranged in 1861 with Macmillan for her first published volume, whose title poem – 'Goblin Market' – he had named.[15] He also designed the book's cover and that of the second edition, in 1865, which appeared with his frontispiece and title page designs – as did her second volume, *The Prince's Progress*, in 1866. With respect to that project she wrote him, 'I foresee you will charitably do the business-details.'[16] Dante Gabriel not only arranged terms, invented titles and pseudonyms, and designed covers and title pages, he also suggested revisions and made selections and arrangements of the poems themselves. Rossetti sent her manuscript to Macmillan by way of Dante Gabriel for his final advice, and he had Macmillan send separate proof sets to him and to her. But though Christina was apparently willing to concede her brother most of the responsibility for the participation of her work in the public literary market, she could on occasion firmly resist his revisions and intervene when he tried to alter her arrangement with Macmillan in a way she did not approve. 'So please wash your hands of the vexatious business; I will settle it now myself with him', she wrote her brother in 1865.[17] In fact, by 1861 she was corresponding directly with Macmillan, despite her willingness to employ Dante Gabriel as a go-between – or at least, to let him believe that he handled her business matters for her.

This combination of apparent reluctance to enter the literary market except under her brother's auspices with a retention of some degree of control over the marketing of her product may have more than one explanation. Certainly Rossetti was not indifferent to the value of her writing as property which might be sold for money; she never resists her brother's efforts to publish her poems and joins gleefully in speculations about earning money from literary production. But her eagerness for publication and its profits is tempered in part by her own scruples against close dealing, reinforced by a not unrealistic estimate of the small commercial value of her work, and in part by a sense that writing is sullied by commercial exchange (a sense she shared with her brother, as well as with many other Victorian artists). Dante Gabriel, for example, drew a sharp distinction between the paintings by which he made his living and the poems which remained until 1870 largely unpublished. The former he often spoke of derogatorily as a prostitution of his talents; the latter, he wrote to a friend in 1860, he had a special regard for as 'depend[ing] mainly on their having no trade associations, and being still a thing of one's own'.[18] Christina catches her brother's tone when she distinguishes between the poems she published in *Macmillan's Magazine*, for which she was directly paid in return for the copyright – her 'potboilers' – and those she saved for her volumes, in which she would have a share in any profits, but did not exchange her property rights for direct cash payments.[19]

But this not uncommon ambivalence toward the commercial market for art is exaggerated by her awareness, often expressed obliquely and ironically, that women's products are undervalued, while they incur particular risks in a public market as agents of exchanges. In a letter to her brother William in 1853, she imagines a comic scenario in which she will reverse a decline in the family fortunes through the publication of her short story 'Nick'. In the letter, the story is accepted because it is accompanied by her portrait, which appears to be the reason why the 'man of business', who is also 'a susceptible individual of great discernment', 'risks the loss of his situation by immediately forwarding me a cheque for £20'.[20] Christina leaves it quite ambiguous whether this is a portrait *of* her (Dante Gabriel had painted her more than once) or *by* her, since she had been trying her hand at portraits that year. If read as a portrait of her, the fantasy suggests it is not her literary talents but her brother's artistic ones (and the lure of a female face) that will sell her work. If she is the artist, her estimate of her talents is more assertively made – though there may still be some ironic note taken of her greater commercial success as a face than as an author or artist. The letter would seem to put all these meanings deliberately into play.

Rossetti had plenty of opportunities to observe that the commercial value of women's faces might be at odds with their ability to get what they wanted in a world structured by an exchange economy. Just a few months before this letter, itself a fantasy partly generated by her failure to sell anything for publication, Dante Gabriel succeeded in selling his painting, *Ecce Ancilla Domina!* (1850), an annunciation for which Christina had been the model for the Virgin (as she had been for the first painting he sold, *The Girlhood of Mary Virgin* [1849]). Perhaps more disturbing, Rossetti was also witness to the fate of her brother's favourite model, Elizabeth Siddal, who by 1853 was herself writing poems and painting pictures (with no commercial success), suffering chronic ill health, and waiting – as she would until 1860 – for Rossetti to redeem his promise to marry her. Christina's poem 'In an Artist's Studio' (dated December 1856) is usually understood to represent her brother's tortuous relations with Lizzie. 'One face looks out from all his canvases', it begins, 'We found her hidden just behind those screens'. The painted face is lovely: 'Fair as the moon and joyful as the light' – not, like the real woman, 'wan with waiting, not with sorrow dim.' The dim, silent, hidden woman has been drained of all vitality by what the poem depicts as the artist's act of consumption: 'He feeds upon her face by day and night.' The woman who perhaps aspired to be an agent of exchange, to negotiate money or love or marriage for the use of her face – even, like Lizzie (and Christina), to author her own exchangeable objects of beauty – has been herself reduced to that object, and consumed.

This memento mori (in 1862, Lizzie was in fact to die), like the silenced, fallen women she observed at St Mary's, underlines the hazards of exchange economies for women and points to the conclusion Rossetti entertains in her 1853 letter to William – women can more easily sell themselves than what they can produce – and to its consequence: if they enter the marketplace, they risk being literally consumed. Rossetti's preoccupation with consumption (to the virtual exclusion of any consideration of women as producers) is evidently strongly shaped by market relations that she perceives as substituting women's bodies for women's productions. Well before Lizzie's death, Rossetti had begun to explore women's precarious relation to production and consumption in a group of poems that considerably extend these speculations on what she could observe in her brother's studio or at St Mary's, Highgate. Though I shall focus on 'Goblin Market' (dated April 1859), I would like to look first at several lesser-known poems written between October 1856 (the year St Mary's opened) and the mid-1860s.

II

The poems I shall be considering allude to but revise two different traditions of poetry about sex and marriage current in the mid-nineteenth century. They can be viewed as responses to the prose idylls made popular in the 1820s and 30s by Mary Russell Mitford and mined as material for poetry by Tennyson, several of whose 'English Idyls' from the 1830s and 40s draw on stories by Mitford. These were sketches of rural English life, short narratives of domestic romance intended for a middle-class reading audience.[21] Both Mitford's tales and Tennyson's poems depict courtships leading to marriage, not seductions and betrayals. Their women are successful at what many Victorians saw as an exchange situation parallel to that of the market in sex: female love and beauty exchanged for the security of a home and family offered by men. Mitford's tales usually end with the achievement of such security, though not always marriage, for the woman, while Tennyson's adaptations of her stories conclude with marriage or, failing that, happy return to a patriarchal family. Mitford's stories reveal a great deal of anxiety about economic security, a subject generally displaced or suppressed in Tennyson's versions, but both portray sentiment as the key to domestic content. For example, in Mitford's 'The Queen of the Meadow', a gentleman farmer falls in love with Katy, the miller's daughter.[22] Though Katy fears that her lover has abandoned her for her beautiful, educated cousin from the city, it turns out that lover and cousin are simply conspiring to bring about his marriage to Katy. In Tennyson's version of this story, 'The Miller's Daughter', class barriers themselves play the role dramatised by the 'cousin': the neighbouring squire falls in love and marries despite the social distance that divides them. The poem is a retrospective account of this idyllic, cross-class rural romance by the husband, after years of 'wedded bliss'.[23]

Rossetti's poems, however, view the marriage of the rural idyll from the perspective of women who fail to achieve emotional or economic security. Seduced and abandoned women contemplate their married rivals as successful competitors in a market they have belatedly learned to recognise. In what might be read as her version of the Mitford–Tennyson story, 'Cousin Kate' (dated November

1859, a few months after 'Goblin Market'), a 'cottage maiden' laments her abandonment by 'a great lord' who has seduced her and then left her for her cousin, who 'grew more fair than I'. Kate gets the wedding ring, the gold, and the land; the speaker is left with a child and very little else. In Rossetti's version of the story, to succeed in this market is to consume, while to fail is to be consumed (the speaker loses her beauty).

Where the sentimental middle-class rural romance excludes the exchange of sexual beauty for money from its account of how marriages are achieved, ballad stories and their remnants in nursery song readily adopt the language of the market. In its franker treatment of money and sex (there are no illegitimate children in Mitford or Tennyson), 'Cousin Kate', like Rossetti's other rural idylls, has much in common with ballad narratives of seduction.[24] But the pragmatic acceptance of economics and gender inequalities that often underlies the ballad stories is missing from Rossetti's. In the popular song 'Where are you going to, my pretty maid?' (published in a number of versions in the eighteenth and nineteenth centuries), for example, the dialogue between milkmaid and gentleman reveals no illusions on either side: seduction is a possibility, but not marriage.

> What if I do lay you down on the ground,
> With your white face and your yellow hair?
>
> I will rise up again, sweet Sir, she said,
> For strawberry leaves make maidens fair.
>
> What if I do bring you with child
> With your white face and your yellow hair?
>
> I will bear it, sweet Sir, she said,
> For strawberry leaves make maidens fair.[25]

Another popular version of the ballad makes the economic and class terms of the transaction equally explicit.

> What is your father, my pretty maid?
> My father's a farmer, sir, she said.
>
> What is your fortune, my pretty maid?
> My face is my fortune, sir, she said.
>
> Then I can't marry you, my pretty maid.
> Nobody asked you, sir, she said.[26]

The song implies that the attempted seduction is legitimate because the girl accepts the bargain she's offered (pleasure, but no prospect of marriage) – though her confidence that nature will always renew the face that is her fortune may be quite unrealistic.

Rossetti's cottage maiden is, by contrast, quite innocent of the need to bargain with her beauty.

> I was a cottage maiden
>   Hardened by sun and air,
> Contented with my cottage mates,
>   Not mindful I was fair.
> Why did a great lord find me out,
>   And praise my flaxen hair?
>   (ll.1–8)

Unlike Cousin Kate, she does not know that her beauty is a commodity, to be guarded until it can be exchanged advantageously. The speaker of 'An Apple-Gathering', who plucked her apple blossoms to wear for her lover only to find herself without lover or fruit at apple-gathering time, is similarly unable to estimate values or obey the economic law (save now to buy later) of courtship.

> Ah Willie, Willie, was my love less worth
>   Than apples with their green leaves piled above?
> I counted rosiest apples on the earth
>   Of far less worth than love.
>   (ll.17–20)

Rossetti's naïve speakers begin with the expectations of the heroines of Mitford's and Tennyson's idylls, and learn – too late – to perceive courtship as an economic transaction, a matter of 'value' and 'worth'. But although the poems may seem to endorse the more realistic views of Cousin Kate and 'plump Gertrude' (who wins Willie), the questions of the naïve speakers linger: 'Was my love less worth?' Or as the speaker asks Cousin Kate: 'Now which of us has tenderer heart? / You had the stronger wing' (ll.31–2).

In fact the poems use each woman's position to criticise the other: the speakers for their sentimental naïveté (and for their misplaced resentments of their rivals, a point to which I shall return), Kate and Gertrude for their too-ready acceptance of gender relations as competitive bargaining, sex for money (or beauty and pleasure for marriage and children). The implied criticism of Kate and

Gertrude, made strong and plump and complacent by their success, is not simply or perhaps not even primarily moral. The poems attempt to unravel the economic logic by which Kate's and Gertrude's actions are justified by showing, not that it is morally repugnant, but that it is faulty. Bargaining for the security of marriage, women become the objects as well as the agents of exchange.

Rossetti's point may be clearer if we contrast her stories with a classic ballad narrative. Both versions of 'Where are you going, my pretty maid?' quoted above appear in collections of nursery songs and are probably fragments. In the longer ballad to which they are related, 'The Knight and Shepherd's Daughter', the seduced maiden runs to the king, protests that she's been robbed of her maidenhead, and is promised the body of her seducer – as a corpse, if he is married, as a husband, if he is not. Rejecting offers of money, she holds out for a fair exchange, his body for hers, and manages – thanks to the king – to turn the tables on her seducer and redeem her loss with marriage.

> 'O I'le have none of your gold,' she said,
> 'Nor I'le have none of your fee;
> But I must have your fair body
> The king hath given me.'[27]

Most other popular ballads of seduction, like 'The Knight and Shepherd's Daughter', conclude by mitigating what first looks like a very unequal transaction by allowing a persistent woman (provided she is neither wanton nor a child murderer) the recompense of revenge or marriage.[28] Such conclusions disguise but do not deny the facts of class and gender inequality that structure the exchange of sex and marriage. The shepherdess who wins the king's support turns out to be herself a king's daughter. While this revelation explains her apparent power, the ballad's final lines reinscribe her within the patriarchal hierarchy of the family. The Knight comes out quite well in the exchange, after all: 'He had both purse and person too, / And all at his command.'

In Rossetti's several versions of the rural seduction story ('Light Love' as well as 'Cousin Kate' and 'An Apple-Gathering') woman's disadvantage in these transactions is exposed but not overcome. Even the apparent successes of Kate or Gertrude are necessarily called into question. Kate and Gertrude seem to illustrate how women can participate in such bargaining and win – even without the hidden capital held by the pseudo-shepherdess – by recognising and obeying economic laws. They prudently withhold their bodies and their beauty until they can exchange them for the security of marriage. But the poems suggest there are at least three things wrong with such advice, quite apart from any moral objections to an economic model for love relationships. Management of commodified sex and beauty depends upon an economy of scarcity that the poems belie. There is always another maid in the cottage for the great lord; the apple orchard is full of maidens (Lilian and Lilias as well as Gertrude). Moreover, as Rossetti's imagery of blossoms and fruit and seasonal change constantly stresses, beauty is a highly perishable commodity (a fact the maid of 'Where are you going' has overlooked). The speaker of 'Cousin Kate' finds the great lord 'changed me like a glove' when Kate 'grew more fair than I'. The male speaker in the dialogue poem 'Light Love' taunts the mistress he is abandoning with her powerlessness in a world where new beauties are abundantly available:

> For nigh at hand there blooms a bride,
>   My bride before the morn;
> Ripe-blooming she, as thou forlorn.
>   (ll.43–5)

Though it may appear that brides are safe from abandonment, the mistress's reply reminds us that all women who bargain for marriage risk being reduced from consumer to consumed. Trading with their beauty, they become wholly identified with it, and hence subject to the inevitable natural process of decay. Wives can also be abandoned when their beauty withers:

> Change new again for new;
>   Pluck up, enjoy – yea, trample too.
>
> Alas for her, poor faded rose,
>   Alas for her, like me,
> Cast down and trampled in the snows.
>   (ll.59–63)

The lover's reply suggests that permanent success in the market depends not on prudent bargains for beauty but on some prior security: 'Like thee? nay, not like thee: / She leans, but from a guarded tree' (ll.64–5). The speaker of 'An Apple-Gathering' associates the cheerful confidence of Lilian and Lilias with the fact that 'their mother's home was near' (l.12). Milly Brandon, who loves her cousin but has lost him to a cottage maiden, 'has no mother', while her successful rival Nelly 'dwells at home beneath her mother's eyes' ('Brandons Both', ll.25, 22). Without protection, Rossetti's stories imply, women cannot participate on equal terms in courtships structured by economic laws of exchange. Unlike the pseudo-shepherdess, they have no independent power as consumers; at best they can manipulate male consumption to avoid becoming consumed themselves. Those who are 'guarded' – for Rossetti, significantly, by a mother's watchfulness, not a father's wealth or authority – have a far better chance of succeeding at even this limited venture. Rossetti's poems show her under no illusions that the markets of sex and marriage can be either avoided or made safe for women.[29]

By pairing abandoned with safely coupled women, Rossetti calls into question both the account of cross-class courtship presented in the sentimental rural tale and that of cross-class seduction found in the ballads. She also draws attention to the way participation in these economic and sexual exchanges affects relations between women. In nearly every one of Rossetti's tales the woman who has failed to find and hold a mate talks about, and often directly addresses, a woman successful in love and marriage ('Cousin Kate', 'An Apple-Gathering', 'Maude Clare', 'The Lowest Room', 'Brandons Both'). In a related group of poems ('Noble Sisters', 'Sister Maude'), one sister blocks the marriage or elopement of another, in the name of family honour. In all of these poems, sisters, cousins, and female friends are the objects of jealousy and barely suppressed resentments that complicate our attitudes toward the otherwise sympathetically presented speakers. Indeed, one might argue that Rossetti's critical focus on the problem of male and class supremacy is at least partially displaced in her poems by that of female competition for a limited supply of male love. Or as Rossetti herself might see it, a second economy of exchange and competition is generated by the first. The lingering questions of 'An Apple-Gathering' and 'Cousin Kate' – 'was my love less worth?' 'which of us has the tenderer heart?' – may move us as the pathos of a wronged speaker, but they are also presented as ungenerous attempts to devalue a rival.

'Maude Clare', Rossetti's reworking of a well-known ballad ('Lord Thomas and Lady Ellinor' in the English version, 'Lord Thomas and Fair Annet' in the Scottish) makes this point quite

204 ELIZABETH K. HELSINGER

clearly.[30] In the original ballad, Lord Thomas loves Fair
Ellinor/Annet but takes the advice of his mother (father, brother)
and marries a 'nut-browne bride' who has the lands and gold his
love does not. Ellinor/Annet, resplendently dressed, confronts the
two at the wedding; Lord Thomas places a rose in her lap, and his
bride stabs her. The wronged heroine has class on her side,
however, and romance, an aristocratic possession, has its revenge
on nut-brown brides and their money when Lord Thomas draw his
sword and kills first his bride and then himself. Rossetti wrote three
progressively more concise versions of the ballad, each focusing on
the confrontation at the wedding between Lord Thomas, Maude
Clare ('like a queen') and Nell ('like a village maid').[31] As in the
ballad, Maude Clare, especially in the first version, is clearly the
suffering wronged woman whose love and romantic, aristocratic
beauty have been valued less than the lands and gold of the rural
middle-class heroine of domesticity (bride and bridegroom are
imagistically linked to mated pigeons). But where the bride of the
ballad taunts and then stabs Ellinor/Annet, in all three versions of
Rossetti's poem Maude Clare taunts both Lord Thomas and Nell.
(In the first version she explicitly tells Nell he's married her for her
gold.) Nell's reply is neither a verbal nor a physical stab but a spirited defence against Maude Clare's accusations. In this poem, Nell
has the last words:

> 'And what you leave,' said Nell, 'I'll take,
>   And what you spurn, I'll wear;
> For he's my lord for better and worse,
>   And him I love, Maude Clare.
>
> Yea, tho' you're taller by the head,
>   More wise, and much more fair;
> I'll love him till he loves me best,
>   Me best of all, Maude Clare.'
>   (ll.41-8)

The traditional ballad turns the gendered marketplace of marriage into a reaffirmation of aristocratic values; Rossetti, however,
lets Lord Thomas keep his middle-class bride. The tale's transformation seems to replicate a literary history in which aristocratic
romance gives way to the middle-class rural idyll, where the squire
does marry the miller's daughter. But in the poem's final version,
Rossetti eliminates Maude Clare's scornful reference to the bride's

material assets. Though she thus uncharacteristically suppresses the economic bargain which underlies the marriage – as Tennyson and Mitford do in 'The Miller's Daughter' and 'The Queen of the Meadow' – the omission helps refocus the poem away from the differences of class and toward the ties of gender, toward what the two women have in common. 'Cousin Kate' or 'An Apple-Gathering' suggest that the rural idyll misrepresents courtship as an affair of sentiment only, and thus fails to depict women's dangerously disadvantaged situation where they must use themselves as currency to purchase security. 'Maude Clare' also emphasises the insidious effects on female relationships of women's powerlessness in the competitive marriage market. Neither Maude Clare nor Nell is allowed moral authority in Rossetti's version of their confrontation, even though Nell has profited from Lord Thomas's faithlessness, and Maude Clare may be a compromised woman (she has exchanged love tokens and waded barefoot in the beck with Lord Thomas). Rossetti refuses to place exclusive value on either purity or wronged beauty. Rather, both women are implicated in the morally dubious enterprise of devaluing each other, the more subtle but equally destructive consequence of their participation in a market of sex and marriage. Though Rossetti's poems implicitly criticise a male-dominated economy in which women are consumed, they can also be read as an account of competition between women as would-be consumers of men. Both these dangers, as Rossetti sees them, are circumvented in her utopian fable of female consumer power. 'Goblin Market' is fantasy not because its men are goblins and its consumer goods magical ('Men sell not such in any town' [l.101], but because, for once, sisterhood intervenes so that women can successfully buy in markets run by merchant men.

III

Like 'Cousin Kate', 'An Apple-Gathering', or 'Maude Clare', Rossetti's 'Goblin Market' responds to a literary representation as well as to its author's own observations of sexual and economic exchange. In Dante Gabriel Rossetti's dramatic monologue, to which Christina's poem alludes, a young student addresses a sleeping prostitute, meditating on the dissimilar fates of two initially like women, the prostitute Jenny and his cousin Nell.[32] The poem's epigraph identifies the eponymous Jenny as a character borrowed from

Shakespeare ('Vengeance of Jenny's case! Fie on her! Never name her, child!'). Despite Mrs Quickly's admonition, Dante Gabriel's speaker ponders over both Jenny and her 'case' for all of one long night. The heroines of Christina Rossetti's poem cannot forget her either:

> She thought of Jeanie in her grave,
> Who should have been a bride;
> But who for joys brides hope to have
> Fell sick and died.
>
> (ll.312–15)

Jenny lives out her fate as whore as she circulates through these authors' texts. She is the shadow figure of the prostitute that haunts 'Goblin Market' and its initially innocent female consumers, Laura and Lizzie. We should not be surprised to find her unexamined presence in another contemporary discussion of consumption, Marx's 1844 manuscript 'On Money'.

Marx too has Shakespeare in mind, and in two passages apostrophising money in *Timon of Athens* he finds concisely expressed the double nature of money as 'Thou common whore of mankind' and 'Thou *visible* God!' Money is a 'visible God' because it is, in Marx's words, 'the alienated *ability of mankind*,' the *truly creative* power' that can transform 'essential powers which are really impotent, which exist only in the imagination of the individual – into *real powers* and *faculties*'; god also because it is an *un*creative power that can change real human abilities into 'tormenting chimeras'. Money is a common whore because it circulates between men, and because it has no intrinsic value – it is a means to an end, not an end in itself. In fact the whore, like the god, is a power whose source is ultimately man; money as whore is a bearer of power or meaning alienated from man that he must constantly struggle to repossess. In Marx's text gender difference appears only to disappear; god, whores, and money alike reduce to one, and that one is man. Yet Marx cannot leave the fascinating scene of prostitution. 'Money's properties are my properties and essential powers – the properties and powers of its possessor. ... I am ugly, but I can buy for myself the most *beautiful* of women. Therefore I am not *ugly*.' Woman as woman has constantly to be reduced to 'the properties and powers of its possessor', to be appropriated as money in the text and yet still to be purchased with money in the world again and again.[33] Marx's text points to money as an objectified human power which in turn threatens him and must be constantly reclaimed as his own. But it also suggests unwittingly that for women the dangers of the marketplace are rather different. What women have to fear is not (or not just) the alienated power of money, but the efforts of men to reappropriate that power by buying women. ¡Male consumption, in other words, takes place through feminised figures. The female consumer, no less than the prostitute, risks being reduced from the agent who consumes to an object to be consumed in a chain of substitutions by which an alienated power is reappropriated by more powerful consumers, usually men. Money is a whore is a woman. Male texts on the marketplace, like Marx's own, repeat this process of substitution, appropriating the power of an alienating representation, money, by refiguring it: money is a woman who can be possessed. 'Goblin Market' sets out to undo this double consumption or erasure of woman, textual and sexual or economic.

Dante Gabriel Rossetti's poem acts out the scenario suggested by Marx's words; it is the text which Christina Rossetti's poem most directly rewrites. As an allusion to Shakespeare's Jenny, the woman in Dante Gabriel's poem is already doubly in circulation, as whore and as a literary property. The poet, however, must exercise countless strategies to deprive her once again of difference. He makes her unconscious throughout the poem; then he articulates her thoughts for her; finally he constantly figures her as money, itself of course both the bearer of and the power for the satisfaction of his own desires.[34] Thus at one point the speaker himself notes that

> Jenny, looking long at you,
> The woman almost fades from view.
> A cipher of man's changeless sum
> Of lust, past, present, and to come,
> Is left.
>
> (ll.276–80)

But even a thoroughly silenced Jenny is not simply the figure of man's lust, another number in a 'changeless sum', and so as the poem ends the speaker must both buy her and replace her with his money yet again:

> I lay among your golden hair
> Perhaps the subject of your dreams,
> These golden coins...
> . . . .

> I think I see you when you wake,
> And rub your eyes for me, and shake
> My gold, in rising, from your hair,
> A Danaë for a moment there.
>   (ll.340–2, 376–9)

As Zeus descending in a shower of gold, the speaker achieves in imagination the sexual climax that pointedly has not occurred in Jenny's room that night. But he also attempts another kind of victory over Jenny; laying the coins in Jenny's golden hair, he signifies that Jenny is for him the gold he claims she dreams of. Money is a whore, and a whore is money.

When the heroine of Christina Rossetti's 'Goblin Market' is 'mindful of Jeanie' (l.364), she is thinking not just of Jenny's sexual fall but of her failure to take her place in the market as a consumer. Laura and Lizzie, the poem's sister protagonists, live in a state of pastoral maidenhood like that enjoyed by Lilian and Lilias in 'An Apple-Gathering', or by the speaker and her cottage mates, before the great lord came along, in 'Cousin Kate'. They sleep at night 'Golden head by golden head, / Like two pigeons in one nest' (ll. 184–5), united in an image of domestic, even conjugal unity (as the image implied in 'Maude Clare') that is guarded by nature: the moon, the stars, the wind, and some solicitous owls. At cock crow, 'neat like bees, as sweet and busy' (l.201) they

> Fetched in honey, milked the cows,
> Aired and set to rights the house,
> Kneaded cakes of whitest wheat,
> Cakes for dainty mouths to eat,
> Next churned butter, whipped up cream,
> Fed their poultry, sat and sewed;
> Talked as modest maidens should.
>   (ll.203–9)

But 'goblin men' have set up their market even in this place of pastoral childhood and 'natural' domestic production. (Christina Rossetti is never under any illusions about the chances of innocence remaining so in the countryside more than in the city.) The luscious fruits these merchants sell are reputed to be harmful to maidens, and Lizzie, mindful of Jeanie's case, refuses to look or listen to the goblin men with their cries of 'Come buy, come buy!' But 'curious Laura' takes her chances, succumbing to the peculiar dangers that beset women in the marketplace. At the goblin men's suggestion,

Laura pays for her purchase with a golden curl of her hair, and in so doing she becomes both the buyer and the bought, the agent and the object of exchange. She uses her body as money – and money, of course, is a whore.)

Rossetti's account of Laura's fall is markedly different from the usual (male) Victorian version, however. Unlike Dante Gabriel's Jenny, (Laura suffers no instant loss of purity. She is not transformed from maiden to fallen woman.[35] Her mind does not become an open sewer ('Jenny' [ll.164–6]). She goes home to the domestic nest and sleeps the sleep of innocence, rises and cheerfully performs her pastoral chores. But having placed her body in circulation, she cannot re-enter the market as consumer or as object of exchange. She can no longer see or hear the goblin men to buy their fruit, but must suffer the debilitating effects of her unsatisfied desires. She begins to pine and wither away. Like Jeanie, it appears that she will die a maiden, without tasting 'joys brides hope to have'. The fairy tale form of the poem suggests that this may be a fable of the passage from childhood to adulthood, where participation in the marketplace of sex and marriage is the task whose successful accomplishment marks the transition) Laura, however, has failed; she will not grow up. Attempting to exercise the power of the consumer, she has been consumed.

Her sister Lizzie succeeds where Laura has failed. But her success (and her 'redemption' of Laura, as her act is usually read) is not, I think, simply a function of her greater moral strength to resist temptation. Lizzie goes to market doubly armed. Unlike Laura, (Lizzie has money in her pocket, and she knows how to use it. She has learned from the examples of Jeanie and Laura enough to know that she must not 'pay too dear'. She does not offer herself as money. With a penny in her purse, 'for the first time in her life' she begins 'to listen and to look'. The goblin men are not to be put off easily. They don't want her to participate in the market on her terms. They insist that she not only buy the fruit that her sister wants, but eat it herself. Lizzie emerges unscathed with her purchase not only because she has money but also because she does not bring her desire – the intellectual or sexual hunger signified by Laura's curiosity – to market with her. She buys for her sister, not herself. The goblin men cannot force her to eat what she has purchased. Lizzie is allowed to triumph all around: the disgusted goblin men throw her back her penny, and its jingle in her purse is 'music to her ear' as she runs home, covered with the juices of the fruit that will prove a bitter but successful antidote to the poisonous desire that is destroying Laura.

Lizzie is the heroine of this poem because she gets what she wants without giving in to the pressure that a male marketplace, like male texts about the marketplace, exerts on women – to become that which is exchanged, to become money. She retains the power of the consumer, but to do so she must limit the meaning of consumption. For Lizzie, consuming is understood in its strictest (and etymologically originating) sense as buying (Latin *consumere*, from the root verb *emere*, to buy). She refuses the ordinary metaphorical extensions of the word: to take wholly, to use, burn, or devour. A linguistic purist, Lizzie resists male pressures to make economic acts express desire. She will not say 'I want', even if resistance means she cannot speak at all:

> The goblins cuffed and caught her,
> . . . .
> Lizzie uttered not a word;
> Would not open lip from lip
> Lest they should cram a mouthful in.
>   (ll.424, 430–2)

The danger she avoids is of course exemplified by Jeanie's fate. For Jeanie and Laura, purchase becomes inseparable from desire. Laura's consumption – her purchase of the luscious fruits from the goblin men – is rendered primarily as a scene of pleasure in eating.

> She clipped a precious golden lock,
> She dropped a tear more rare than pearl,
> Then sucked their fruit globes fair or red:
> Sweeter than honey from the rock,
> Stronger than man-rejoicing wine,
> Clearer than water flowed that juice;
> She never tasted such before,
> How should it cloy with length of use?
> She sucked and sucked and sucked the more . . .
>   (ll.126–34)

To consume in this extended sense, however, is to expose oneself to the same uses – not only to risk becoming the object rather than the subject of exchange, but also to risk becoming the devoured rather than the devourer. So both Jeanie and Laura waste away, self-consumed by their own desire, the desire that is fed by participation in the marketplace:

> But when the noon waxed bright
> Her hair grew thin and grey;
> She dwindled, as the fair full moon doth turn
> To swift decay and burn
> Her fire away.
>
> (ll.276–80)

Lizzie arrests the horrifying, or 'soul-consuming' (l.512), progress of desire by re-establishing a necessary separation between acts of economic exchange and the expression of desire. She buys but does not consume; Laura is then allowed to consume what she has not bought but been given. The second scene of Laura's eating is fully as passionate as the first, as many readers have noticed, sometimes with embarrassment:

> She clung about her sister
> Kissed and kissed and kissed her:
>
> . . . .
>
> She kissed and kissed her with a hungry mouth.
>
> (ll.485–6, 492)

But this is the first scene played in reverse: as the kiss replaces her voracious sucking, so the luscious juice becomes 'wormwood to her tongue' (l.494); 'She gorged on bitterness without a name' (l.510). Wasted Laura is purged and restored to health. The desire to consume which made her long to buy again became a smouldering fire consuming her, but in this scene it is overcome by a stronger fire:

> Swift fire spread thro' her veins, knocked at her heart,
> Met the fire smouldering there
> And overbore its lesser flame.
>
> (ll.507–9)

What is this stronger fire? As the poem would have it, love between women. Love, that is, as mutual care and support, surviving and defeating the competitive ethos of the market. The play of desire has been reprivatised, divorced from the play of money, and hence no longer, according to the logic of the poem, an issue of consuming or being consumed.

The poem has its happy fairy tale ending. (Lizzie and Laura, having learned to operate successfully in the marketplace of sex and marriage, both grow up. Their reciprocal aid – Lizzie learns from Laura and uses what she learns to help her – enables them to get all the rewards of participating in both the money and the sexual economies, without succumbing fatally to their dangers. Unlike the Jennys of the world, they live to know 'the joys brides hope to have', though significantly, the joys of marriage are in this poem the joys of motherhood. This conflation of terms is significant because heterosexual desire is banished from the poem. (Lizzie can get her money back because she does not want to enjoy the fruits of merchant men. To achieve power as a consumer, she leaves desire at home, not, for Rossetti, a place of heterosexual desire.

In 'Goblin Market' home is a place for love between women. The startling passion with which Laura receives from Lizzie the antidote to goblin fruit suggests that such love may be sexual, though consumption, in the literal as well as the economic sense, is to be interdicted after this moment (luscious juice turns to wormwood in Laura's mouth). The narrative seems to assure us that this scene of sexual passion is the first and last in the sisters' lives, serving to guarantee the passage into marriage and maternity. But Rossetti may be insisting on a different conception of desire altogether: desire not expressed in special acts of passionate, literal consumption, but in the daily sensuous relationships of nurturance that mark the pastoral childhood of the sisters ('Golden head by golden head, / Like two pigeons in one nest / Folded in each other's wings') and their adult experience of maternity ('Their lives bound up in tender lives'). This world of sisters and mothers without fathers (conspicuously absent in the poem) is utopian – as is the 'distant place' of the Christian afterlife (the 'home' of 'From House to Home') to which woman's desire is displaced in much of Rossetti's poetry, when that desire is not, as in her other fairy tale 'The Prince's Progress', perpetually deferred.[36] Whether displaced to another world or located in a wholly feminised domestic space, women's desire is withdrawn from sexual and money economies dominated by merchant men.

'Goblin Market' is a tale of women's survival in a world where 'the market offers itself to women and girls as a stage for the production of themselves as public beings, [but] on particularly unfavourable terms'.[37] However qualified its happy ending may turn out to be, on closer examination, it depicts with considerable acuteness the terms on which girls succeed or fail to reach adulthood. To become adults they must enter a marketplace in which they are always at risk. As the texts of Shakespeare, Marx, and Dante Gabriel Rossetti all suggest, women in the marketplace have not only to reclaim the power of money as their own, but also to resist the tendency of men to exercise their mastery of money through women. The key to this resistance is the separation of economic acts from consuming desires. What makes it possible is the mutual support of women for women. Christina Rossetti reads Jenny's silence as death: reduced to money, the maiden dies. Her death also marks the suppression of gender in the marketplace. The story of survival offered in 'Goblin Market' – consumer power achieved by withholding female desire – culminates in the production of its heroines as 'public beings' who can publish female difference. Laura lives not only to marry and have children, but to tell her story:

> Days, weeks, months, years
> Afterwards, when both were wives
> With children of their own;
>
> . . . .
> Laura would call the little ones
> And tell them of her early prime,
>
> . . . .
> Would talk about the haunted glen,
> The wicked, quaint fruit-merchant men,
>
> . . . .
> Would tell them how her sister stood
> In deadly peril to do her good,
>
> . . . .
> Would bid them cling together,
> 'For there is no friend like a sister ...'
> (ll.543–5, 548–9, 552–3, 557–8, 561–2)

The access to adulthood is also an access to speech – for Laura, to speech within the family, the extent of her sphere, but for her author, Christina Rossetti, to the published speech of literature. Like Lizzie and Laura, Rossetti avoided Jenny's fate in the market of sex and marriage. She did not allow her body to circulate as the currency of exchange between men. The story of 'Goblin Market' is in this respect its author's story as well. Nor did she engage in competitive consumption with other women that was, for Rossetti, the equal or greater danger posed by a heterosexual exchange economy. The poem was dedicated to Christina's sister Maria, who was later to become a Sister in an Anglican religious order, and thus, like Christina through the lay Sisterhood at St Mary Magdalene's, to affirm the mutual ties of women to women, both inside and outside the family, as a refuge from the double threat of an exchange economy.[38] Laura's concluding celebration of a sister's act, telling the tale to others, mimics her author's efforts to save sisters from the consuming passions of the marketplace.

As my reading of 'Goblin Market' should make clear, Rossetti herself is finally less interested in exposing the fictions of separate spheres through the transgressive figure of the female consumer (and her shadow sister, the prostitute), than in rescuing the possibility of a utopian place for women outside the marketplace. The fantasy of consumer power and the retreat to a utopia of desire is, however, powerfully attractive to feminist readers. I want to urge that we resist this attraction in order to retain the critical power of the poem. The resistance might begin with a critique like this.

'Goblin Market' 's conclusion may be altogether too self-congratulating – for feminist critics as much as for Christina Rossetti. The triumphant jingle of Lizzie's coin, like the reiteration of Jeanie's name, jars on the ears, suggesting as it does that Lizzie, her author, and her author's critics embrace the laws of exchange and use that whore, money, as long as we do not become it. The apparent displacement of desire from the marketplace to no-place or *utopia* perhaps conceals a greater investment in a political economy, both sexual and literary, than this interpretation of the poem's ending admits. Rossetti's heroines, one might argue, are never really outside the economies from which they appear to triumphantly withdraw, because they are always participants in production that presumes exchange. The butter, milk, and honey of their pastoral childhood, the babies of their adult lives, and, in a different sense, even the femininity or female sexuality that they bring to the goblin market, all belie the possibility of women's work or a woman's sphere untouched by the political economy of the dominant, 'male' world. Rossetti herself was, of course, an economic agent, whose books, as well as her face, were for sale – however mediated and disguised her relations with the literary market. The shadowy figure of the prostitute, so named because she shows herself in the public market rather than staying home (*prostituere*, to place before, expose publicly, offer for sale), may after all be an inescapable meaning of the feminine as it is constructed in a market economy.

The withdrawal from the marketplace that 'Goblin Market' re-commends, even were it possible, would have the unwanted conse-quence of silencing women as totally as Jenny is silenced: Lizzie, refusing to open her lips to consume the goblins' fruit, cannot utter a word. But neither Rossetti nor her heroines mean to swallow their words permanently. Perhaps the fantasy of withdrawal from ex-change relations played out in 'Goblin Market' conceals the desire, not to give and nurture, but to hoard – goods, words, sex, children, and even money (Lizzie's jingling coin). This hoarding becomes itself a kind of power, but only in the context of the exchange rela-tions that women might – a teasing possibility – choose at moments to re-enter. Consumer power is then dependent on the power to produce, and ultimately, of course, on the intertwined systems of production and exchange that Rossetti would keep separate for women. Although Rossetti's fable imagines that women who suc-cessfully exercise consumer power can then leave the marketplace for the privacy of sisterhood or marriage and motherhood, that withdrawal hardly describes her own activity as author, and it does not describe ours. We would be deluding ourselves if we confused the utopia constructed by Rossetti's strategy for survival, the with-holding of desire (which, on closer inspection, turns out to be the reinvestment of desire in hoarding what we have produced) with any real retreat from the public marketplace. Not only is Jenny's case always potentially ours. We also remain invested in the politi-cal economies of production and exchange that make utopian desire both necessary – and utopian.

From *English Literary History*, 58 (1991), 903–33.

NOTES

[Elizabeth K. Helsinger's detailed analysis of 'Goblin Market' is a major contribution to forms of feminist literary criticism that connect with devel-opments in contemporary cultural studies. The extensive and helpful notes to the essay indicate how this discussion of Rossetti's engagement with con-sumer capital adapts theoretical perspectives which employ a variety of Marxist methodologies to analyse mass culture. In this respect, Helsinger's work has an affinity with the research of Terry Lovell (note 5) and Tania Modeleski (note 9). Her distinctive analysis of Victorian consumer rela-tions should be compared with Elizabeth Campbell's essay, 'Of Mothers and Merchants: Female Economics in Christina Rossetti's "Goblin Market" ', *Victorian Studies*, 30:3 (1990), 393–410.

Helsinger's essay, especially in her notes, does much to relate 'Goblin Market' to another area of popular culture: namely, the tradition of nursery rhyme, ballads and folk-song which shape and define many of Christina Rossetti's poems. In terms of its methods, the essay has a great deal in common with historicist approaches, such as McGann's (pp. 167–88) which seek to locate literary works in the specific conditions of their cultural production. Ed.]

My special thanks to Lauren Berlant, an acute critic of many versions of this essay.

1. Though Rossetti later insisted 'Goblin Market' was only a nursery tale, she published it as the title poem in a volume of serious verse (1862). Among the 550 rhymes collected by Iona and Peter Opie in *The Oxford Dictionary of Nursery Rhymes* (Oxford, 1951) – taken from late eighteenth- and nineteenth-century published collections – almost a fifth concern buying and selling. One continuing favourite in Mother Goose collections goes: 'To market, to market, to buy a fat pig,/ Home again, home again, jiggety-jig;/ To market, to market, to buy a fat hog,/ Home again, home again, jiggety-jog.' Robert Browning describes the purchase of the Old Yellow Book at a street market in Florence in detail in the first book of *The Ring and the Book* (1868–9). That poem, like Dante Gabriel Rossetti's 'Jenny' (see discussion below), is also concerned with the figurative prostitution of the artist for money and its relation to women's participation in such exchanges. Other poems by Browning and Dante Gabriel Rossetti explore related themes; see Browning's 'Andrea del Sarto' and 'Fra Lippo Lippi' (from *Men and Women* [1855]), for example, and, more obliquely, the introductory poem 'The Sonnet', to Dante Gabriel Rossetti's *House of Life* (1870, 1881) (where the poem is a coin). Elsewhere in Victorian literary poetry, however, markets, whether of sex or other commodities, are rare.

2. Thus Jerome McGann, opening his discussion of the poem, can state: 'Everyone agrees that the poem contains the story of temptation, fall, and redemption, and some go so far as to say that the work is fundamentally a Christian allegory' ('Christina Rossetti's Poems: A New Edition and a Revaluation', *Victorian Studies*, 23 [1980], 247). A variant of this common reading interprets the temptation in terms of Rossetti's internal spiritual history or psychodrama; thus Dorothy Mermin begins her discussion: '*Goblin Market* is usually read as an allegory of the poet's self-division that shows, in Lionel Stevenson's representative summary, the conflict between "the two sides of Christina's own character, the sensuous and the ascetic", and demonstrates "the evil of self-indulgence, the fraudulence of sensuous beauty, and the supreme duty of renunciation"' ('Heroic Sisterhood in *Goblin Market*',

Victorian Poetry, 21 [1983], 107; the Stevenson quotation is from his *The Pre-Raphaelite Poets* [Chapter Hill, NC, 1972], p. 105). Many critics also recognise that the spiritual narrative has a social referent in the Victorian fallen woman, perhaps specifically those Christina encountered in her association with the Diocesan Penitentiary, St Mary Magdalene's, Highgate, a home for fallen women. A recent example that argues that the poem may have been actually read aloud at the home is D.M.R. Bentley's 'The Meretricious and the Meretorious in *Goblin Market*: A Conjecture and an Analysis', in David A. Kent (ed.), *The Achievement of Christina Rossetti* (Ithaca, NY, 1987), pp. 57–81.

3. Market relations in nursery rhymes are not especially gendered: neither the little piggy who went to market ('This little piggy went to market/ This little piggy stayed at home . . .') nor the fat pig who was sold there ('To market, to market, to buy a fat pig') is assigned a gender. Little old women feature as often as merchant men among the sellers in nursery lore (as they surely did at village markets). The ideology of separate spheres apparently is not reflected in Mother Goose – whose origins, after all, are neither Victorian nor middle-class. On the historicity of the distinction between public and private, see Jürgen Habermas, *The Structural Transformation of the Public Sphere: An Inquiry into the Category of Bourgeois Society* (Cambridge, MA, 1989). The critical literature on the gendering of the public and private in Victorian discourses is extensive; for an excellent recent discussion, see Mary Poovey, *Uneven Developments: The Ideological Work of Gender in Mid-Victorian England* (Chicago, IL, 1988).

4. For English attacks on novel reading as a feminine vice, see Terry Lovell, *Consuming Fiction* (London, 1987), especially pp. 8–11; also John Tinnon Taylor, *Early Opposition to the English Novel* (New York, 1943). For the attacks on women as patrons and consumers of rococo art in France, see Erica Rand, 'Boucher, David, and the French Revolution: Politics and Gender in Eighteenth-Century French History Painting', PhD dissertation, University of Chicago, 1988, especially chs 2 and 3.

5. See Lovell, *Consuming Fiction*, pp. 9 and 36–44, and Rand, 'Boucher, David, and the French Revolution'. Lovell points out not only that the novel was far from an exclusively feminine province, but that perceptions of women readers as 'leisured' or 'idle' have also been strongly challenged by recent scholarship. For a similarly debunking account of women's relation to rococo art, see, besides Rand, Danielle Rice, 'Women and the Visual Arts', in Samia L. Spencer (ed.), *French Women and the Age of Enlightenment* (Bloomington, IN, 1985), pp. 242–55.

6. For analyses of how women's desires are employed in contemporary advertising and popular culture, see Judith Williamson, *Decoding Advertisements: Ideology and Meaning in Advertising* (London, 1978),

and *Consuming Passions: The Dynamics of Popular Culture* (London, 1986); and Rosalind Coward, *Female Desires: How They Are Sought, Bought and Packaged* (New York, 1985).

7. Karl Marx, 'Economic and Philosphic Manuscripts', in Robert C. Tucker (ed.), *The Marx–Engels Reader*, revised edition (New York, 1978), pp. 93–4.

8. Max Horkheimer and Theodor W. Adorno, 'The Culture Industry: Enlightenment as Mass Deception', in *The Dialectic of Enlightenment*, trans. John Cumming (New York, 1987), p. 153.

9. Tania Modelski, 'Femininity as Mas[s]querade: A Feminist Approach to Mass Culture', in Colin MacCabe (ed.), *High Theory/Low Culture: Analysing Popular Television and Film* (New York, 1986), pp. 37–52.

10. Catherine Gallagher has pointed out the way Henry Mayhew rejects a whole political economy embodied in the figure of the Victorian costermonger; one might argue that 'Goblin Market' starts from a similar point, but Mayhew's costermongers (female as well as male) have become Rossetti's goblin *men*. See Gallagher, 'The Body Versus the Social Body in the Works of Thomas Malthus and Henry Mayhew', *Representations*, 14 (1986), especially on 98–106.

11. This is the argument made by Joan Riviere in 'Womanliness as Masquerade', in Victor Burgin, James Donald, and Cora Kaplan (eds), *Formations of Fantasy* (London, 1986).

12. Mary Poovey and Catherine Gallagher have written illuminatingly on the place of authorship within a Victorian ideology of separate spheres; Gallagher discusses the association between production for a market economy and prostitution as a special danger for women authors. See Poovey, *Uneven Developments*, especially ch. 4; and Gallagher, 'George Eliot and *Daniel Deronda*: The Prostitute and the Jewish Question', in Ruth Bernard Yeazell (ed.), *Sex, Politics, and Science in the Nineteenth-Century Novel* (Baltimore, MD, 1986), pp. 39–62.

13. William Michael Rossetti is the source for this information; see Mackenzie Bell, *Christina Rossetti: A Biographical and Critical Study* (Boston, 1898), p. 60; *The Poetical Works of Christina Georgina Rossetti*, ed. William Michael Rossetti (London, 1904), p. 485; and *The Family Letters of Christina Georgina Rossetti*, ed. William Michael Rossetti (London, 1908, reprinted New York, 1969), p. 26. The most recent discussions of Rossetti's association with St Mary's are D.M.R. Bentley, 'The Meretricious and the Meretorious in *Goblin Market*', and Diane D'Amico, 'Christina Rossetti and Highgate Penitentiary: Working among Fallen Women' (paper delivered at the Victorians Institute Conference, University of North Carolina at Chapel Hill, 17 October 1987). I have drawn especially on the latter.

14. The phrase is quoted by D'Amico from Thomas Carter, *A Memoir of John Armstrong* (London, 1859), p. 199. Armstrong and Carter were both central figures in the movement to establish penitentiaries for fallen women. On the reforming role of the penitentiary, see John B. Bender, *Imagining the Penitentiary* (Chicago, IL, 1987), and Michel Foucault, *Discipline and Punish*, trans. Alan Sheridan (London, 1977).

15. Christina Rossetti had originally called it 'A Peep at Goblins'; Dante Gabriel Rossetti, she later recorded, 'substituted the greatly improved title as it now stands'. See her note in an 1893 copy of the volume (Iowa State Department of History and Archives, Des Moines), which concludes, 'And here I like to acknowledge the general indebtedness of my first and second volumes to his suggestive wit and revising hand' (note quoted by R.W. Crump in the textual notes to her edition, *The Complete Poems of Christina Rossetti*, 3 vols [Baton Rouge, LA, 1979–90], I, p. 234). Unless otherwise noted, all quotations from Christina Rossetti's poems will be taken from this edition; line numbers will be given in the text.

16. Letter to Dante Gabriel Rossetti, 3 March 1865, *The Rossetti–Macmillan Letters*, ed. Lona Mosk Packer (Berkeley, CA, 1963), p. 44. The Macmillan correspondence provides much of the information I have drawn on in this paragraph. For pre-1860 publication, see also *The Family Letters of Christina Georgina Rossetti*, ed. William Michael Rossetti.

17. Letter to Dante Gabriel Rossetti, April–May 1865, *The Rossetti–Macmillan Letters*, p. 51.

18. Letter to William Allingham, September–October 1860, in *Letters of Dante Gabriel Rossetti*, ed. Oswald Doughty and John Robert Wahl, 2 vols (Oxford, 1965), I, p. 377.

19. For the reference to 'pot-boilers', see *The Rossetti–Macmillan Letters*, p. 46. For Christina Rossetti's decided wish to retain copyright for her published volumes, see especially her letter to Alexander Macmillan, 20 April 1881, ibid., pp. 133–4. One could argue that Christina's insistence on retaining copyright to her volumes came as much from shrewd business sense as from distaste for selling poems. No doubt both motives were at work.

20. Quoted by Antony H. Harrison, 'Eighteen Early Letters by Christina Rossetti', in Kent (ed.), *The Achievement of Christina Rossetti*, p. 198.

21. See A. Dwight Culler's discussion of prose and poetic idylls in the early nineteenth century, in *The Poetry of Tennyson* (New Haven, CT, 1977), pp. 114–16.

22. Collected in vol. 3 of Mary Russell Mitford's *Our Village* (1828); cited here from *Our Village*, 2 vols (1828; reprinted London, 1865), II, pp. 70–84.

23. First published in *Poems, Chiefly Lyrical* (1830). That it was influenced by Mitford's story is generally acknowledged. See *The Poems of Tennyson*, ed. Christopher Ricks, second edn, 3 vols (Berkeley, CA, 1987), I, pp. 406–17.

24. Her choice of form suggests as much. Most of her rural poems use ballad stanza or more complex combinations of alternately rhymed tetrameter or trimeter lines, together with frequent repetitions, a good deal of dialogue or direct speech, and concise, minimal narration. All the Rossettis seem to have been very interested in ballads, from the 1840s. Dante Gabriel Rossetti, who avidly read Bishop Percy's *Reliques of Ancient English Poetry*, experimented with ballad stories and ballad forms throughout his poetic career. Christina Rossetti did so too.

25. Opie, *The Oxford Dictionary of Nursery Rhymes*, p. 282.

26. Ibid.

27. Quoted from Francis James Child (ed.), *The English and Scottish Popular Ballads*, 5 vols (1882–98; reprinted New York, 1965), II, p. 460. This, the English version of the ballad, was published in Bishop Percy's *Reliques of Ancient English Poetry*, 3 vols (London, 1765), III, p. 75. Closely related Scottish versions appeared in several eighteenth- and nineteenth-century publications (see Child [ed], *The English and Scottish Popular Ballads*, II, pp. 457–9). As Child notes, the ballad has many parallels with the tales in Gower and Chaucer ('The Wife of Bath's Tale'). The ballad version seems to have been popular in Elizabeth I's time; a stanza was quoted in Fletcher's comedy, *The Pilgrim* (1621).

28. See, for example, 'Fair Annie' and 'Child Waters' (in Child [ed.], *The English and Scottish Ballads*, II, pp. 63, 83); 'Mary Hamilton' gets nothing, but she is both wanton and a child murderer (III, p. 379).

29. Rossetti's conviction that women are always at a disadvantage in dealing with men seems to be one consequence she drew from the Biblical injunction (that woman is the helpmeet to man) that she accepted. In her prose work, *The Face of the Deep* (London, 1892), she concluded: 'Society may be personified as a human figure whose right hand is man, whose left woman; in one sense equal, in another sense unequal. The right hand is labourer, acquirer, achiever: the left hand helps, but has little independence, and is more apt at carrying than executing. The right hand runs the risks, fights the battles; the left hand abides in comparative quiet and safety: except (a material exception) that in the *mutual* relationship of the twain it is in some ways far more liable to undergo than to inflict hurt, to be cut (for instance) than to cut' (p. 410); quoted by Diana D'Amico, 'Eve, Mary, and Mary Magdalene: Christina Rossetti's Feminine Triptych', in Kent (ed.), *The Achievement of Christina Rossetti*, p. 181.

30. Both versions were published in Percy's *Reliques*. Christina Rossetti appears to have followed the English version (which has the explicit comparison of the second woman to a queen, as does her poem); this would also have been available in several other late eighteenth- and nineteenth-century published collections. See Child (ed.), *The English and Scottish Ballads*, II, pp. 179–99. To my knowledge, no one has noted that 'Maude Clare' is based on an existing popular ballad.

31. Antony H. Harrison discusses the differences between the three versions in his *Christina Rossetti in Context* (Chapel Hill, NC, 1988), pp. 4–8. See *The Complete Poems of Christina Rossetti*, ed. Crump, I, pp. 244–7 for the manuscript and first published versions.

32. First published in Dante Gabriel Rossetti's *Poems* of 1870, but begun more than twenty years earlier. Rossetti worked on it in the late 1850s, when Christina was composing her poem.

33. Karl Marx, 'The Power of Money in Bourgeois Society', from 'Economic and Philosophic Manuscripts of 1844', in Tucker (ed.), *The Marx–Engels Reader*, pp. 102–5.

34. Of the many recent critical essays on Dante Gabriel Rossetti's 'Jenny', only one to my knowledge discusses the mutual figuring of woman as money and money as woman in the text. See Daniel A. Harris's suggestive piece, 'D.G. Rossetti's "Jenny": Sex, Money, and the Interior Monologue', *Victorian Poetry*, 22 (1984), 197–215. Harris, however, reads the poems as a much more radical statement than I do.

35. This assertion of the initial innocence of female desire is maintained by Rossetti in her interpretation of the fall of Eve. As Diane D'Amico has pointed out, not only is Eve presented sympathetically in Rossetti's poetry; her commentary on the scriptural event in *Letters and Spirit* (London, 1883) insists: 'It is in no degree at variance with the Sacred Record to picture to ourselves Eve, that first and typical woman, as indulging quite innocently sundry refined tastes and aspirations, a castle-building spirit (if so it may be called), a feminine boldness and directness of aim combined with no less feminine guessiness as to means. Her very virtues may have opened the door to temptation' (pp. 17–18). Eve's desire is 'prideful, not lustful', as D'Amico puts it. Sexual desire is her punishment, not her sin. 'Eve, the representative woman, received as part of her sentence "desire": the assigned object of her desire being such that satisfaction must depend not on herself but on one stronger than she, who might grant or deny', Rossetti wrote in another of her prose works, *The Face of the Deep* (1892). See D'Amico's 'Eve, Mary, and Magdalene', which quotes these passages, especially pp. 175–80. The sequence of sexually innocent desire, disobedience, and punishment through desire is exactly followed in Laura's story.

36. Dorothy Mermin, in a particularly sensible essay, argues that 'Goblin Market' is a utopian fantasy of 'female potency and exclusively female

happiness' – disputing Gilbert and Gubar's influential reading of it as conveying 'bitter repressive wisdom'. See Mermin, 'Heroic Sisterhood in Goblin Market', 116, and Sandra M. Gilbert and Susan Gubar, *The Madwoman in the Attic: The Woman Writer and the Nineteenth-Century Literary Imagination* (New Haven, CT, 1979), p. 573. 'From House to Home' (composed November 1858) is a good example of a poem about the need to relocate desire to 'a distant place', not in this world but the next.

37. Erica Carter, 'Alice in Consumer Wonderland: West German Case Studies in Gender and Consumer Culture', in Angela McRobbie and Mica Nava (eds), *Gender and Generation* (London, 1984), p. 198.

38. For the dedication, deleted in the published version, see *The Complete Poems of Christina Rossetti*, ed. Crump, I, p. 234.

8

'Because men made the laws': The Fallen Woman and the Woman Poet

ANGELA LEIGHTON

I

In 1851, from her vantage point in Florence at the windows of Casa Guidi, Elizabeth Barrett Browning looked towards an England that was confident and powerful; an 'Imperial England' (*Casa Guidi Windows*, II.578),[1] that had come through the Hungry Forties, and was embarking on the new decade with a Great Exhibition. Instead of rejoicing, however, she issued accusations:

> no light
> Of teaching, liberal nations, for the poor
>   Who sit in darkness when it is not night?
> No cure for wicked children? Christ, – no cure!
>   No help for women sobbing out of sight
> Because men made the laws?
>   (II.634–9)

Quick to take up the cause of the downtrodden – the poor, children, and women – she points accusingly to the dark underside of economic expansion, an underside of ignorance, crime, and prostitution. The glittering facade of commercial prosperity only hides the need for 'God's justice to be done' (II.655).

Barrett Browning's message is neither new nor unusual. The Victorians were the first to acknowledge their double vision, as well

223

as their double standards. The age which so thoroughly explored the underlying reaches of the individual subconscious was also one haunted by the social underworld of class. Doubleness was of its very nature. In some ways, Barrett Browning sounds a note of characteristically middle-class concern. She is conscience-stricken at the plight of the poor, and uses them to castigate the materialism of the age. Yet the last two lines mark a sharpening of her attitude. Her social criticism turns into a specific grievance over the condition of women in England's cities: 'No help for women sobbing out of sight / Because men made the laws?' The figure of the fallen woman elicits from the woman poet her most pointed accusation.

Yet, prostitution at this time was not associated with specific laws. It was not a criminal offence, unless it entailed disorderly behaviour. The age of consent was twelve, until in 1875 it went up to thirteen. Only in 1885, partly as a result of W.T. Stead's sensational exposure of the white slave trade in the pages of the *Pall Mall Gazette*, did it become sixteen. Spooner's Bill, introduced in 1847 to suppress trading in seduction and prostitution, was itself quickly suppressed in the House of Commons, when the names of 'some of the highest and noblest in the land'[2] were in danger of being made public in it. The Contagious Diseases Acts, by which suspect prostitutes were subjected to forced medical examinations, and against which Josephine Butler waged her fierce campaign of repeal, were not passed until the 1860s. In general, as historians have often pointed out, 'prostitution does not seem to have threatened any fundamental principle of the state',[3] and on the whole the law tended to let it alone if only for the reason that 'some of the highest and noblest in the land' had an interest in it.

When the French romantic socialist, Flora Tristan, visited England in 1839, she was astonished at the numbers of prostitutes to be seen 'everywhere at any time of day'.[4] In her *London Journal* she describes how they collected round the taverns and gin palaces – the 'finishes', as they were called – and she recounts in some detail the lurid sport that was enjoyed at their expense. The Englishman, she notes with disgust, is a sober prude by day and a drunken lecher by night (p. 87). She herself showed none of the shrinking horror of the middle-class Englishwoman in her investigations. She availed herself of some stout protectors, and went to the 'finishes' to have a look.

Tristan is passionate in her denunciations of two aspects of English life, which she blames for the prevalence of prostitution: the inequality of wealth between the classes, and the social and legal inequality between the sexes. She is full of indignation, above all, at the legal dependence of the married Englishwoman, who, at this time, had no right to sue for a divorce, to own property, to make a will, to keep her earnings, to refuse her conjugal services, to leave the conjugal home, or to have custody of her children if separated. Such overwhelming legal dispossession leads Tristan to a quite surprising conclusion in her defence of woman as a class: 'As long as she remains the slave of man and the victim of prejudice, as long as she is refused training in a profession, as long as she is deprived of her civil rights, there can be no moral law for her' (p. 82).

However, it is precisely in the area of the 'moral law' that the Victorian woman holds power. Deprived of 'civil rights' by the law of the land, hers are the compensatory rights of morality. She is the chief upholder and representer of morality, and also its most satisfying symbol. Thus, angel or demon, virgin or whore, Mary or Magdalen, woman is the stage on which the age enacts its own enduring morality play. The struggle between good and evil, virtue and vice, takes up its old story on the scene of the woman's sexual body. The 'moral law', as a result, has a glamorous simplicity as well as a fascinating secretiveness. Its simplicity is mythic, and its secrets sexual.

Yet this 'moral law' of woman's sexuality also relies on a hard core of technical fact. The woman's virginity on which, as Engels points out,[5] the whole social and familial system depends, is not a spiritual virtue, which can be constantly reclaimed, but a physical virtue, subject to proof. If, on the one hand, woman represents a last remaining absolute good in a world of threatening expediency and enterprise, she also, on the other hand, represents a perishable good, the misuse of which diminishes the value. The 'moral law' is not only feminised, but economised, and thus comes very close to the law of commodity.

The broad implications of this 'economising' of sexuality are brought out in a notorious passage from William Lecky's *History of European Morals*, published in 1869: 'That unhappy being whose very name is a shame to speak ... appears in every age as the perpetual symbol of degradation and sinfulness of man. Herself the supreme type of vice, she is ultimately the most efficient guardian of virtue.'[6] It is in the interests of the very principle of morality to keep the 'type of vice' separate from the type of 'virtue'. The moral stakes of Lecky's opposition are high. The individual 'type' carries the burden of a whole system. Unsurprisingly then, for the

Victorians the fallen woman is a type which ranges from the successful courtesan to the passionate adulteress, from the destitute
streetwalker to the seduced innocent, from the unscrupulous pro-
curess to the raped child. To fall, for woman, is simply to fall short.

The logic of Lecky's statement is manifestly not moral; it is
economic. The unspoken fact which makes women either types of
'vice' or types of 'virtue' is the unquestioned fact of male sexual
need. Such a need justifies the supply and demand, by which the
'type of vice' offers what the type of 'virtue' necessarily abhors.
Thus the 'moral law' erects its mythology of good and bad on a
laissez-faire economics of male sexuality, which relies on a social
apartheid between women. 'No cure for women sobbing out of
sight / Because men made the laws?'

More than any other poet, Barrett Browning probes the notion of
the moral law as the mythologised superstructure of social inequality. In *Aurora Leigh*, the sexual fall of Marian Erle constantly
entails a quarrel with that law. At times Marian's innocence seems
too white to be true. However, the purpose of that innocence is not
to indulge the squeamishness of the reader, but to deflect moral
judgement from the personal to the social. The idea of the law, re-
curring throughout the poem, provides the connection between
those two separate spheres.

Thus, for instance, in Book 3, Barrett Browning describes the
birth of Marian, in a mud shack, liable, 'Like any other anthill'
(3.836),[7] to be levelled by a ruthless landlord. The defiant mixture
of physical detail and political reproach is typical:

> No place for her,
> By man's law! born an outlaw was this babe;
> Her first cry in our strange and strangling air,
> When cast in spasms out by the shuddering womb.
> Was wrong against the social code, – forced wrong: –
> What business had the baby to cry there?
> (3.841–6)

Here, 'man's law' is unequivocally the law of property rights, land
ownership, and class difference. This law casts out, from the start,
the girl child born in poverty. The poor have no business to be
giving birth to girls on other people's land. The 'social code' of
wealth, class, and, by implication, sex, makes Marian's life a kind
of 'wrong' from the beginning.

The story of Marian Erle charts, every step of the way, the
complicity between 'man's law' and moral law. For instance, the

description of the mother's attempt to prostitute her daughter to that same 'squire' who also owns the land, is a continued indictment of 'the social code', as well as a rare reference in nineteenth-century literature to the scandal publicised in the *Pall Mall Gazette*. The trade in children for prostitution, both at home and abroad, was a thriving one, and one which had a singular appeal to the male customer afraid of catching venereal disease and willing to pay extra for virginity. As Flora Tristan noted: 'The demand for children is ... enormous' (p. 97). Yet, noticeably, even while Barrett Browning blames the mother, she traces her motives back to yet another kind of violence: 'Her mother had been badly beat, and felt / The bruises sore about her wretched soul' (3.1041–2). The temptation to 'Make offal of [our] daughters' (7.866) finds its originating cause in all men's violence: squires' or fathers'. Only because Marian Erle is 'poor and of the people' (4.845) is she more readily tradable than her wealthier sisters.

Marian's rape in a French brothel thus only continues a theme begun early. If Barrett Browning's account of the rape seems sensational, this is not because it is improbable. The trade in girls to continental brothels may have been exaggerated by Stead in 1885, but it was nonetheless a fact, and he witnessed the use of chloroform. Marian's unconsciousness is not a pretext to prove her innocent, but a truth to prove the guilt of the system. Barrett Browning constantly emphasises the culpability of the system, and particularly, of course, the class system, involving 'some of the highest and noblest in the land'. Although she finally exonerates Lady Waldemar, her possible responsibility for Marian's fate lurks behind the story till the end.

Barrett Browning's deflection of moral responsibility from the personal to the social is then made clear in the dramatic encounter between Aurora and Marian in Paris: Accused by Aurora of being corrupt, Marian snatches up her child, and fiercely repudiates the morality by which she has been judged:

> 'Mine, mine,' she said. 'I have as sure a right
> As any glad proud mother in the world,
> Who sets her darling down to cut his teeth
> Upon her church-ring. If she talks of law,
> I talk of law! I claim my mother-dues
> By law – the law which now is paramount, –
> The common law, by which the poor and weak
> Are trodden underfoot by vicious men,
> And loathed for ever after by the good.'
>
> (6.661–9)

Marian's self-defence consists in making a radical connection between the church law of marriage and the common law of oppression, between legalisation of motherhood in a 'church-ring' and legalisation of poverty by an accepted system. As law thus comes to seem less of a moral absolute, and more of a social commodity affordable by the rich, the very nature of virtue and vice becomes uncertain. Furthermore, there is an explicit gender shift to parallel the shift from sexual to social. The 'types of vice', here, are those 'vicious men' who tread the poor 'underfoot'. Thus the terms of Marian's own rape, 'being beaten down / By hoofs of maddened oxen into a ditch' (6.676–7), subtly echo the language of a more general beating down of a whole class of 'poor and weak'.

Against this continuing social protest one must read the end of *Aurora Leigh*, when Marian rejects Romney's offer of marriage, his '"gift"' (9.255) of law to her, as Aurora puts it, ironically echoing that earlier '"gift"' (2.1085) of money to herself, when Romney had tried to trap her in marriage, and make her family inheritance 'Inviolable with law' (2.1111). Both women repudiate the male gift that comes not as love but law. Against it, Aurora asserts her right to work. Now Marian asserts her right to live by a morality free of any Christian or social legitimacy: 'Here's a hand shall keep / For ever clean without a marriage-ring' (9.431–2). For all her adulation of Romney, she denies the law which he can confer, and rejects the fathering he offers. Her own child, she once asserted, is '"Not much worse off in being fatherless / Than I was, fathered"' (6.646–7). The law of the father is associated in her memory with the law of violence. Conveniently for Aurora, Marian has good reason to do without.

Once again, Barrett Browning is drawing general conclusions. The legalism of inheritance, property, and blood is present in the best-minded of men. Even Romney, Marian declares, in marrying her, would be haunted by the law of birthright. The children on his knee would never be equal. '"He is ours, the child"' (9.409), she insists with passion, meaning mother's and God's. Fathers, even the best of them, will always have a taint of the other system, a system which excludes women: 'Because men made the laws.' It is interesting to remember that, at this time, by Victorian law, the fallen woman had automatic custody of her children; the legitimate wife did not. '"He is ours, the child"' gains added determination from the fact.

However, it is the actual encounter between Aurora and Marian which represents Barrett Browning's most obvious flouting of the moral law. The 'type of vice' and the type of 'virtue' meet and go together, in a liaison which is stressed at various levels in the text. Simply in terms of narrative, Aurora and Marian defy the conventions of class difference, sexual rivalry, and moral discrimination which should separate them. This social alignment is then doubled by an alignment of voice, by which the virtuous poet and her vicious subject share a first-person narrative which is intimately gendered from the start. The speech of *Aurora Leigh* passes from woman to woman – from Barrett Browning to Aurora to Marian to Lady Waldemar. Each interrupts, and sometimes disproves, the authority of the others. This strategy of shared and relativised speech leaves little room for moral mediations, for charity, or disapprobation. The first person of this dramatic monologue secures her identity, not in opposition to, but in association with, the other women whose speech becomes closely allied to her own.

Thus *Aurora Leigh* asserts an identity of social and aesthetic purpose against the laws of difference between women. To say '"my sister" to the lowest drab' (5.789), as Lady Waldemar must in Romney's phalanstery, is a greeting repeated throughout this text. By the end, Aurora has sistered Marian: '"Come with me, sweetest sister"' (7.117), and even Lady Waldemar is begging to be recognised, as not so bad a sister as she has been judged. The class divisions which Romney so notably fails to bridge are bridged by this implicit sisterhood of women who, although they are rivals for the same man, are drawn to each other from a common bond of sexual powerlessness. As Sally Mitchell has pointed out, upper and middle-class women in the nineteenth century had more in common with working-class women than with the men from their own class (p. 101). The trio of heroines in *Aurora Leigh*, though separated by class, share the common vulnerability of their sex.

The idea of sisterhood as a social liaison between women was given an impetus during the 1850s from a somewhat unexpected quarter. At this time, amid considerable controversy and opposition, the first Anglican Sisterhoods were established. Among those prominent in their support were Mrs Jameson and Florence Nightingale. Often the argument in favour of religious Sisterhoods in fact turns on the question of women's rights to education and to work, an argument which became all the more urgent as, from the middle of the century, the numbers of women rapidly outgrew the numbers of men. Mrs Jameson's lecture on *Sisters of Charity*, given in 1855, is a barely disguised advocacy of some 'well-organised system of work for women'.[8] Florence Nightingale, who gave her support to the new nursing Sisterhoods, roundly answered criticism of convent rules by declaring them preferable to 'the petty grinding tyranny of a good English family'.[9] The first issue of Emily Faithfull's *Victoria Magazine*, which was set up as an enterprise run entirely by women, carried an article unequivocally in favour of Sisterhoods.[10]

Conservative opposition pointed not only to the Popish connotations of convents but also to the risk of moral contamination in those Houses which undertook social work among the poor, the sick, or the fallen. An early article on 'Female Penitentiaries' in *The Quarterly Review* of 1848 gives a foretaste of the arguments to come. In general the reviewer lends his support to penitentiaries, but he balks at the idea of middle-class women undertaking any practical running of them. At this point his language becomes alluringly pious: 'We may express a doubt whether it is advisable for pure-minded women to put themselves in the way of such knowledge of evil as must be learnt in dealing with the fallen members of their sex.'[11] If the 'type of vice' meets the type of 'virtue', moral chaos might be loosed upon the world. The much more likely, and more injurious, contact between 'pure-minded women' and their rather less pure-minded husbands, fathers, brothers, or sons, is a reality which never affects the myth. The scandal lies in the myth, in imagining the pure and the impure, nuns and prostitutes, living together. Such proximity seems a moral contradiction in terms.

II

'And whilst it may truly be urged that unless white could be black and Heaven Hell my experience (thank God) precludes me from hers, I yet don't see why "the Poet mind" should be less able to construct her from its own inner consciousness than a hundred other unknown quantities', wrote Christina Rossetti to Dante Gabriel, who had cautioned his sister against the inclusion of a particular poem in her new volume.[12] 'Under the Rose' is about an unmarried mother and her illegitimate child, a subject which, according to Dante Gabriel, might not be suitable for a woman. Licentious as he was in his own life, his moral protectiveness is roused by the possible impropriety of such a subject for a woman poet. Moral contamination, contrary to all the facts, is transmitted only from woman to woman, even when one of them is an imaginary creation. Christina insisted with due circumlocution on keeping the poem in her volume, and in later editions changed the title, perhaps pointedly, to 'The Iniquity of the Fathers upon the Children'. Her reply at the time, however, clearly acknowledges the source of Dante Gabriel's anxiety: 'Unless white could be black and Heaven Hell.' Between herself and the unmarried mother of her poem there is a gulf as wide as heaven and hell. Yet the very extremity of these moral terms only throws into relief the nature of the task facing '"the Poet mind"'. In one place the bleak opposition between 'white' and 'black', 'Heaven' and 'Hell' might be overcome: '"The Poet mind" should be ... able to construct her from its own inner consciousness.' The 'inner consciousness' of a woman poet, as Dante Gabriel might have suspected, will be especially apt for the task.

Not only Christina's work in the refuge run by the Sisterhood of All Saints during the 1850s brought her into contact with the other sort of woman; her own imagination was unruly enough to throw into doubt and confusion the moral certainties of her own religious temperament. The clash in Rossetti's work between the fixed moral reference of heaven and hell and the derangement of that reference by an imaginative identification so strong it is anarchic, is the hallmark of her greatness as a poet. All her best poems have the intensity of a contradiction between the believer's knowledge and the imagination's desires:

> There's blood between us, love, my love,
> There's father's blood, there's brother's blood;
> And blood's a bar I cannot pass:
> I choose the stairs that mount above,
> Stair after golden skyward stair,
> To city and to sea of glass.
> My lily feet are soiled with mud,
> With scarlet mud which tells a tale
> Of hope that was, of guilt that was,
> Of love that shall not yet avail;
> Alas, my heart, if I could bare
> My heart, this selfsame stain is there.
> (ll.1–12)[13]

Christina Rossetti wrote 'The Convent Threshold' in 1858. Like so many poems about the fallen woman by women poets, it is a dramatic monologue, in which the single speaking voice is both the self's and the other's, both the poet's and the character's. The 'inner consciousness' of the text is a shared one. Such an identification, however, entails, for Rossetti, a larger, terrifying loss of bearings. Her poem sensationally blurs the distinctions, not only between nun and lover, poet and fallen woman, but also, in the end, between heaven and hell. Alice Meynell caught something of the emotional paradox of the work when she called it 'a song of penitence for love that yet praises love more fervently than would a chorus hymeneal'.[14] But it is not only love which is at stake in this poem. On the threshold of the convent, torn between sin and grace, world and refuge, earth and heaven, passion and renunciation, the woman stands on a fine line between moral opposites she can barely keep apart.

Such a border placing becomes radically displacing. This is the threshold, not only of a convent, but of consciousness; it is a consciousness tormented by white and black, heaven and hell, the 'skyward stair' and the 'scarlet mud'. Whatever brought Rossetti's imagination to this pass, 'The Convent Threshold' suggests that to cross from earth to sky, mud to stair, love to grace, lover to nun, is to risk a passage into confusion and hallucination, in which the 'inner consciousness' is wrecked by difference. This poem is rife with a sensuality more lovely, but also more damnable, than anything in Dante Gabriel. Rossetti's female imagination must always bear the cost of its Romantic desires. To 'construct' the other is to yield the 'inner consciousness' to the moral opposite which that other represents.

Thus, although 'The Convent Threshold' seems to offer a choice between going in or staying out, that choice is soon lost in a disturbingly surreal narrative of visions and dreams, past and future, death and life. The threshold is not a single step, but a shifting subliminal line; it is not a place, but a boundary. This poem is full of thresholds, and consequently full of 'faults' of level and register. To cross into the convent is not, for Rossetti, a step into safety, but a nightmare plunge into vague, unconnected territories of the mind.

The penultimate section of the poem, which is spoken from within the convent, luridly contradicts the religious aspiration of the work. Having chosen the 'skyward stair', the nun dreams of being dragged down in mud. Having chosen eternal life, she hallucinates endless death. Having chosen renunciation, she enters a nightmare of lost love. Yet, the language of this section, contrary to all the moral purpose of the poem, sounds like a true homing of Rossetti's imagination:

I tell you what I dreamed last night:
It was not dark, it was not light,
Cold dews had drenched my plenteous hair
Thro' clay; you came to seek me there.
And 'Do you dream of me?' you said.
My heart was dust that used to leap
To you; I answered half asleep:
'My pillow is damp, my sheets are red,
There's a leaden tester to my bed:
Find you a warmer playfellow,
A warmer pillow for your head,
A kinder love to love than mine.'
You wrung your hands; while I, like lead
Crushed downwards thro' the sodden earth:
You smote your hands but not in mirth,
And reeled but were not drunk with wine.
                    (ll.110–25)

'The Convent Threshold' seems to stage a sinner's progress on the way to grace; but in effect the poem founders in a hellish fantasy of decay and death. Distorted time and deranged dreams torment this latter-day Héloïse.

Yet Rossetti's sense of the macabre has a playful shiftiness about it. The thresholds of dream and waking, death and life, are unnervingly unstable in this poem. 'The Convent Threshold' opens up a strange hall of mirrors in which, by some bewildering logic, the living woman dreams of being dead and of dreaming nonetheless of him who asks: '"Do you dream?"' Instead of leading up to heaven, the poem leads downwards and inwards, to that typically Rossettian state of semi-consciousness, which is both heartless and fixated, both capricious and afraid. Certainly some deep and terrible doubt underlies this poem of religious penitence. Its passionate hallucinations seem closer to the imagination of an Emily Brontë than to that of the 'over-scrupulous'[15] Anglican, who, in her later years, would pick up pieces of paper in the street in case the name of God was written on them.[16] 'The "Poet mind" should be ... able to construct her from its own inner consciousness.' The evidence of 'The Convent Threshold' is that the 'inner consciousness' suffers as a result from some profound and brilliant incoherence.

The scene of encounter between fallen and unfallen woman, which 'The Convent Threshold' telescopes into the single figure of the lover-nun, recurs like an obsession in women's poetry. Its most obvious purpose is to forge a forbidden social liaison across the divisions of moral law and sexual myth. In a poem by Dora Greenwell called 'Christina',[17] the fallen speaker remembers her childhood friend Christina, with whom she still feels a sympathetic kinship: 'Across the world-wide gulf betwixt us set / My soul stretched out a bridge.'[18] The poem tells of a chance meeting between two women over the grave of Christina's dead child. In an interesting substitution of identities, Christina urges her fallen friend to come home, and take the place of her child: 'I call thee not my Sister, as of old' (but) 'Daughter' (p. 13). However, the 'world-wide gulf' proves too wide to cross, and the unnamed Penitent returns to die in a refuge.

The religious sentimentality of Greenwell's poem keeps it from being anything more than a failed gesture of philanthropy. However, for other poets, the encounter between fallen and un-fallen achieves the intensity of a recognition scene. The political sister is the psychic double, the social underworld into which the fallen disappear becoming associated with the subconscious in which the fallen re-emerge as the other self.

In a strange poem by Adelaide Procter, 'A Legend of Provence', a young nun runs off with a soldier, who then betrays and abandons her. After many years she returns to her convent, only to meet her double at the door:

> She raised her head; she saw – she seemed to know –
> A face that came from long, long years ago:
> Herself.[19]

This is not a spectre from the past, but a real, other self, who has been living, all the while, in an unfallen state personated by the Virgin Mary. At the convent door, the two halves come together. Once again, the threshold of the convent seems to be a threshold of the self, marking a split of consciousness which echoes the moral di-visions of the age. If the place of the Romantic imagination is that of a border-line between the known and the unknown, the border-line of the Victorian female imagination is the same, but fraught with social and sexual anxieties.

In *Aurora Leigh* the meeting between Aurora and Marian, as critics have noted,[20] has all the emotional urgency and narrative doubling of a recognition scene:

> What face is that?
> What a face, what a look, what a likeness! Full on mine

The sudden blow of it came down, till all
My blood swam, my eyes dazzled.
(6.231–4)

Marian returns like the dead, but also like the repressed. When the two women finally meet, their uncanny doubling movements suggest a twinning of purpose beyond all the charities of social aid. First Aurora leads, and Marian 'followed closely where I went, / As if I led her by a narrow plank / Across devouring waters' (6.481–3). But a few lines later, as the moral authority is transferred to Marian 'she led / The way, and I, as by a narrow plank / Across devouring waters, followed her' (6.500–2). These 'devouring waters' are another 'world-wide gulf'. Unlike Greenwell, however, Barrett Browning goes across. That it is a crossing both ways emphasises the egalitarian nature of the relationship. This is not rescue work. It is self recognition.

Such doubling effects are taken a stage further in Rossetti's 'Goblin Market'. Not only are the two sisters, Lizzie and Laura, hard to distinguish; they also enact the same drama though with different intentions. Laura pays for goblin fruit with a curl of her hair, and pines away. Lizzie gets fruit without paying, and so revives her sister. 'The moral is hardly intelligible', Alice Meynell complained.[21] Rossetti herself, it seems, did not intend a moral.[22] Certainly, as Jerome McGann has argued, a 'middle-class ideology of love and marriage' underlies the story,[23] and the cautionary figure of the fallen woman, Jeanie; 'who for joys brides hope to have / Fell sick and died' (ll.314–15), casts a realistic shadow across the fairy tale.[24] Nonetheless, 'Goblin Market' singularly fails to press home the moral of Jeanie. Laura knows she should not loiter and look, but she does. Lizzie knows she should not take without paying, but she does. The only rule pertaining at the end is that sisters should stick together. Only together will they be a match for the goblins. Jeanie died, not because she ate the fruit, but because she had no sister to rescue her.

If 'Goblin Market' is a feminised myth of Christian redemption, it is redemption through a willed confusion of fallen and unfallen. 'Undone in mine undoing / And ruined in my ruin', Laura wails (ll.482–3). Yet, it is precisely through this shared fall, this transgression of the rule of difference, that sisterhood becomes a match for brotherhood, and the goblins are beaten at their own tricks. 'We may express a doubt whether it is advisable for pure-minded women to put themselves in the way of such knowledge of evil as must be learnt in dealing with the fallen members of their sex', wrote the *Quarterly* reviewer. Such 'knowledge of evil', for Christina Rossetti, is not only advisable, but also awakening and saving. Lizzie, the rescuing sister, goes 'At twilight, halted by the brook: / And for the first time in her life / Began to listen and look' (ll.326–8). The two girls desire, loiter and look, in a gesture that combines a Romantic hovering on the threshold of strange knowledge with the purposeful delay of the streetwalker.

In the end, it seems that Rossetti brilliantly displaces the message of this poem onto the two terms of the title. 'Goblin Market' is the place of magic and marketing. Far from being representers of the moral seriousness of the Fall, these mischievous and childish creatures play by the rules of magic and money. They thus uncannily echo the commodity morality of nineteenth-century myths of sexuality. Moral downfall is linked to market exchange. By not paying, Lizzie tricks the market and resists not so much the fruit as the law by which fruit turns to poison because, Rossetti seems to say, goblins made the laws. There is a sense in which 'Goblin Market' hoodwinks the moralisers as well.

'After much hesitation and many misgivings, we have undertaken to speak of so dismal and delicate a matter', writes W.R. Greg.[25] He begins his 1850 article on 'Prostitution' with elaborate cautions and apologies. Even William Lecky slips at times into coy circumlocutions: 'That unhappy being whose very name is a shame to speak.' When it comes to speaking, 'shame' is a constant obstruction. When it comes to women speaking, a whole complicated magic of sin and contamination comes into play. 'I am grateful to you as a woman for having so treated such a subject', wrote Barrett Browning to Elizabeth Gaskell, on the publication of *Ruth*, as if she were speaking as one of the fallen herself.[26] Certainly, the connection between writing and sinning is a close and involved one. The doubling of sisters in these texts hints at the way in which the poet is verbally implicated in the fall. Writing and sexuality double each other. 'There has always been a vague connection', writes Simone de Beauvoir, 'between prostitution and art.'[27] Such a connection is both more probable and more inadmissible when the artist is a woman. A sign of the sheer inhibitory power of the taboo imposed on women is that, as late as 1929, Virginia Woolf, in *A Room of One's Own*, looks forward to a time when the woman writer will be able to meet 'the courtesan' and 'the harlot' without 'that self-

consciousness in the presence of "sin" which is the legacy of our
sexual barbarity'.[28] Woolf looks forward, but she might also have
looked back.

One voice from the nineteenth century which speaks out with
brave shamelessness on the subject of the fallen is a voice which has
been unaccountably lost to the poetic canon. 'By-the-by', wrote
Christina Rossetti to a friend, 'did not Mr Gladstone omit from his
list of poetesses the one name which *I* incline to feel as by far the
most formidable of those known to me.'[29] The name she gave was
that of Augusta Webster.

Webster's poem, 'A Castaway', was published in 1870, in her
volume *Portraits*, and was almost certainly known to Rossetti. A
long dramatic monologue, spoken by a relatively high-class courtesan who muses on the strange course of her life, the poem becomes
a magnificent and panoramic indictment of contemporary society.
Webster makes the connection between the moral and the mercantile overtly and persistently, so that all trades are levelled to the
same kind of value: that of profit and loss. In a narrative that is
strikingly free of myths and metaphors, the Castaway judges the
ways of the world. Hers is a stark and literal language, a language
of the market without any goblins:

> And, for me,
> I say let no one be above her trade;
> I own my kindredship with any drab
> Who sells herself as I, although she crouch
> In fetid garrets and I have a home
> All velvet and marqueterie and pastilles,
> Although she hide her skeleton in rags
> And I set fashions and wear cobweb lace;
> The difference lies but in my choicer ware,
> That I sell beauty and she ugliness;
> Our traffic's one – I'm no sweet slaver-tongue
> To gloze upon it and explain myself
> A sort of fractious angel misconceived –
> Our traffic's one: I own it. And what then?
> I know of worse that are called honourable.
> Our lawyers, who with noble eloquence
> And virtuous outbursts lie to hang a man,
> Or lie to save him, which way goes the fee:
> Our preachers, gloating on your future hell
> For not believing what they doubt themselves:
> Our doctors, who sort poisons out by chance
> And wonder how they'll answer, and grow rich:

Our journalists, whose business is to fib
And juggle truths and falsehoods to and fro:
Our tradesmen, who must keep unspotted names
And cheat the least like stealing that they can:
Our – all of them, the virtuous worthy men
Who feed on the world's follies, vices, wants,
And do their businesses of lies and shams
Honestly, reputably, while the world
Claps hands and cries 'good luck', which of their trades,
Their honourable trades, barefaced like mine,
All secrets brazened out, would shew more white?[30]

'A Castaway' presents the fact of prostitution bare of any myth or magic. Its causes are unremittingly social, and so are its effects – penury, poor education, an imbalance of the numbers of women against those of men, and a shortage of work for both sexes. Webster, who was a lifelong campaigner for women's suffrage (though she failed to convert Christina Rossetti to her cause) as well as for women's education, issues a moving reminder in this poem of how the education of girls is stinted to pay for the training of their luckier brothers: 'The lesson girls with brothers all must learn, / To do without' (p. 56). Never having been fitted for anything except marriage, what can girls do to keep alive except carry out that trade which so darkly resembles marriage, and yet is its moral opposite.

Most of the fallen women who play any prominent role in nine-teenth-century literature are only variations on the real theme. Seduced, raped, betrayed, or simply fickle, they are either innocent girls led astray, or sensational adulteresses. Their actions thus remain largely within the parameters of romance. They are moti-vated by feeling, not by economic exigency. But Augusta Webster gives us the professional. As a result, she can point to the real un-mentionable of Victorian prostitution: the male client. The endlessly elaborated discourse on the tantalising secret of female sexuality, like any other taboo, in fact serves to disguise another, more deep-seated taboo which creates the silence on the other side of all this speech. Sexuality is not just, as Michel Foucault claims, the well ex-ploited 'secret' of the modern age;[31] woman's sexuality provides a gratifying decoy from the thing that is no secret at all and yet remains curiously unspoken. Gladstone, who was himself, like Dickens, a keen rescuer of fallen women, inclined to take them home to talk with his wife, confessed in his diary that his motives were suspect: he feared in himself some '"dangerous curiosity & filthiness of spirit"'.[32] By writing about the professional courtesan,

Webster dares to mention the men who in reality provide the rationale of prostitution. These are not the figures of literary romance,
dark seducers or passionate rakes. These are, quite simply, other
women's husbands, for whom the illicit is routine:

> And whom do I hurt more than they? as much?
> The wives? Poor fools, what do I take from them
> Worth crying for or keeping? If they knew
> What their fine husbands look like seen by eyes
> That may perceive there are more men than one!
> But, if they can, let them just take the pains
> To keep them: 'tis not such a mighty task
> To pin an idiot to your apron-strings;
> And wives have an advantage over us,
> (The good and blind ones have) the smile or pout
> Leaves them no secret nausea at odd times.
> Oh, they could keep their husbands if they cared,
> But 'tis an easier life to let them go,
> And whimper at it for morality.
>
> (pp. 39–40)

Webster exposes, with scornful simplicity, the other hidden and
forbidden topic which lies behind the Victorians' obsession with
fallen women. If men are the arbiters of virtue and vice, they are
also the go-betweens. For them the passage from one to the other is
a secret passage between separate spheres. But for women the difference is not so certain. The passage which divides the 'type of
virtue' from the type of 'vice' can turn into a mirror, to reflect the
self. The very nature of womanhood is split by a mirror stage, man-
dated by man's law. Thus, the doubleness of the social order serves
to match a doubleness within. The very nature of female subjectivity is founded and wrecked on this law of opposites. Not only is the
pure woman divided from 'the other'; the very self is split from its
own history.

At one point, the Castaway remembers her girlhood:

> So long since:
> And now it seems a jest to talk of me
> As if I could be one with her, of me
> Who am ... me.
>
> (p. 36)

When she looks in the mirror it seems to reproduce the doubleness.
Between 'me' and 'me' falls the shadow of the moral law. Against

that law, however, the dramatic monologue asserts its single voice. The pronoun doubles poet and outcast, speaker and actor, in a drama which is transgressively sistering from the start. The voice of the poem is both act and consciousness, both object and subject, both 'me' and 'me'. The gender-specific nature of this poet's voice makes a common cause of the fact of womanhood.

One of the saddest poems on the fallen woman is Amy Levy's 'Magdalen'. In reality a poem of seduction, its note of bitter and sceptical despair as the girl prepares to die in a refuge is a sign of the continuing power of the myth as late as the 1880s. Like Rossetti before her, Levy finds in the event of the fall a mockery of all creeds and of all ethical systems:

> Death do I trust no more than life.
> For one thing is like one arrayed,
> And there is neither false nor true;
> But in a hideous masquerade
> All things dance on, the ages through.
> And good is evil, evil good;
> Nothing is known or understood
> Save only Pain.[33]

Levy was only twenty-eight when, five years after the publication of this poem, she killed herself in her parents' house without explanation. Her 'Magdalen' is an immature poem, and its language is too limply melancholy; it does, nonetheless, betray the strain of that social morality which founds its whole system of good and evil on the sexual propriety of women.

Charlotte Mew – a poet who was, in many ways, herself a last Victorian – was one of the last poets to write about the Magdalen. In 1894, Mew published a story in *The Yellow Book* called 'Passed', describing an encounter between the narrator and a destitute young girl whom she meets in a church, and whose sister has killed herself following some sexual betrayal. Behind the vivid melodrama of Mew's language, the narrative traces a rather interesting psychological story. The moment when the narrator takes the girl in her arms is one of extreme bewilderment and hallucination. Thinking of her home, she finds it 'desolate'; imagining a mirror, she sees no 'reflection'; opening a book, she finds the pages 'blank'.[34] All the usual signs of her sheltered identity have been erased. In this encounter with the homeless, distraught girl, she seems to have lost her own self. In terror, she cruelly throws the girl

off, and makes her escape; but when, many months later, she
glimpses the girl on the arm of the same man who betrayed her
sister, the meaning of the encounter flashes on her mind. The last
lines of the story confirm the suspicion that the girl is the speaker's
lost reflection, her alter ego, forfeited to the differences of moral
law and class division: 'I heard a laugh, mounting to a cry. ... Did it
proceed from some defeated angel? or the woman's mouth? or
mine? (p. 78).

The 'woman's mouth or mine?' The sound of that confused
'laugh' or 'cry' comes from an 'inner consciousness' which is
woman's, in general, not hers or mine, but both. Sexual morality
and social difference have split the very nature of female subjectivity. For women in the nineteenth century, the Romantic split, 'I is
another', carries the added penalty of a sexual transgression: 'I is
the other.' The mirror, for women, is also a gulf. Yet to pass from
one side of the gulf to the other is to undertake an act of social
protest which is also an act of daring self-recovery.

By the time Mew came to write her own dramatic monologue of
the fallen woman, the schizophrenia of Victorian morality had
largely been overcome. 'Madeleine in Church' was published in
1916, and is, in spite of its title, an uninhibited love poem. The idea
of the fall as a psycho-sexual event which splits subjectivity into
'me' and 'me' is missing in it. Instead, its rich evocation of passion
affirms that the self is consistent with itself, and coherent with its
history:

> We are what we are: when I was half a child I could not sit
> Watching black shadows on green lawns and red carnations burning
> in the sun,
> Without paying so heavily for it
> That joy and pain, like any mother and her unborn child were
> almost one.
> I could hardly bear
> The dreams upon the eyes of white geraniums in the dusk,
> The thick, close voice of musk,
> The jessamine music on the thin night air,
> Or, sometimes, my own hands about me anywhere –
> The sight of my own face (for it was lovely then) even the scent of
> my own hair,
> Oh! there was nothing, nothing that did not sweep to the high seat
> Of laughing gods, and then blow down and beat
> My soul into the highway dust, as hoofs do the dropped roses of the
> street.

> I think my body was my soul,
>   And when we are made thus
>   Who shall control
> Our hands, our eyes, the wandering passion of our feet.
> (pp. 23–4)

This poem, in some ways, marks the end of a tradition. By the time women come to write openly about sexual passion, the figure of the fallen woman ceases to haunt their imaginations. For she is the ghost of what has been forbidden, denied, divided. She is the Victorian woman poet's familiar, the double that returns like herself, the other that beats against the internalised social barriers of the mind. She is the vivid emblem of a social and sexual secrecy which is still clamorous with self-discovery.

The figure of the fallen woman is also, however, a sign for women of the power of writing. Her wandering, outcast state seductively expresses the poet's restlessness and desire. To summon her is not only to assert a political purpose which breaks the moral law, but also to claim the power of writing as necessarily free of control, of rule. The fallen woman is the muse, the beloved – the lost sister, mother, daughter, whose self was one's own. In poetry, above all, the social gesture of reclamation and solidarity becomes also an imaginative gesture of integration and identity.

Barrett Browning, at the beginning of this tradition, invokes the fallen woman, not only as her sister, but also as her muse. Only if the poet takes the 'part' of the other, and speaks with her cries, will she find her own voice. The political other is the poetic self. To speak from the 'inner consciousness' of being a woman is to speak from that which has been divided, disenfranchised, but which, for that very reason, needs to be recovered. The 'depths of womanhood' may have been kept 'out of sight', but only from such 'depths' can the poet challenge men's laws:

> 'Therefore,' the voice said, 'shalt thou write
>   My curse to-night.
> Some women weep and curse, I say
> (And no one marvels), night and day.
>
> 'And thou shalt take their part to-night,
>   Weep and write.
> A curse from the depths of womanhood
> Is very salt, and bitter, and good'
> ('A Curse for a Nation', ll.41–8)[35]

NOTES

[Angela Leighton has conducted pioneering research into the broad field of nineteenth-century poetry by women. Her study, *Victorian Women Poets: Writing against the Heart* (Hemel Hempstead, 1992), is a standard work of reference. Combining biographical information with exacting analyses of a wide range of poems, Leighton's research defines the contours of a changing tradition of poetry that begins with Felicia Hemans and ends with Charlotte Mew.

The present essay is the first sustained exploration of how and why the controversial issue of female prostitution preoccupied many women poets over the course of four decades. To comprehend the broader cultural context of women's responses to debates about prostitution in the Victorian period, readers should consult Judith Walkowitz, *Prostitution and Victorian Society: Women, Class, and the State* (New York, 1980), and Lynda Nead, *Myths of Sexuality: Representations of Women in Victorian Britain* (Oxford, 1988), chs 3–5. Ed.]

1. Elizabeth Barrett Browning, *Casa Guidi Windows*, in *The Complete Works of Elizabeth Barrett Browning*, ed. Charlotte Porter and Helen A. Clarke, 6 vols (New York, 1900), III, pp. 249–313.

2. Quoted in Sally Mitchell, *The Fallen Angel: Chastity, Class, and Women's Reading 1835–1880* (Bowling Green, 1981), p. 340.

3. Vern Bullough and Bonnie Bullough, *Women and Prostitution: A Social History* (New York, 1987), p. 197.

4. *The London Journal of Flora Tristan 1842 or The Aristocracy and the Working Class of England*, trans. Jean Hawkes (London, 1982), p. 83.

5. Frederick Engels, *The Origin of the Family, Private Property and the State*, introduced by Eleanor Leacock (London, 1972), pp. 125–46.

6. William Lecky, *History of European Morals*, 2 vols in one (New York, 1855), II, p. 283.

7. Barrett Browning, *Aurora Leigh and Other Poems*, introduced by Cora Kaplan (London, 1978).

8. Mrs [Anna] Jameson, *Sisters of Charity: Catholic and Protestant, Abroad and at Home* (London, 1855), p. 13.

9. Quoted in A.M. Allchin, *The Silent Rebellion: Anglican Religious Communities 1845–1900* (London, 1958), p. 115.

10. Rev. F.D. Maurice, 'On Sisterhoods', *Victorian Magazine*, 1 (1863), 289–301.

11. 'Female Penitentiaries', *Quarterly Review*, 83 (1848), 375–6.

12. Christina Rossetti to Dante Gabriel Rossetti, 13 March 1865, in *Three Rossettis: Unpublished Letters to and from Dante Gabriel, Christina, William*, ed. Janet Camp Troxell (Cambridge, MA, 1937), p. 143.

13. Christina Rossetti, 'The Convent Threshold', in *The Complete Poems of Christina Rossetti*, ed. R.W. Crump, 3 vols (Baton Rouge, LA, 1979–90), I, pp. 61–5.

14. Alice Meynell, 'Christina Rossetti', *New Review*, NS 12 (1895), 203.

15. William Michael Rossetti, 'Memoir', in *The Poetical Works of Christina Georgina Rossetti* (London, 1904), p. 1xvii.

16. Katharine Tynan, *Twenty-Five Years: Reminiscences* (London, 1913), p. 161.

17. The poem was written in 1851, almost certainly before Greenwell had met Rossetti or had read any of her poems.

18. Dora Greenwell, 'Christina', in *Poems* (Edinburgh, 1861), p. 4.

19. Adelaide Anne Procter, 'A Legend of Provence', in *The Poems of Adelaide A. Procter* (Boston, 1877), p. 189.

20. See, for instance, Dolores Rosenblum, 'Face to Face: Elizabeth Barrett Browning's *Aurora Leigh* and Nineteenth-Century Poetry', *Victorian Studies*, 26 (1983), 321–38; and Angela Leighton, *Elizabeth Barrett Browning* (Brighton, 1986), ch. 7.

21. Meynell, 'Christina Rossetti', in *Prose and Poetry*, introduced by V. Sackville-West (London, 1947), p. 147.

22. Note to 'Goblin Market', by William Michael Rossetti, in *The Poetical Works of Christina Georgina Rossetti*, p. 459.

23. Jerome J. McGann, 'Christina Rossetti's Poems: A New Edition and a Revaluation', *Victorian Studies*, 23 (1980), 248.

24. Christina Rossetti, 'Goblin Market', *The Complete Poems of Christina Rossetti*, I. pp. 11–26.

25. [W.R. Greg] 'Prostitution', *Westminster Review*, 53 (1850), 448.

26. *Letters Addressed to Mrs Gaskell by Celebrated Contemporaries*, ed. Ross D. Waller (Manchester, 1935), p. 42.

27. Simone de Beauvoir, *The Second Sex*, trans, H.M. Parshley (Harmondsworth, 1972), p. 579.

28. Virginia Woolf, *A Room of One's Own* (Harmondsworth, 1945), p. 88.

29. Christina Rossetti to William Michael Rossetti, 22 January 1890, in *The Family Letters of Christina Georgina Rossetti*, ed. William Michael Rossetti (London, 1908), p. 175.

30. Augusta Webster, 'A Castaway', in *Portraits*, third edn (London, 1893), pp. 38–9.

31. Michel Foucault, *The History of Sexuality: An Introduction*, trans, Robert Hurley (Harmondsworth, 1981), p. 35.

32. *The Gladstone Diaries*, ed. M.R.D. Foot and H.G.C. Matthew (Oxford, 1968–86), IV, p. 41.

33. Amy Levy, 'Magdalen', in *A Minor Poet and Other Verse* (London, 1884), p. 71.

34. Charlotte Mew, 'Passed', in *Collected Poems and Prose*, ed. Val Warner (Manchester, 1981), p. 71. Hereafter this edition is cited by page number in the text.

35. Barrett Browning, 'A Curse for a Nation', *Aurora Leigh and Other Poems*, pp. 401–6.

Further Reading

The critical reconstruction of the detailed shape and pattern of poetry by Victorian women is still very much in progress. The fact that there is no annotated edition of the complete works of a writer as distinguished as Elizabeth Barrett Browning testifies to how much more solid editorial scholarship needs to be undertaken in this neglected field of inquiry. It is, indeed, surprising to discover how little research has been conducted on the substantial canon of poetry by a figure as well-known as Emily Brontë. Even if Christina Rossetti's poetry has been published in a distinguished variorum edition, her prose works have long been out of print. Several women poets whose work displays special intellectual strengths and creative ambition – Mathilde Blind, Caroline Clive, Mary Coleridge, Michael Field, Amy Levy, Adelaide Anne Procter, and Augusta Webster immediately come to mind – have yet to receive the critical and editorial attention they surely deserve. But, as this volume shows, there have in recent decades been significant scholarly contributions to our knowledge of the diverse kinds of poetry – devotional, dramatic, lyric, epic – produced by women writers between 1830 and 1900. Two major anthologies currently in preparation – one by Isobel Armstrong and Joseph Bristow, another by Angela Leighton and Margaret Reynolds – will assuredly throw much-needed light on the range and scope of the available printed sources.

The notes accompanying each of the essays in this volume indicate which books and essays have exerted greatest influence on our current critical understanding of Victorian women poets. Methods of feminist critical inquiry have certainly led the field. Especially significant in this respect are the relevant short sections and chapters in Ellen Moers, *Literary Women* (New York: Doubleday, 1977), Sandra M. Gilbert and Susan Gubar, *The Madwoman in the Attic: The Woman Writer and the Nineteenth-Century Literary Imagination* (New Haven: Yale University Press, 1979), and the relevant essays collected in Cora Kaplan, *Sea Changes: Culture and Feminism* (London: Verso, 1986). Such work has enabled several major studies to emerge, notably Dolores Rosenblum, *Christina Rossetti: The Poetry of Endurance* (Carbondale: Southern Illinois University Press, 1986), Helen Cooper, *Elizabeth Barrett Browning: Woman and Artist* (Chapel Hill: University of North Carolina Press, 1988), Dorothy Mermin, *Elizabeth Barrett Browning: The Origins of a New Poetry* (Chicago: University of

246

Chicago Press, 1989) and Angela Leighton, *Victorian Women Poets: Writing against the Heart* (Hemel Hempstead: Harvester–Wheatsheaf, 1982). Leighton's study provides the most complete picture to date of the achievements of women poets writing at different moments within the Victorian period. Individual chapters examine the work of Felicia Hemans, Letitia Elizabeth Landon, Elizabeth Barrett Browning, Christina Rossetti, Augusta Webster, Michael Field, Alice Meynell, and Charlotte Mew. Leighton's book broadens the range of writings explored in Margaret Homans's pioneering study, *Women Writers and Poetic Identity: Dorothy Wordsworth, Emily Brontë, and Emily Dickinson* (Princeton, NJ: Princeton University Press, 1980), an extract from which is published in this volume, pp. 84–107. Homans's study of Brontë's poetry can be usefully compared to the analysis presented in Irene Tayler's *Holy Ghosts: The Male Muses of Emily and Charlotte Brontë* (New York: Columbia University Press, 1990).

Two short and stimulating essays on Emily Brontë's poetry are Emma Francis, 'Is Emily Brontë a Woman? Femininity, Feminism and the Paranoid Critical Subject', and Kathryn Burlinson, '"What Language Can Utter the Feeling": Identity in the Poetry of Emily Brontë', both in Philip Shaw and Peter Stockwell (eds), *Subjectivity and Literature from the Romantics to the Present Day* (London: Pinter, 1991), pp. 28–48. Francis's essay provides the most sustained exploration of Brontë's work in the light of modern critical theory.

The corpus of feminist-inspired criticism of Elizabeth Barrett Browning's poetry has extended rapidly in the 1980s and 1990s, often focusing on *Aurora Leigh*. Particularly influential have been Cora Kaplan's introduction to her edition of *Aurora Leigh and Other Poems* (London: Women's Press, 1978), pp. 5–36, and Dolores Rosenblum, 'Face to Face: Elizabeth Barrett Browning's *Aurora Leigh* and Nineteenth-Century Poetry', *Victorian Studies*, 26 (1983), 321–38. Sustained studies of Barrett Browning's *magnum opus* can be found in Rod Edmond, *Affairs of the Hearth: Victorian Poetry and Domestic Narrative* (London: Routledge, 1988) and Amanda S. Anderson, *Tainted Souls and Painted Faces: The Rhetoric of Fallenness in Victorian Culture* (Ithaca, NY: Cornell University Press, 1993) – both of which examine aspects of the Victorian 'woman question' in this poem. Hardly as much attention has been given to Barrett Browning's other substantial works, such as *Sonnets from the Portuguese* and *Casa Guidi Windows*. One important exception, in this respect, is Dorothy Mermin, 'The Female Poet and the Embarrassed Reader: Elizabeth Barrett Browning's *Sonnets from the Portuguese*', *ELH*, 48 (1981), 351–67. One of the few essays to employ psychoanalytic categories to analyse structures of desire in Barrett Browning's work is John Fletcher, 'Poetry, Gender, and Primal Fantasy', in Victor Burgin, James Donald, and Cora Kaplan (eds), *Formations of Fantasy* (London: Methuen, 1986). For comprehensive overviews of Barrett Browning's large canon of poetry, see Angela Leighton, *Elizabeth Barrett Browning* (Brighton: Harvester, 1986), and ch. 3, *Victorian Women Poets: Writing against the Heart* (Hemel Hempstead: Harvester–Wheatsheaf, 1992).

Since the 1970s, Christina Rossetti's 'Goblin Market' has received more critical attention than any of her other poems. The richness of its religious, sexual, and economic meanings has prompted some very exacting readings. Notable among them are Dorothy Mermin, 'Heroic Sisterhood in *Goblin Market*', *Victorian Poetry*, 21 (1983), 107–18, Rod Edmond, 'Who Needs Men? Christina Rossetti's *Goblin Market*', in his *Affairs of the Hearth: Victorian Poetry and Domestic Narrative* (London: Routledge, 1988), and Elizabeth Campbell, 'Of Mothers and Merchants: Female Economics in Christina Rossetti's "Goblin Market"', *Victorian Studies*, 33:3 (1990), 393–410. Isobel Armstrong writes on the transformation of Christina Rossetti's reputation in the 1950s for the 'simplicity' and 'delicacy' of her work to a poet whose writing in the 1970s and 1980s benefited from feminist rereading in 'Christina Rossetti: Diary of a Feminist Reading', in Sue Roe (ed.), *Women Reading Women's Writing* (Brighton: Harvester, 1987). Notable recent critical explorations of representations of femininity in Rossetti's poetry are Sharon Smulders, 'Woman's Enfranchisement in Christina Rossetti's Poetry', *Texas Studies in Language and Literature*, 34:4 (1992), 568–88, and Kathy Alexis Psomiades, 'Feminine and Portic Privacy in Christina Rossetti's "Autumn" and "A Royal Princess"', *Victorian Poetry*, 31 (1993), 187–202. A substantial collection of essays that situates Rossetti's poetry in relation to a range of contexts – including the significance of the devotional tradition to which much of her work belongs – is David A. Kent (ed.), *The Achievement of Christina Rossetti* (Ithaca, NY: Cornell University Press, 1987). As a counter to some of the claims made by Jerome J. McGann in 'The Religious Poetry of Christina Rossetti' (reprinted in this volume, pp. 167–88), it is useful to consult Linda E. Marshall, 'What the Dead Are Doing Underground: Hades and Heaven in the Writings of Christina Rossetti', *Victorian Newsletter*, 72 (1987), 55–9. Equally informative is Dolores Rosenblum, 'Christina Rossetti's Religious Poetry: Watching, Looking, Keeping Vigil', *Victorian Poetry*, 19 (1981), 33–49. Complementary to McGann's historicist methods is Antony H. Harrison, *Christina Rossetti in Context* (Brighton: Harvester, 1988). Harrison's detailed study examines Rossetti's position within debates about the Pre-Raphaelite movement, aestheticism, and Victorian devotional poetry.

The poetry of Emily Brontë, Elizabeth Barrett Browning, and Christina Rossetti has been the subject of major editorial work. Most recently, Janet Gezari has edited Brontë's *Complete Poems* (Harmondsworth: Penguin, 1992). This edition, which contains copious explanatory notes, adopts different editorial procedures from C.W. Hatfield's *Complete Poems of Emily Jane Brontë* (New York, Columbia University Press, 1941). Gezari's detailed introduction discusses the specific problems involved in selecting a copy text for Brontë's poems in manuscript. It should be noted that Charlotte Brontë's extensive corpus of poetry has received exacting critical attention in recent years, first by Tom Winnifrith in *The Poems of Charlotte Brontë: A New Annotated and Enlarged Edition of the Shakepeare Head Brontë* (Oxford: Blackwell, 1984), and second by Victor A. Neufeldt, *The Poems of Charlotte Brontë: A New Text and Commentary* (New York, Garland, 1985).

An annotated edition of Barrett Browning's complete poetical works is sorely needed. Margaret Reynolds's variorum edition of *Aurora Leigh* by Elizabeth Barrett Browning (Athens, OH: Ohio University Press, 1992) has done more than justice to this major poem. Indeed, Reynolds has accomplished one of most impressive feats of scholarship in recent Victorian studies, and she furnishes this meticulously detailed edition with very full critical and editorial introductions, which include masses of information about the publishing history, reception, and critical tradition surrounding Barrett Browning's *magnum opus*.

R.W. Crump has edited an indispensable variorum edition of *The Complete Poems of Christina Rossetti*, 3 vols (Baton Rouge, LA: Louisiana State University Press, 1979–90), although the explanatory notes are limited. Crump is also the editor of two helpful bibliographies: *Christina Rossetti: A Reference Guide* (Boston: G.K. Hall, 1976), and *Charlotte and Emily Brontë, 1846–1915: A Reference Guide* (Boston: G.K. Hall, 1982). An Oxford Authors' edition of selected poems by Christina Rossetti is being prepared by Emma Francis.

Given the unabated popularity of biography, it is not surprising that Emily Brontë, Elizabeth Barrett Browning, and Christina Rossetti have had many different versions of their lives published over the years. Winifred Gérin's *Emily Brontë: A Biography* (London: Oxford University Press, 1971) is still the definitive work, despite several successors including Edward Chitham, *A Life of Emily Brontë* (Oxford: Blackwell, 1987). Margaret Forster's distinguished *Elizabeth Barrett Browning* (London: Chatto & Windus, 1988) pays scant attention to her subject's poetry while probing many of the less discussed aspects of Barrett Browning's personal life. No uncertain controversy has raged around the life of Christina Rossetti. Lona Mosk Packer's weighty *Christina Rossetti* (Berkeley, CA: University of California Press, 1963), which draws on a great deal of archival material, makes the unsubstantiated assertion that her subject was romantically involved with the poet and painter, William Bell Scott. Subsequent biographers, notably Georgina Battiscombe in *Christina Rossetti: A Divided Life* (London: Constable, 1982), have contested Packer's hypothesis. A more recent biography, *Learning Not to Be First* by Kathleen Jones (Oxford: Oxford University Press, 1992), interweaves life and work in a readable manner. To mark the centenary of Rossetti's death, Jan Marsh has published a substantial and detailed account of the poet's life: *Christina Rossetti: A Literary Biography* (London: Jonathan Cape, 1994).

Notes on Contributors

Isobel Armstrong is Professor of English at Birkbeck College, University of London. She is the author of several major studies of nineteenth-century poetry, including *Victorian Scrutinies: Reviews of Poetry 1830–1870* (1972), *Language as Living Form in Nineteenth-Century Poetry* (1982), and *Victorian Poetry: Poetry, Poetics and Politics* (1993). She has also edited *The Major Victorian Poets: Reconsiderations* (1969), *New Feminist Discourses: Critical Essays on Theories and Texts* (1992), and (with Helen Carr) a journal, *Women: A Cultural Review*.

Deirdre David, Professor of English at Temple University, is author of *Intellectual Women and Victorian Patriarchy: Harriet Martineau, Elizabeth Barrett Browning, George Eliot* (1987), and recent essays on Victorian imperialism. Her forthcoming book is entitled '*Grilled Alive in Calcutta': Women, Empire, and Victorian Writing*, a study of the part played by women in the writing of the Victorian colonial and imperial nation.

Sandra M. Gilbert, a Professor of English at the University of California, Davis, has, with Susan Gubar (a Professor of English at Indiana University), co-authored *The Madwoman in the Attic: The Woman Writer and the Nineteenth-Century Literary Imagination* (1979), and *No Man's Land: The Place of the Woman Writer in the Twentieth Century*, vols 1, 2, and 3: *The War of the Words* (1987), *Sexchanges* (1989) and *Letters from the Front*. In addition, Gilbert and Gubar have co-edited *Shakespeare's Sisters: Feminist Essays on Women Poets* (1979) and *The Norton Anthology of Literature by Women: The Tradition in English* (1985).

Elizabeth K. Helsinger, Professor of English at the University of Chicago, is the author of *Ruskin and the Art of the Beholder* (1982) and co-author (with Robin Sheets and William Veeder) of *The Woman Question: Society and Literature in Britain and America, 1837–1883* (1983, 1989). She is completing *Rural Scenes and National Representation: Britain 1820–1850*, and working on a collection of essays on art, gender, and commodity culture in Victorian Britain.

Margaret Homans is Professor of English at Yale University, where she also chairs the Women's Studies Program. She is the author of *Women Writers and Poetic Identity: Dorothy Wordsworth, Emily Brontë, and Emily Dickinson* (1980), *Bearing the Word: Language and Female Experience in Nineteenth-Century Women's Writing* (1986), essays on nineteenth-century literature and culture, and essays on contemporary feminist theory. She is currently working on a book on Queen Victoria and Victorian culture.

Angela Leighton is a Reader in English at the University of Hull. She is the author of *Shelley and the Sublime* (1984), *Elizabeth Barrett Browning* (1986), and *Victorian Women Poets: Writing against the Heart* (1992), as well as articles on Romantic and Victorian poetry.

Jerome J. McGann is the John Stewart Bryan Professor of English, University of Virginia. He is currently designing and building *The Complete Writings and Pictures of Dante Gabriel Rossetti: A Hypermedia Research Archive.*

Dorothy Mermin, Professor of English at Cornell University, is the author of *The Audience in the Poem: Five Victorian Poets* (1983), *Elizabeth Barrett Browning: The Origins of a New Poetry* (1989), and *Godiva's Ride: Women of Letters in England 1830–1880* (1993).

Index

Helsinger, Elizabeth K., 24–6, 28
n7, 189–222
Hemans, Felicia, 4, 32, 37, 60
Henderson, Philip, 106 n3
Herbert, George, 74, 167–8, 173–4
Héring, J., 187 n21
Homans, Margaret, 84–107, 18,
22, 82 n10
Hopkins, Gerard Manley, 25,
169–70, 172–3
Horkheimer, Max, 192, 218 n8

Ingelow, Jean, 38, 40, 63 n54; 'The
High Tide on the Coast of
Lincolnshire', 58; 'Requiescat in
Pace!', 58–9

James, Henry, 133, 135
Jameson, Anna, 45, 154, 229–30,
243 n8
Johnson, E.D.H., 30 n44

Kaplan, Cora, 12, 16, 30 n35, 82
n10, 108–9, 111, 124, 130 n1,
165 n41
Keats, John, 49, 135
Keble, John, 25, 31 n54, 42–3, 52,
55, 62 n15, 169
Krieger, Murray, 185 n6
Kristeva, Julia, 43, 62 n16

Landon, Letitia Elizabeth, see
L.E.L.
Law, Joe K., 187 n17
Lawrence, D.H., 135, 158, 161,
166 n59
Lecky, William, 225–6, 236, 243
n6
Le Gallienne, Richard, 11
Leighton, Angela, 4, 26, 28 n10,
223–45
L.E.L. [Letitia Elizabeth Landon],
4–6, 32, 37, 60
Lewes, George Henry, 42, 62 n13
Lewis, C. Day, 106 n5
Levy, Amy, 4, 240
Lonsdale, Roger, 4, 28 n9
Lootens, Tricia, 28 n10
Lovell, Terry, 217 n4

Loxterman, Alan 106 n9

McGann, Jerome J., 24–5, 167–88,
216 n2, 235, 244 n23
Marchand, Leslie, 165 n45
Markus, Julia, 143
Marshall, Linda, H., 31 n51
Martineau, Harriet, 109–10
Marx, Karl, 25, 192, 206–7, 213,
218 n7, 221 n33
Maurice, F.D., 243 n10
Mermin, Dorothy, 1, 20–2, 27, 31
n57, 64–83, 216 n2, 221 n36
Mew, Charlotte, 240–1; 'Madeleine
in Church', 241–2
Meynell, Alice, 235, 244 n14
Mill, John Stuart, 20, 30 n38, 42,
45
Miller, J. Hillis, 106 n10
Miller, Nan, 186 n17
Milton, John, 54
Mitchell, Sally, 229, 243 n2
Mitford, Mary Russell, 115, 198–9,
205
Modleski, Tania, 193, 218 n9
Moers, Ellen, 12, 29 n26, 81 n7,
139, 164 n29
Moi, Toril, 14–15, 30 n31,
Morgan, Charles, 106 n10
Murray, Janet Horowitz, 28 n7

Nightingale, Florence, 133, 160,
229–30

Ohmann, Carol, 106 n4
Ostriker, Alicia, 82 n10
Ouida, 136

Packer, Lona Mosk, 186 n8
Parkes, Bessie Rayner, 3
Patmore, Coventry, 21, 30 n40
Peel, Ellen, 164 n29
Plath, Sylvia, 79
Poe, Edgar Allan, 68
Poovey, Mary, 217 n3, 218 n12
Procter, Adelaide Anne, 26, 32,
36–40; 'Envy', 37–8; 'Homeward
Bound', 38; 'A Legend of
Bregenz', 39; 'A Legend of